I0760124

27th BRITISH COMMONWEALTH BRIGADE IN KOREA 1950 – 1951

27th BRITISH COMMONWEALTH BRIGADE IN KOREA 1950 – 1951

THE FIRE BRIGADE

DAVID ALLISON

Pen & Sword
MILITARY
AN IMPRINT OF PEN & SWORD BOOKS LTD.
YORKSHIRE – PHILADELPHIA

First published in Great Britain in 2025 by
Pen & Sword Military
An imprint of
Pen & Sword Books Ltd
Yorkshire - Philadelphia

ISBN 978 1 03613 602 4

A CIP catalogue record for this book is available from the British Library.

Typeset in INDIA by IMPEC eSolutions
Printed and bound in the England by CPI Group (UK) Ltd, Croydon, CRO 4YY

The Publisher's authorised representative in the EU for product safety is Authorised Rep Compliance Ltd., Ground Floor, 71 Lower Baggot Street, Dublin D02 P593, Ireland.
www.arccompliance.com

For a complete list of Pen & Sword titles please contact:

PEN & SWORD BOOKS LIMITED
George House, Units 12 & 13, Beevor Street, Off Pontefract Road,
Barnsley, S71 1HN, UK
E-mail: enquiries@pen-and-sword.co.uk
Website: www.pen-and-sword.co.uk

or

PEN AND SWORD BOOKS
1950 Lawrence Rd, Havertown, PA 19083, USA
E-mail: Uspen-and-sword@casematepublishers.com
Website: www.penandswordbooks.com

For Sasha

Contents

The Canadians

The Indians

Kapyong

Foreword

It is a privilege to be able to write a foreword to this excellent book. My introduction to David Allison came with his stand-out account of the Battle of Sangshak, one of the key early engagements of the Imphal campaign during the Japanese invasion of India in late March 1944. David's effective research among some confusing sources and his detailed stitching together of the story of the battle was as good as anything I have read. This battle certainly deserved rescuing from both obscurity and controversy. David did it brilliantly.

This new book is equally as good, fluently written and a powerful tribute to that remarkable conglomeration of people from across the Commonwealth which formed, during the Korean War, 27 Commonwealth Brigade. This so-called 'fire brigade' was cobbled together at short notice from two British battalions undertaking garrison duty in Hong Kong, its ranks a mix of long-service regulars wearing medal ribbons from the Second World War and men undergoing National Service. It's a testament to the soldiering skills of this brigade – and its officers – that in the event there was little to show in combat between the origins of each type of soldier. Nor was there much to show between the countries that eventually offered up troops for this brigade: Britain, Australia, India, New Zealand and Canada. The disparate units, forced together by circumstance, created a formation of unique power and effectiveness.

The two-battalion British 27 Brigade – named 'Commonwealth' by is commander, Brigadier Basil Coad, following the arrival of 3rd Battalion, Royal Australian Regiment – created something unusual in the history of the British Empire and Commonwealth, certainly since the departure of the British from India in 1947. Brigades in the Indian Army had routinely joined together Indian and British battalions: the evidence of the Second World War – in North Africa, Italy and Burma – demonstrated the efficacy of this arrangement in respect of combat performance. British and Indian troops who worked together regularly observed the mutual benefit gained by all units through this arrangement. In the case of 27 Brigade, the addition of the Australians, followed by New Zealand artillery units, Indian medics and later a Canadian battalion, resurrected this old Indian Army practice. The Commonwealth Brigade emerged as the product of serendipity, but over eight months of combat deployment in Korea between 1950 and 1951, a formation of unique power and effectiveness was created. It is no exaggeration to suggest that 27 Commonwealth Brigade, which would later transition into the

Commonwealth Division, was one of the most capable formations in the whole of the United Nations command. David Allison certainly thinks so, and I agree with him. After reading this fine book, I am certain that you will too.

Dr Robert Lyman MBE FRHistS
Author, with General Lord Dannatt, of *Korea, War Without End* (Osprey, 2025)

Preface

The 'Commonwealth of Nations', or the 'British Commonwealth' as it was more popularly known in the 1950s,[1] is a curious child of the British Empire. It in the main comprises former British colonies and is styled as an 'association of independent states', each of which have equal status. To this day, the Commonwealth remains an important international organization, focusing on issues common to all member nations, such as law, human rights, the environment and the economy.

There was one significant arena, however, with which the Commonwealth was never envisaged as dealing, and that was the military sphere. While the Commonwealth Charter lists the advancement of international peace and security as foundational values and aspirations, it is clear that the Commonwealth was not established to be a military alliance of any sort, and discussion of military matters is largely absent from the work of the Commonwealth and all its institutions.

In the early 1950s, following North Korea's brutal surprise attack on South Korea, various Commonwealth governments quickly joined together to raise a number of combined military units under the Commonwealth banner. The first unit raised and fielded was 27 British Commonwealth Brigade, to be superseded in mid-1951 by the larger 1st Commonwealth Division. The Brigade, comprising soldiers from Britain, Australia, New Zealand, Canada and India, quickly welded into an extremely effective fighting force.

Over the years, several excellent histories of individual national units that formed the Commonwealth forces have been written, but there are scant few that look at the contributions of all five member countries *as a whole*. This is unfortunate, as the previous histories fail to adequately recognize that the stunning successes of the Commonwealth forces was due in large part to the combination of units and countries which comprised the Commonwealth brigades and divisions.

In this book, I take a close look at 27 British Commonwealth Brigade during its eight-month tour in Korea during the initial stages of the war. Covering such a long period of intense fighting, with extended movement up and down the entire length of the Korean peninsula, it is not possible to examine each and every attack or battle undertaken by the brigade in minute detail. Rather, I explore the makeup of each of the units which comprised the brigade and focus on their key battles or encounters in order to give the reader a sense of the Commonwealth Brigade as a whole. My aim is to show that it was their combined strength which made them so formidable and such an effective part of the UN's fight to repel the North Korean (and later Chinese) invaders in 1950 and 1951.

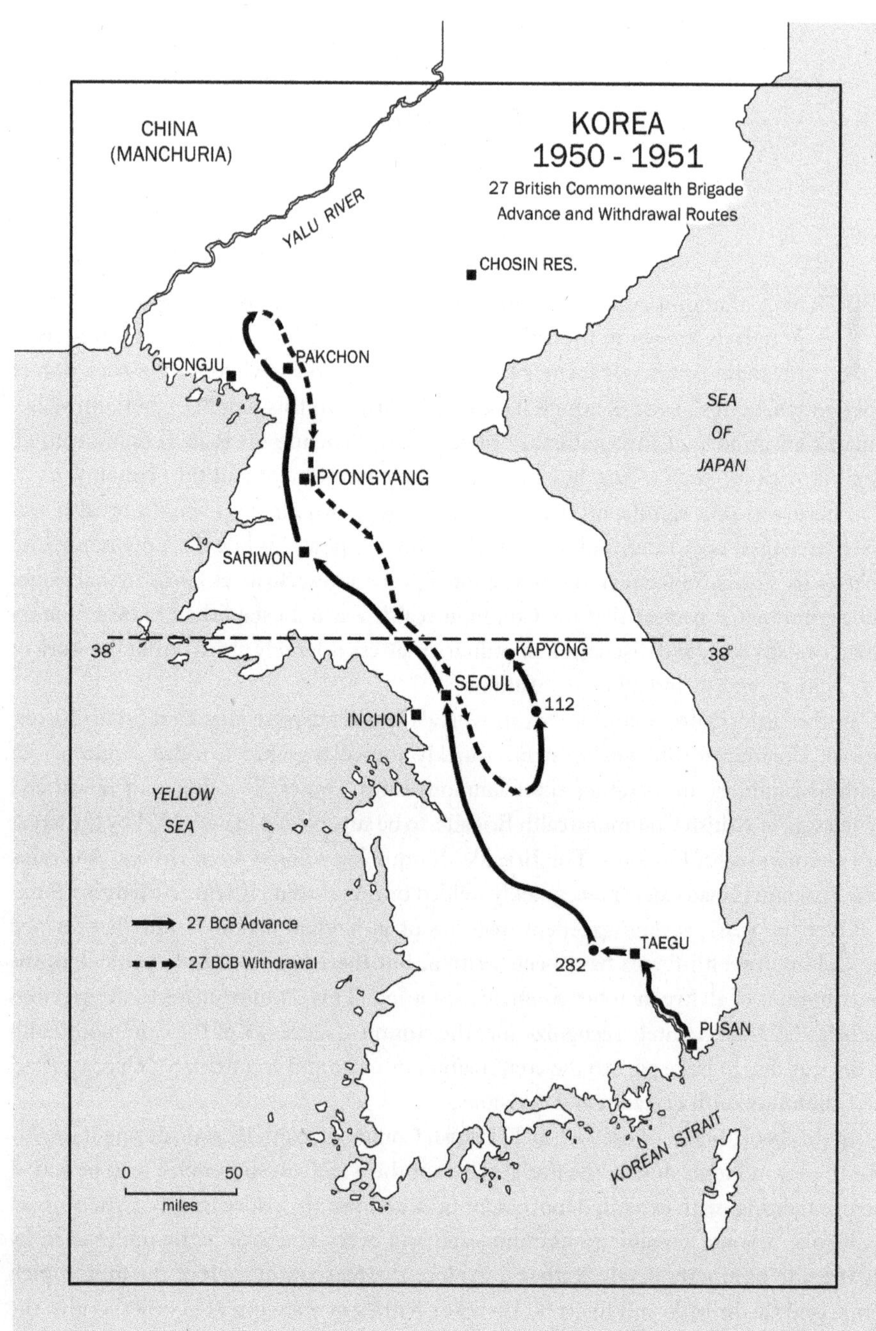
KOREA
1950 - 1951
27 British Commonwealth Brigade
Advance and Withdrawal Routes
CHINA
(MANCHURIA)
YALU RIVER
CHOSIN RES.
PAKCHON
CHONGJU
SEA
OF
JAPAN
PYONGYANG
SARIWON
38°
KAPYONG
38°
SEOUL
112
INCHON
YELLOW
SEA
27 BCB Advance
27 BCB Withdrawal
TAEGU
282
PUSAN
KOREAN STRAIT
0
50
miles

Timeline

Date	Event
25 June 1950	North Korea invades the South
25 June 1950	UNSC Resolution 82 – calls for North to withdraw
27 June 1950	UNSC Resolution 83 – authorizes military action to support the South
28 June 1950	Seoul falls to the Communists
18 August 1950	Brigadier Coad receives signal to mount Operation Graduate
25 August 1950	1 MX & 1 ASH depart Hong Kong for Korea
12 September 1950	North Korea's furthest gains into South Korea
15 September 1950	Operation Chromite – Inchon Landing
17 September	UN forces break out from Pusan perimeter
23 September 1950	Battle for Hill 282
25 September 1950	Seoul Liberated
27 September 1950	3 RAR depart Australia for Pusan
1 October 1950	3 RAR joins 27 Commonwealth Brigade
17 October 1950	Brigade action at Sariwon
19 October 1950	UN forces capture Pyongyang and continue north towards Chinese border
25 October 1950	China crosses the Yalu River and enters the war
25–26 October 1950	3 RAR and Battle at Broken Bridge, Pakchon
1 November 1950	3 RAR CO, Lieutenant Colonel Green, killed
5 November 1950	2nd Battle at Pakchon. 3 RAR CO Lieutenant Colonel Walsh relieved of command
29 November 1950	60 Fd Ambulance arrive Pyongyang
December 1950	The 'Great Bug Out' – withdrawal of UN forces from North Korea
18 Dec 1950	2 PPCLI arrive in Pusan
4 January 1951	Communists capture Seoul

Date	Event
20 January 1951	16 RNZA join 27 Commonwealth Brigade
11 February 1951	China launches 4th Offensive
13–15 February 1951	Defence of Chipyong-ni
14–15 February 1951	1 MX defence at point 112
18 February 1951	2 PPCLI join 27 Commonwealth Brigade
14 March 1951	UN recaptures Seoul
23 March 1951	Operation Tomahawk – 60 Fd Ambulance takes part in paradrop
23 March 1951	Brigadier Coad departs brigade, replaced by Burke
11 April 1951	MacArthur relieved of command of UN forces, replaced by Ridgeway
22 April 1951	China commences its 'Spring Offensive'
22–26 April 1951	Battle of Kapyong
26 April 1951	27 British Commonwealth Brigade rebadged as 28 British Commonwealth Brigade
27 July 1953	Armistice agreement signed

Prologue: Operation Storm[2]

The T-34 was one of the standout tanks of the Second World War. Built by the Soviet Union, equipped with aggressively sloped armour capable of deflecting all but the most accurate anti-tank rounds and armed with a brutally effective 76mm main gun, the T-34 was the nemesis of the German Army in the Second World War. Its broad tracks could cope with the most difficult terrain, including mud or snow, allowing it to keep advancing in even the most hostile of conditions. The Germans derisively called the T-34 'Mickey Mouse' due to the shape of the twin round hatches mounted on the turret – but there was nothing cartoonish about the deadly efficiency of this Soviet monster. It had been feared by the Germans on the Eastern Front; now, a mere five years after the end of the war, 200 of them were at the head of North Korean troops driving deep into South Korean territory.

It was the shock effect of the T-34s that did the most damage on that first day of the invasion, 25 June 1950. General Paik, the young but already highly experienced commander of the 1st Republic of Korea Division (1st ROK Division) guarding the south bank of the Imjin River and north-west approaches to Seoul, noted the difficulties his hastily assembled troops faced on that first day of fighting:

> 'Despite having an anti-tank platoon, ROK soldiers did not have sufficient anti-tank training or weapons and had never seen a tank. This contributed greatly to the "T-34 disease" that gripped our troops on the first day of the war. The symptoms of the disease were straightforward. As soon as men even heard the word "tank" they fell into a state of terror.'[3]

A few months later, the T-34 disease would dissipate as UN troops gained familiarity in fighting the Communists and brought to bear effective anti-tank weapons and air support. But this knowledge lay in the future, and on this first day of the war, the T-34 disease hastened the loss of the strategic town of Kaesong within hours of the invasion. The disease spread quickly, heralding a full-scale retreat of both ROK (Republic of Korea) and US forces, all of them streaming south in a desperate bid to outrun the advancing Communist armour.

Paik's 1st ROK Division was badly mauled on the first day of fighting, with one of his three regiments effectively 'shattered' within hours of the NKPA (North Korean People's

Army) advance. However, with the coming of the next day, Paik was able to assemble and deploy some badly needed reinforcements and his pitifully small, but nevertheless very welcome, artillery.[4] Shaking off the shock of the first day, the ROK soldiers' resistance stiffened and, from their trench lines and prepared defensive positions, they were able to slow down and resist the advancing tide of NKPA troops, tanks and guns.

While the ROK troops were inevitably pushed south from their initial positions to a secondary defensive line, individual and small-unit bravery managed to make minor dents in the NKPA's onslaught, at times slowing the advance. But such gains were too small and far too localized to make a meaningful difference to the overall outcome of the invasion. While Paik's men were holding on and gaining a few small victories, reports of an accidental bombing of South Korean troops by US aircraft soured some of the hastily assembled men towards the efforts of their 'allies' and erstwhile military mentors. Yet still, the ROK men now located just north of the capital, Seoul, tried to dig in, often helped by shovel-wielding students from a local school, and offer some resistance against the advancing NKPA juggernaut.

With streams of civilian refugees already rapidly moving past Paik's position in an attempt to flee the fighting, and with his men already occupying their fallback defensive positions north of Seoul, Paik received the following dreaded order from the ROK high command: 'Fight to the death in your present positions.'[5] It was a hateful order, senseless really, given both the scale of the enemy forces and the pitiful lack of weapons or support that the ROK soldiers possessed. Yet Paik and his men tried to hang on.

Just a day later, Paik learned that the NKPA had already brushed past all resistance on the eastern flank and occupied Seoul behind Paik's defensive positions. It had taken only three days and the capital of South Korea had already fallen. NKPA troops and vehicles were filling the capital, while the bridge over the Han River, and 1st ROK Division's only means of escape, had already been destroyed.

After three days of fighting, Paik and his men had been abandoned. He later wrote: 'The series of shocks had come too fast and too strong for me to handle. I was seized by a strong feeling that I was living out the last moments of my life. I felt like I no longer had control of events, and there wasn't a damn thing I could do about it.'[6]

***

Origins of the Korean War

The massive surprise attack launched by North Korea on 25 June 1950 not only stunned General Paik and his men with its speed and savagery, but also deeply shocked the whole world. Newspaper headlines on that day conveyed the mood: 'Reds Invading Korea', declared the Sunday morning edition of the *Los Angeles Times*, and similar headlines greeted readers of major newspapers around the globe. It was a surprise to many readers, just as it was to most of the world's leaders, who had had little prior knowledge or interest in South Korea or any inkling that these actions in that far-off land would soon engulf many of them.

In early 1950, it would have been a very astute and well-read politician – let alone an ordinary citizen of the Western world – who could even identify Korea on the map, much less speak knowledgably about its recent history. This was understandable, given both its history and geography.

Korea lies on the north-east tip of the Asian landmass, bordered by China and Russia to the north, and with Japan its nearest neighbour to the south and east, located across the narrow straits of the Sea of Japan. In 1910, Korea had been annexed by Japan, and both its manpower and resources were used heavily in support of Japan's wartime efforts in the first half of the 20th century. There was also an intensive effort on the part of Japan during the colonial period to promote the Japanese language and institutions, while simultaneously deemphasizing or delegitimizing Korea's language, culture and traditions.

Following the end of the Second World War and the withdrawal of the Japanese colonial government, the Korean peninsula was divided roughly along the line of the 38th parallel, with a trustee administration arranged under the auspices of the United Nations. The Soviet Union assumed control in the north and the Americans were given trusteeship of the south. It was only ever intended to be a temporary arrangement, with control of the two halves quickly devolving to local administration and then, following elections, a possible reunification.

No discussion of modern Korea can be made without frequent reference to the '38th parallel'. What is curious, however, is that there is no real logic, much less magic, as to the selection of the 38th parallel as the line dividing North from South Korea. The line does not correspond to any historical division of the two Koreas. Rather, it was a purely administrative and arbitrary division of the peninsula following the Second World War, a line of convenience to separate the northern, Soviet-dominated half from the US-administered south.

In any event, in 1948 the administration period ended, with the establishment of the respective North and South Korean governments on both sides of the parallel. While only lasting three years, the trustee and administration period had left a deep mark on both countries, leading to the establishment of a Communist-controlled North whereas the South was nominally a Western-style democratic country.

What followed was much political wrangling and posturing from Korean politicians on both sides of the border, each claiming that the division of the country was a temporary measure and that they were the true leaders of a united Korea. There were discussions at the United Nations regarding country-wide elections, but such efforts fell down in the face of politics in both parts of the peninsula. The Americans were eager to leave

Korea, quickly winding down their civil and military presence in the country after 1948. By 1950, the Americans would only have a small presence of several hundred military advisers in the country, the so-called KMAG (the Korean Military Advisory Group). This left the South Korean Army in a very poor state, lightly equipped with only simple infantry weapons and very little in the way of artillery or armour. The South Koreans also had no aircraft of any type. It was, in fact, little more than a constabulary outfit rather than a fully equipped modern army.

On the other side of the border, things couldn't have been more different. Stalin and the Soviet Union had worked quickly to help develop a Korean one-party Communist state, backed by a large, well-equipped, Soviet-style modern army. At the outbreak of the war, North Korea had an army in excess of 100,000 troops, many of whom had previously fought with the Chinese communists in the Second World War. The Soviet Union had been lavish in providing the North Korean regime with modern arms and training, including 200 T-34 tanks, a large supply of artillery and self-propelled guns as well as a quantity of fighter and ground-attack aircraft.

Accordingly, by the time the North Korean leadership under Kim Il-Sung made the decision to invade the South in June 1950 (with the explicit support of Stalin), it was pitting a relatively modern army against little more than a beefed-up police force. Of course, the modernization process was not yet complete in the North at the time of the invasion, and not all Communist troops travelled south by tank or truck. It still fielded units mounted on stout Mongolian ponies and many infantrymen had no choice but to march to the front. That said, both qualitatively and quantitatively, there was little doubt that the NKPA was initially superior to its adversaries in the South. Added to this, the shock of the invasion and the mass of tanks involved contributed to the initial confusion, damage and destruction of the South Korean defenders. It is little wonder that Seoul was lost in a mere three days of fighting, with the South Koreans effectively routed.

***

Besides the armoured support wielded by the Communists, another reason for the North's initial successes was the total failure of both the South Korean and American governments to accept that the North really would attack. Despite clear intelligence warnings of an invasion, as well as some limited incursions and firefights along the border in 1949, no one believed that the North Koreans would mount a full scale invasion. '[W]e gave too much weight to our own interpretation of the enemy's intentions and too little to the facts we knew about his capability', was how General Matthew Ridgeway, the man who would eventually lead UN forces in 1951, described these failings.[7]

And what of US forces, the unchallenged victors of the Second World War and the superpower whose troops were currently garrisoning a defeated Japan? How was the previous administrator of South Korea positioned to support the South in their hour of need? 'Woefully unready' would be the general verdict. At the time of the invasion, the United States only had several hundred US troops in the entire country. These KMAG soldiers were part of a mentoring and training mission, and as such were not prepared or equipped for a high-intensity fight. When the first North Korean troops smashed their way south, there was little these troops could do. Despite some individual and small-unit heroics, they too had no choice but to retreat before the rampaging Communist forces.

There were of course sizeable US forces nearby in Japan, but these troops were not the hardened veterans of the Pacific fighting who had occupied Japan at the end of the war five years beforehand. Rather, the men now in Japan were occupying troops, used to the comfortable life of post-war Japan. Many of the veterans of the war had already returned to the US; instead, the garrison troops were largely new joiners and untested troops, leavened with a small number of veterans now considerably softer than they were at the end of the Second World War. Total numbers were also much reduced, since the US – like most Western nations – had aggressively cut its armed forces following the end of the war, anxious to return their men to civilian duties and reap the 'peace dividend'.

The result was that there were less than two divisions of troops available in Japan for mobilization, and even these were not regarded as tier-one combat troops. Despite these handicaps, the US quickly scrambled what soldiers it had available and committed them to the defence of South Korea, in the hope that there would still be some territory left to defend.

***

Almost immediately after the North's invasion, an intense diplomatic battle played out in the major capitals of the world, and crucially in the recently established United Nations. The United States immediately called for a resolution of the UN Security Council condemning the North Korean attack, with an immediate end of hostilities and the withdrawal of all North Korean troops.[8] The resolution was passed on 25 June 1950 by all members of the Security Council, with one abstention from Yugoslavia.

A second resolution (UN Security Council Resolution No 83) quickly followed on 27 July 1950. The new resolution largely reiterated the precepts of the initial one, but critically added the following wording: 'Recommends that the Members of the United Nations furnish such assistance to the Republic of Korea as may be necessary to repel the armed attack and to restore international peace and security in the area.'[9] It would be these two resolutions which provided the legal basis for the United States and UN forces generally to actively assist the South Koreans on a military basis. The resolutions are relatively rare in the annals of the United Nations, and a similar resolution would almost certainly fail today given that any one of the five permanent members (the USA, Great Britain, USSR/Russia, China and France) can veto any resolution.

In 1950, two factors were critical in getting the resolutions passed, both of which (ironically, as future events would show) related to China. In October 1949, the Chinese Communists had just won the Chinese Civil War and had declared the establishment of the People's Republic of China in Beijing. Nevertheless, the losers of the civil war, the fiercely anti-Communist Chinese Nationalists, still retained their seat at the UN as one of the five permanent members of the Security Council. Unsurprisingly, the Chinese Nationalists voted in favour of the Korea resolutions.

Meanwhile, the USSR had temporarily absented itself from the United Nations in protest against the failure of the UN to immediately transfer China's seat on the Security Council to the newly established People's Republic. The Soviets were keen to have another large Communist country join it on the Security Council to balance the overwhelming presence of Western powers on the body, and it was thought that its absence and boycott could move the world body to vote in favour of the Chinese Communists. However, it was not to be and the Soviets' absence prevented them from exercising their veto power. Consequently, the resolutions were passed. From the Soviet perspective, it was a costly mistake which allowed a large UN-sanctioned military force to be raised and go to the aid of South Korea. But for this failure on the Russian part, it is highly unlikely that international forces could have been raised in such a short period of time to prevent the South's collapse. It was a mistake that Russia would never make again; henceforth, it would never be absent from the Security Council when major decisions and resolutions were being debated.

By the time the Soviets realized their mistake, the 'damage' (in their eyes at least) had already been done. Passage of these two crucial UN resolutions led to the establishment of a joint UN Command and provided the legal basis for the despatch of international troops to assist the South and repel the Communist attack.

But while the UN resolutions and the diplomatic cover were welcome, the situation on the ground was becoming increasingly desperate. After the loss of Seoul, ROK and newly arrived US forces – which at this time were still relatively small in number but growing daily – were being relentlessly driven south. By August 1950, the situation for the UN troops on the peninsula was dire. A thinly held perimeter, less than 100 miles west of the last southern port of Pusan, was being held along the eastern bank of the Naktong River.

There was, however, one bit of good news to cheer the South Korean defenders. Concurrent with passing the UN resolutions authorizing member countries to assist the South, the US President, Harry Truman, appointed General Douglas MacArthur – the hero of the Pacific campaign in the Second World War – to take overall command of UN forces operating in Korea. As General Paik remarked:

> '[T]he war situation wasn't pessimistic; it was hopeless. A single rumour however, completely reversed everybody's spirits. The word was that five-star

> General Douglas MacArthur himself was to tour the front. At that time General MacArthur was regarded by Korean soldiers and civilians alike as almost a god. He was the hero of World War II and had accepted the surrender of the Emperor of Japan. People today can't imagine the extent of his prestige.'[10]

Following the appointment of General MacArthur, the Americans started to deploy more units from Japan into Korea in an attempt to stem the tide. By 2 August 1950, just over a week after the surprise invasion, it had contributed three understrength infantry divisions, two regimental combat teams and a US Marine division. More troops were being mobilized and trained in the United States. While this was a mighty effort, it is important to stress that in 1950, the United States military only vaguely resembled the mighty juggernaut that it was at the end of the Second World War. Immediately following the end of the conflict, the US went through a period of rapid demobilization. While it still possessed vast stockpiles of war materiel left over from the war, it did not have a limitless supply of combat-ready troops to call upon for Korea. The five-plus divisions that MacArthur was able to assemble in the month or so after the invasion already represented a large portion of the United States' total available combat power. But it was clearly not enough. While the US would rapidly mobilize and train additional troops over the next year, with the North looking poised to drive the UN forces into the sea, there remained a pressing and urgent need for extra troops now.

So the Americans called on their wartime ally, the British, to join the fight.

The British

1st Battalion, the Middlesex Regiment
1st Battalion, the Argyll and Sutherland Highlanders

Chapter 1

On the Border of 'Red China'

As North Korean tanks raced towards Seoul, the officers and men of the 1st Battalion, The Middlesex Regiment (1 MX) had their eyes firmly fixed on another set of Communists – the Chinese. In one of the many trenches and recently dug defensive positions lining the northern hills of Hong Kong's New Territories, Second Lieutenant David Harrop adjusted his binoculars to focus on the Chinese Communist positions in 'Red China' on the other side of the Shenzhen River. There was not a lot to see; just a simple shack-like border checkpoint on the north bank of the river, a flagpole topped with the fluttering red flag of the Chinese communists and the odd group of soldiers. Beyond that was farmland – paddy fields, vegetable gardens and some small farmers' homes for as far as the eye could see into the limitless expanse of the newly formed Communist country.

But the idyllic rural scene could be deceiving. Harrop knew that somewhere in the Chinese hinterland, there were more than a million regular Communist troops, fresh from their victories over the Chinese Nationalist armies. Some were still actively engaged in fighting and mopping up the last pockets of resistance in southern China. The threat of an enormous Chinese Communist army on Hong Kong's doorstep sent waves of concern through both the Hong Kong and British governments, spurring them to action and the hasty despatch of several understrength infantry battalions to Hong Kong to bolster the defences of the Crown Colony.

It was for this reason that Harrop, a newly trained officer undertaking his compulsory National Service obligation, joined the rest of his battalion in March 1950 and was now intently looking at the Communists on the other side of the border. Days were spent in hard training over the hot and humid hills, interspaced with week-long periods of garrison duties in the newly constructed trenches and dugouts lining the hills and facing north.

The men of 1 MX worked hard in the muggy heat of a Hong Kong summer, their time split between patrols on the border and standard infantry training when in camp. Each day started early in the relatively cool, but still humid, morning. First parade would see the men standing to attention in ranks, wearing only their boots, shorts and hats, but with no shirts. They would also sport their standard-issue Lee Enfield rifle, together with a bayonet on their belt. Thus dressed for morning parade, each man would then be issued with a daily dose of paludrine to keep malaria at bay, washed down with a half-cup of salty water to ward off the effects of heat exhaustion.

The work Harrop and his men did in northern Hong Kong was hard, invigorating and interesting. To the young second lieutenant, it was an excellent way to see out his National Service commitment and infinitely better than one spent in the cold and wet camps of England or garrison duties in Germany.

Harrop, like most of his fellow officers, didn't know a lot about Korea, its internal troubles or why the North Koreans had attacked. However, as an intelligent junior officer, he maintained a soldier's interest, in a general way, about the progress of a major war which had just commenced in the 'neighbourhood'. Apart from this, Harrop had little reason to think or believe that his battalion would ever be deployed to South Korea, having been told that the Middlesex's vital role was to protect Hong Kong.

So Harrop spent the bulk of his days lazily scanning the Chinese positions through his binoculars and making notes in his log book of what he saw, all the while thinking to himself that Hong Kong was an exciting posting and an excellent place to see out two years before he returned to England.

Chapter 2

From One Fragrant Harbour to Another[11]

Harrop's unit was an infantry battalion with a long and proud tradition. It was also known by its nickname, 'The Diehards', which the regiment gained in 1811 during the Napoleonic Wars when a commanding officer, mortally wounded, had exhorted his men to keep fighting with the words, 'Die hard, the 57th, Die hard'.[12] Ever since, the name had stuck.

The Middlesex Battalion had a long association with Hong Kong, having courageously fought against the Japanese when they launched their surprise attack on the colony on 8 December 1941 until it surrendered a little over a fortnight later on Christmas Day. After spending the rest of the war as prisoners, it was amazing that in mid-1950 there were still several former POWs serving in the ranks of the battalion. Chief among them was the Drum Major, Charles 'Drummie' Holdford, who commanded the battalion band. As with most Commonwealth forces of the time, the band had a double role, seeing them play their instruments during peacetime soldiering but then being deployed as stretcher bearers and medics during active service.

In early August 1950, just like Harrop, neither Drummie Holford nor any of the other men of the battalion even remotely suspected that within a week, they would be actively fighting the Communist North Koreans.

The men in Hong Kong were certainly aware of the war in Korea, but did not think it would affect them at all. They were convinced that the US troops would handle it and it was unlikely that UK soldiers would be needed. As the days passed following the invasion with no hint of a British involvement, their supposition appeared proven. Korea slipped further into the back corners of the men's minds as they continued with their patrolling of the border. On 16 July 1950, while on duty manning a border observation post, Harrop noted that: 'The war here or rather in Korea seems to drag on. I don't expect it will affect us. I can give you first-hand information that no attack is building up across the border here, although there does seem to be a big build-up of petrol drums, however we shall see.'[13] It was a sentiment shared by most of the men in the battalion.

A month later, on 20 August, the battalion was enjoying a relaxing Sunday afternoon swimming carnival against a rival battalion at the Victoria Recreation Club. The Diehards were reportedly faring well, besting their rivals at water polo, when the Commanding Officer, Lieutenant Colonel Andrew Man, was called to the phone to receive an important message from the brigadier.

Major John Willoughby, one of Man's subordinate company commanders, records in his diary that when Man was suddenly called away, rumours already started to circulate that the battalion might be called up for Korea. Briefly noting the relaxing swimming carnival, Willoughby presciently recalled a similar social situation preceding a battle over a hundred years previously, writing in bold: 'The Duchess of Richmond's Ball!'[14]

Brigadier Coad – 27 Brigade

It was the brigade commander, Brigadier Basil Aubrey Coad, DSO, who had mysteriously called Man away from the battalion's games that Sunday afternoon.

Born in 1906, Coad was a professional soldier, having held a series of posts in India, Shanghai and Palestine prior to the war. In the Second World War, he saw active service in Normandy and then through Europe, winning not one but two Distinguished Service Orders. Coad rose to the temporary rank of major general during the war before reverting to brigadier when he was posted to Hong Kong in 1949.

Coad was regarded as an officer who took his soldiering seriously, one who excelled at the administrative side of his business as well as displaying personal courage and bravery in battle. Even at this relatively senior level, he was not afraid to conduct reconnaissance forward of his troops himself, demonstrating both his commitment and physical courage. Likewise, Coad was known to be forceful when defending his men's interests; there were many instances recorded during the Korean War when he spoke up quite strongly, and in opposition to his American superiors, in order to protect the interests of his soldiers.

In all, Coad was an excellent brigade commander. Experienced, committed and with a very dry sense of humour, he was universally respected and admired by all members of his brigade. Even the Australians, whom he would command later in Korea, and who were not known for uncritical respect for rank, universally acknowledged Coad's qualities. In their uniquely playfully and affectionate manner, they referred to Coad as the 'grey headed old bastard' – despite the fact that he was only 45 years old when deployed to Korea.

***

Coad commanded 27 Infantry Brigade (27 Bde), which was part of the United Kingdom's Strategic Reserve. It was sent to Hong Kong in early 1950 to bolster the Crown Colony's defences when it looked to a nervous UK government highly likely that the advancing Chinese Communist Army could threaten Hong Kong. Coad noted in correspondence after the war that 27 Bde's task was 'to be at 10 days' notice to proceed anywhere!! As a result of this, we were known by some people as the Fire Brigade!'"[15]

Developing the Fire Brigade theme, 27 Bde's formation sign was an inverted triangle in navy blue, superimposed with three 'nines' in red. Coad noted that: 'Three "nines" equals "27" and in England, if you are in trouble and require either Police – Ambulance or Fire Brigade, you dial 999 at any telephone!'.[16] Later events would prove this to be a very apt sign, accurately describing the brigade and its role throughout the Korean campaign.

Coad received with tremendous surprise a message on 20 August 1950 from the UK Minister of Defence that his brigade would sail to Korea forthwith. As recently as July 1950, 'The Minister of Defence stated categorically that neither the garrisons of Hong Kong or Malaya would be weakened and so the news that the Battalion had been selected, together with the Argylls, came as rather a surprise.'[17]

While Britain had committed air and naval assets to the UN Command almost immediately after passage of the UN resolutions, it had been less keen in agreeing to commit ground forces, stretched as it was with its own commitments in Europe, Malaya and Hong Kong. When it was eventually decided that a British infantry brigade should sail to join the UN forces, the unit selected was 29 Brigade, currently stationed in Britain. This was a heavy brigade, still in the process of being brought up to full strength. It was to receive the full complement of supporting arms and weapons, modern clothing, communications and other equipment, as well as tanks and artillery, which would allow it to act and fight as a fully independent combat organization.

But as early August saw the situation in the Naktong bridgehead becoming even more desperate, the Americans once more urged the British to act with all possible haste. They repeatedly stressed that the immediate deployment of even understrength forces would be immeasurably more useful than a perfectly equipped and trained brigade deployed in a month's time – when there may well be nothing left to defend.

So Coad's 27 Bde was activated and told that it would have to sail for Korea in a weeks' time. While the brigade may have theoretically been required to respond to any emergency within ten days, in reality the logistics of assembling the men and equipment and providing orders and directions for major combat operations several thousand miles to the north was a task that would stretch even the finest and most highly trained troops anywhere in the world.

What ensued was a ferocious effort to marshal the men, prepare the equipment and assemble the necessary supplies prior to embarkation. Initial secrecy probably contributed to some delays, since only the commanding officers of the two contributing battalions, Lieutenant Colonel Andrew Man of 1 MX and Lieutenant Colonel (George) Leslie Neilson of the 1st Battalion, Argyll and Sutherland Highlanders (1 ASH) were initially being told of the deployment. A day later, however, the news was out. The men were assembled and told that they would sail to Korea to join the United Nations effort in just a few days' time.

While Coad and his battalion commanders were surprised by the order, Harrop and his fellow National Service officers and soldiers would have been genuinely stunned. Nevertheless, it appears that once the initial surprise wore off, most of the men were excited at the prospect of being deployed. Even those who were less enthusiastic had little time to dwell on the future as what now ensued was a prodigious effort of the entire military establishment of Hong Kong to get the two fighting battalions ready in time to sail on 25 August.

***

Both 1 MX and 1 ASH were typical representatives of post-war British infantry units in terms of their composition. Both were made up of a hard core of company commanders and senior NCOs who had seen service in the Second World War, whereas the junior officers and soldiers were a mixture of recent volunteers and National Service troops.

The Diehards were lucky to have a cadre of extremely experienced officers. For example, Major John Willoughby, in command of D Company, had previously been a temporary battalion commander during the war, but like many officers had reverted to his substantive rank at the conclusion of the conflict. Not only was Willoughby a very capable soldier and commander, he was also well educated, had an excellent command of the English language and apparently attracted the media, who liked to interview him. Fortunately for history, Willoughby has also left behind an excellent series of diaries chronicling his experiences in Korea.

***

While senior officers and NCOs were experienced regulars, a large proportion of the junior officers and rank and file soldiers were National Servicemen. National Service, introduced in Britain in 1947, mandated that all able-bodied men aged 17–21 were required to spend eighteen months in the Armed Forces. These young men were frequently sent overseas to garrison Britain's remaining imperial possessions as well as to fight in both Malaya and, in 1950, Korea. With the Korean War placing great demands on the British Army for additional manpower, in late 1950 it was decided to increase the length of service from eighteen months to two years.

National Service was and remains a contentious programme. On the one hand, the British Armed Forces desperately needed a large number of troops to satisfy its numerous post-war worldwide obligations since the pool of regular soldiers was clearly insufficient. On the other hand, Britain had an acute labour shortage at home in the immediate post-war period, and the diversion of so many young men for National Service naturally reduced the number of available workers for industry.

For the young men themselves, calls to undertake National Service produced a wide range of feelings and emotions. Some were not happy with the scheme, believing that it wasted a man's time doing unproductive activities, but there were also a large number of young men, brought up in the immediate post-war world, which saw National Service as a necessary, patriotic and useful contribution to society.

The regular soldiers were also conflicted about their National Service comrades. For example, Major John Willoughby complained that their training was not as good as it could have been, as the men were often detailed for 'general duties' work (often boring, uninteresting but necessary peacetime soldiering duties) instead of hard training. When the order for Korea came out, Willoughby for one was concerned about the level of training of his National Service soldiers: 'Wonderfully willing as are our National Servicemen, many are at best half trained and I expect they are all as frightened of being pitchforked into battle as I am. May we have time to learn without too many casualties.'[18]

This was unkind of Willoughby, and time would prove that the vast majority of 27 Bde's National Service troops did just as well as their regular counterparts when it mattered on the battlefield in Korea.

A good example was Second Lieutenant Barry Reed, who would command 10 Platoon, D Company, under Willoughby. Reed took up the position in late September 1950 when the original commander, Lieutenant Geoff White, was killed. Reed was a well-educated young man who had a great future in the family's fashion retail business. He had already secured a place at Cambridge when his National Service obligation came to an end, but rather than looking at his stint in the Army as a waste of his time, he claimed that he enjoyed the experience and even seriously considered staying on as a regular soldier after his commitment concluded. As Reed's actions in Korea would later show, his ability to lead men and command them in combat was every bit as good as a regular with several years' experience of peacetime soldiering under his belt. Reed would leave Korea with his men's and Willoughby's respect, as well as a Military Cross for his courage and coolness under fire in April 1951.

***

While such concerns about the quality of his National Service soldiers may have crossed Willoughby's mind during quiet periods patrolling the border with China, now there was simply no time to dwell on such matters. The men needed to be ready within a single week.

Coad's brigade would sail on a very light scale indeed. Besides 1 MX, Coad would also have the services of 1 ASH, which, like 1 MX, was also understrength. To add to Coad's troubles, he then received a message from London, telling him that no National Service soldier under 19 years of age could be sent, nor could any man who was in his last three months of service. This had an enormous effect on the strength of the battalions, immediately rendering at least 25 per cent of the posted strength ineligible for deployment. This included Harrop, who was disappointed not to be able to go.

To make up the strength, a call was put out for volunteers from other units stationed in Hong Kong. A good many put up their hand, many of whom were not even infantry-trained. For example, several quickly drafted platoon commanders were not trained as infantry, but rather were ordinance (i.e. supply) officers. This desperate recruitment exercise was not at all ideal as it provided no time for the men to get to know each other, much less provide the critical pre-deployment and collective training which usually precedes any significant overseas deployment.

But needs must, and sufficient men were soon found to fill three rifle companies for each battalion. This was clearly the bare minimum, as a full-strength battalion would ordinarily be comprised of four companies, together with a support company of heavy weapons (e.g. machine-gun, anti-tank and mortar specialists).

Equipping the Brigade

While securing sufficient manning for the brigade within five days was difficult, gathering enough equipment to allow it to fight when it got to Korea would prove even more of a challenge.

Coad's key initial concerns were focussed on logistics and supply. Having previously commanded large bodies of troops in the field, he was painfully aware that without the necessary equipment and supplies, even a force despatched promptly could have little to no significant effect on the enemy. Worse still, the lack of the right equipment, weapons or ammunition would very likely put the men's lives in danger.

Unfortunately, the 'come as you are' approach to logistics had been a recurring feature of British expeditionary warfare for centuries. It was frequently the case that the first contingent of British forces despatched anywhere – often in great haste – while long on grit and daring, lacked the essentials to allow them to survive and succeed on the battlefield. The initial British deployment to Korea would not break from this wretched tradition.

Coad noted that detailed orders from England regarding the move to Korea were almost non-existent. Writing a few years after the war, Coad said: 'I can remember NO Administrative Directive as such. It was all rather confusing.'[19] With no clear direction from higher headquarters, Coad was on his own, unable to give much in the way of detailed guidance or direction to his battalion commanders. Accordingly, each just proceeded to draw all the standard weapons and kit that they had on hand, pack it and prepare it for the sea voyage to Korea.

The basic weapons of 27 Bde would have been instantly recognizable to any British soldier from the Second World War, having hardly changed at all in the intervening years. The standard British rifle remained the venerable .303 Lee Enfield, a single-shot, bolt action weapon which had seen service with all Commonwealth armies for the duration of the war. Enthusiasts (or apologists) for the Lee Enfield frequently noted its range, accuracy and stopping power, but there was no disguising the fact that it was a relatively heavy weapon (approximately 4kg), with a small magazine capacity of a mere ten rounds, and its manual-operated bolt action limited its rate of fire compared to the semi-automatic M1 Garand sported by US troops. Nevertheless, in the hands of trained soldiers, the Lee Enfield was still capable of up to twenty shots per minute. It could also be fitted with a bayonet, which for 1 MX and 1 ASH was the 'spike-type' bayonet, a simple long steel rod, known by many soldiers as the 'pig sticker'. Lieutenant Colonel James Stone, commander of the Canadian contingent who arrived in Korea in late 1950, said of the .303 (with which his battalion was also equipped): 'Mud and frost shows the advantages of having a hand operated rifle, and I do not think a change to an automatic is desirable. Men who had acquired the US Garand rifles … have since discarded them in favour of the Enfield No. 4.'[20] It is unknown whether Stone's comments were made to make a virtue of necessity or reflected his heartfelt preference for the Lee Enfield.

Arguably the most important weapon in the rifle platoons, however, was the Bren light machine gun. The Bren was a standout weapon of the Second World War, ubiquitous throughout all Commonwealth armies, the main firepower and anchor of every section and platoon. The Bren sported a distinctive curved box magazine mounted on top of the weapon, which allowed the thirty rounds in the magazine to be fed cleanly and with the assistance of gravity into the body of the gun. It fired the punchy .303 calibre round and was usually employed to fire bursts of fire to supress the enemy, who would become all too familiar with the distinctive 'knock, knock, knock' sound of a Bren three-round burst.

Despite the vintage of the British small arms, most of the troops were happy to be going into combat with weapons that were battle-tested and with which they were intimately acquainted. There was, however, one glaring deficiency, and this was in relation to platoon- and company-level anti-tank weapons. All had read the headlines about angry columns of T-34 tanks streaming towards Seoul and realized that their ancient PIAT anti-tank weapons would be of no use in stopping them. Fortunately, Coad was able to arrange for some of the new American 3.5in bazookas (a rocket-propelled anti-tank weapon) to be flown to Hong Kong, together with a team of American instructors. Hasty instruction was carried out and a few rounds were fired by the eager British troops just prior to embarkation. This last-minute training would be repaid many times over in the months to follow when the newly arrived British troops were forced to face Soviet armour at close quarters.

***

Rounding out the men's personal kit was their clothing and web equipment. As it was summer, all of the troops were still dressed in their regular tropical 'jungle green' uniform. Little had changed from those worn in Burma at the end of the war. Headwear was the floppy bush hat rather than the steel helmet, although there are many photographs of the Argylls wearing their distinctive Scottish tam o' shanter (a type of Scottish bonnet, similar to a beret, with a large pom-pom in the centre). While certainly lightweight, practical and welcome when the men first arrived in Korea during the region's short, hot summer, the jungle green uniforms were soon found wanting when inclement weather hit. With some foresight that their tour might stray into winter, each man also packed a kit bag with his winter serge battle dress uniforms.

As with all other items quickly assembled and stored for the voyage to Korea, personal field kit and webbing was also of Second World War vintage. All men wore the standard Type 37 pattern webbing, which consisted of a belt, two cross straps worn over the shoulders, two large pouches on the front of the webbing for carrying Bren gun magazines, a water bottle and a number of smaller pouches for items such as binoculars or compasses. A small pack and an entrenching tool rounded off the webbing, providing just enough space for a mess tin, some food, a blanket and a spare pair of socks. Very lightweight indeed.

***

While the men's personal weapons and kit were adequate, the same could not be said for their vehicles and transport. Given the speed and urgency with which the brigade had been stood up, it was told that they could hand back all vehicles currently held as they would be supplied with everything they required from the Americans upon arrival in Pusan. In retrospect, this was a particularly short-sighted order. While the US Army *as a whole* had an overwhelmingly large and efficient supply system, at that point in Korea – where its forces had been pushed back to a limited defensive perimeter – it had hardly enough for its own purposes, let alone to supply every need of its newly arrived and needy cousins in the Commonwealth Brigade.

Much too late, someone realized that failure to bring vehicles would be a mistake and seriously limit the ability of the brigade to conduct mobile operations. It would only be on the very last day prior to sailing that the original order was reversed and 27 Bde was told to bring its own complement of vehicles. Given that only one day remained to pack the waiting ships, very few brigade vehicles were able to be sourced, checked and loaded on board in time, with priority given to a number of jeeps for reconnaissance and liaison work.

This lack of integral transport would have implications for the mobility of 27 Bde and would dog it for many months. Limited to a small hodgepodge of barely serviceable vehicles, the demands of mobile warfare could only be met by overuse and eventual ruin of the small number of British vehicles, supplemented – and in the main compensated for – by expenditure of prodigious amounts of boot leather on the part of the foot-weary infantrymen. Again, the British troops would, as had happened many times in their history, just have to make do with what they had.

Nevertheless, Coad did have the foresight to pack some essentials for his British battalions to ensure that they had sufficient supplies to keep morale high: 'I always knew that the Americans were to ration us, so I took the precaution to take six months' tea and rum rations for my Brigade from Hong Kong.'[21] In his post-war report, Coad dryly noted: 'Rum is popular, but only the Brigade Commander authorises this issue.'[22] Not only was it popular with the troops, but the infrequent supply of alcohol to the British troops would also prove to be a useful and valuable barter item, particularly when dealing with Americans (who were theoretically 'dry' during their time in the field) and trading for high-value military equipment which the British needed but did not have.

Journey to Pusan

The effort to select, equip, train and embark an entire infantry brigade upon two large Royal Navy warships within five days was a feat for which Coad could be justifiably proud. Following a brigade parade and various pep talks by senior officers, including General Harding, who dispensed such invaluable wisdom as 'shoot straight and shoot to kill',[23] the aircraft carrier HMS *Unicorn* and cruiser HMS *Ceylon* steamed out of Hong Kong waters in the early hours of 25 August, heading towards Korea.

In one way, Brigade Headquarters and 1 MX had the better voyage as the aircraft carrier had significantly more room to accommodate the troops, as well as ample space on deck for exercise and training. The Argylls, on the other hand, found the *Ceylon* cramped and difficult, quartered on hammocks well below deck. It did, however, have one significant advantage as far as the troops were concerned. Whether by luck or good design, the *Ceylon* had the lion's share of good beer and whisky packed on board, all of which made for a pleasant voyage and compensated somewhat for the less-than-spacious quarters.

***

Three days later, on 27 August, 27 Bde landed at the South Korean port of Pusan. The dock was lined with a large group of cheering Korean dignitaries, civilians and a children's choir who gave a wobbly but heartfelt rendition of 'God Save the King' as the troops struggled down the gangplank with kitbags perched on their shoulders. The children were then very much surpassed by an extremely enthusiastic American Army band, noted by the British troops to be comprised exclusively of black American soldiers, who played a variety of tunes including the 1950 hit song 'If I'd known you were coming I'd have baked a cake'! It was a memorable welcome, still fondly remembered by all British veterans.

Pusan was at this time an extremely dilapidated and crowded city, swollen by refugees from the north. The sudden influx of thousands of US, and now British soldiers, together with the vast quantities of equipment, stores and supplies required to keep a modern army in the field, placed further pressure on Pusan's infrastructure. The city buckled under the strain, and as a result its streets were dirty, crowded and crammed with makeshift shanties and shacks.

While disembarkation was taking place, a new sensation was remarked upon by almost every member of the brigade – the awful smell of the place. General Matthew Ridgeway, who would later command the US Eighth Army in Korea, would pay a special tribute to the smells of Pusan: 'There is one feature that every fighting man will remember – the smell. The use of human excrement – night soil – to fertilize the fields, the husbanding of that commodity in pails and barrels, and in leaky wagons, give to the atmosphere of the country a fragrance so overpowering that the soul at first rebels.'[24]

Yet there was little time to get used to the sights and smells of Pusan. Nor was there much opportunity for acclimatization or any other training, as the thinly held perimeter around Pusan was still being hard pressed by the North Koreas. So after a quick meal of fresh bread, golden syrup and tea supplied by the Royal Navy, the newly arrived troops were herded onto old and filthy train carriages to commence their journey towards the front. What followed was a slow and uncomfortable six-hour journey north towards the railhead at Kyongsan, where 27 Bde spent a few days shaking out and making their final preparations. Then, on 3 September, the brigade moved up to its front-line positions on the Naktong River, the final barrier between UN forces and the North Korean Communists holding the far bank.

Chapter 3

Bridgehead on the Naktong River

US Army trucks bumped and rattled over the rough and winding dirt track, throwing up a cloud of yellow dust, coating both the trucks that followed and the British troops sitting on the hard benches of the open-topped vehicles. They were winding their way up onto the ridgeline which overlooked the lazy Naktong River, twinkling below them in the sunlight. The brigade was on its way to relieve a US unit which had been holding this part of the line. As the trucks bumped their way forward, the officers and men were able to survey the land that would be both their home, and their potential battlefield, over the weeks to come.

From their vantage point up in the hills, they could see that the land in front of them sloped relatively gently downwards, north and west, towards the river. The low-lying land between their ridgeline position and the river was carpeted by a series of rice and cotton fields. Here and there were scattered hamlets, mostly deserted now. Many of them were destroyed, with a number still emitting smoke – sending the newly arrived troops a clear message that intense fighting had very recently been conducted in this area. The river itself was not particularly deep but could not be waded, and thus formed a formidable barrier to advancing troops, a major reason that the Communists were still camped on the other side of the river. The other side of the Naktong was essentially the same type of land but in reverse – farmland and ruined villages abutting the foothills, which rose into larger mountains to the north, where the British knew that thousands of enemy soldiers, tanks and artillery were waiting for them.

As the British troops came forward, the US soldiers currently manning the trenches and positions along the ridgeline appeared to be in a very great hurry to leave and get back towards Pusan. There was very little in the way of a formal handover, an apparent lack of professionalism on the part of the Americans that did not impress Coad. Not for the first time, he would look disapprovingly upon the American allies whom he was relieving. The 27 Bde men taking over the defences also found that many of the trenches and defensive works were only half-built, dilapidated, filthy and filled with rubbish and refuse. The newly arriving British soldiers were quickly sent to work clearing the positions, improving trenches and laying communications wire between the various command posts.

While the state of the current defences was less than ideal Coad knew that these could be improved relatively quickly with some hard work. Of much more concern to Coad and his battalion commanders were the huge gaps of several thousand yards between each of his battalions and the flanking units on either side. With such a large perimeter and relatively few men, it was simply impossible to cover every square foot of ground with either manpower or firepower. Attempts were made to cover gaps in the line by artillery coverage. UN superiority in airpower was also useful, but the fact remained that the poor infantryman on the ground often felt quite isolated. No infantryman wants his flanks exposed and open to a surprise assault from the enemy. But the gaps were there, and all Coad could do to mitigate the risk was to cover the ground by the use of frequent foot patrols and through pre-registering artillery fire on likely enemy assault routes. It was not ideal, and the situation continued to worry Coad. On the other hand, the men appeared to be generally happy, their morale was high and they were quietly, albeit a little nervously, looking forward to testing themselves against the enemy.

Although Coad fretted about the gaps in his defences, the brigade was actually very lucky in terms of timing when it arrived on the Naktong. While the first artillery or mortar round arching over their positions caused men to run for their trenches and gave everyone a fright, the first few days otherwise saw little direct contact with the enemy. It was a relatively gentle introduction to combat and soldiering on the front lines, allowing 27 Bde to shake out and get into the rhythm of soldiering in a combat zone. Meanwhile, those few soldiers who were anxious at the thought of being in Korea had time to face and overcome their fears.

The 27 Bde War Diary is all very upbeat and positive at this time, and you can sense the very earnest and slightly excited atmosphere which pervaded the entire formation. Willoughby, with his cultured and artistic eye, notes in his diary that he was very happy to have found a clump of persimmon trees to site his D Company HQ, 'a bit of shelter from the rain'. Of more practical importance were the eight field telephones and bundles of wire that his 2IC (second-in-command) had 'liberated' from somewhere, making it possible to run telephones to all of his platoons and thus stay in regular contact with them.

Nevertheless, while the brigade was bedding in a low-level anxiety remained, hovering over everyone. They knew the enemy was close by and were wondering when the blow would fall. Night was the worst for exercising men's fears: 'In the front lines nights are always hateful, they last for ever and trees whisper to each other in perpetual disquiet, bushes seem to move and here starving dogs from deserted villages roam amongst them.'[25]

While the bulk of the North Korean forces on the far side of the Naktong were being suspiciously quiet, Communist guerrillas were making a nuisance of themselves to Coad's rear. There were thought to be up to several thousand Communist guerrillas inside the Pusan pocket and behind the front lines. In typical guerrilla fashion, these small bands often raided isolated outposts, destroyed military equipment and conducted propaganda activities. The task of eradicating these bands was given to the South Korean police, who were neither properly equipped nor trained to winkle out guerrillas in the countryside. A programme was thus set up to team the local police with an infantry unit to give the police more firepower.

Willoughby and his D Company were given the task of liaising with the local police forces. While the local police chief had nearly a hundred men at his disposal, they were not an impressive lot: poorly armed, ill-trained and appearing to even lack sufficient food to feed themselves. It was not an inspiring start, and Willoughby was quickly bombarded with requests for weapons, ammunition and food, which he tried to source through brigade and divisional channels. Besides lack of basic equipment, Willoughby also discovered that there was a distinct lack of leadership and very little will among the police to go up into the hills and seek out the guerrillas. Accordingly, Willoughby and his men soon found themselves taking the lead in organizing patrols, setting ambushes and getting after the guerrilla bands. They had some successes; his platoons were engaged in a number of minor actions which had the effect of both disrupting the Communists and encouraging the police. These actions also gave confidence to his men, for most of whom this was their first taste of combat.

Willoughby became less and less impressed with the police commander the more he got to know him (he was suspected of siphoning off a large portion of the weapons and food provided to him – likely sold to the guerrillas themselves for profit). Nevertheless, the D Company commander enjoyed the freedom that independent operations with the police gave him. It was far better than being stuck manning the trenches above the Naktong.

***

The brigade's idyll on the Naktong was never expected to last, and on 15 September it was 'warned out' to be ready to take part in the upcoming 'breakout' from the perimeter. Willoughby expressed some concern that the police guerrilla sweeps to their rear were not yet complete, so there was a risk of leaving enemy groups behind them. But this was a very minor consideration and soon all of the officers and men of 1 MX who were advising the police were brought back to their units to make preparations for the breakout.

Unfortunately, the planned breakout did not materialize. As all too frequently happens in war, orders were changed at the last minute, much to the frustration of the officers and men who were preparing to carry them out. While soldiers will often grumble and grouse about such 'hurry up and wait' situations, it is a regular and expected part of war.

With the orders rescinded, the 27 Bde resumed its defence of the Naktong and general patrolling of the area. Willoughby's men were permitted to return to their police comrades to finish the job of eradicating the guerrilla menace.

***

These initial weeks on the Naktong, manning the defensive positions, gave the British troops an opportunity to find out something about their enemy, their equipment and habits. This was critical, as there had been almost no time to properly evaluate who they were going to fight during the rushed preparations for departure from Hong Kong.

In terms of dress and equipment, the North Koreans had benefitted greatly from their five years of Soviet tutelage. While the hard core of the NKPA had seen fighting in China during both the Second World War and Chinese Civil War, at the end of the latter conflict they were still organized mainly on guerrilla lines and equipped with captured Japanese weapons, along with a small number of American and British weapons. With the end of the war, however, the Soviets had spent a great deal of time and resources equipping the NKPA with modern Soviet equipment. Besides heavy items such as T-34 tanks and self-propelled artillery, infantry down at the platoon level were now equipped with Soviet rifles, light machine guns and the ubiquitous 'burp guns' that would soon be familiar to all UN forces who faced a NKPA attack.

The burp gun – the M1941 PPsh Shpagin sub-machine gun – was a 7.62mm light sub-machine gun which made a distinctive 'burp' sound when fired, thus earning it its nickname. It had a round drum magazine, similar in shape to a small side plate, and was capable of emitting a high rate of fire. Despite its inaccuracy, it was a fearsome weapon in close-quarter combat and assaults. Unlike UN forces, who tended to have more rifles than sub-machine guns in a typical infantry platoon, the NKPA issued the burp gun in great quantities, usually more than the stock of standard rifles, as the NKPA philosophy gave great emphasis to the weight of fire during an assault rather than single soldier's accuracy.

As for fighting qualities, an experienced Argyll company commander described the North Korean soldiers thus: 'He was not unlike the Japanese in his habits, but I would say he is about 33 percent as good by day, and only 50 percent as good by night … his positions, though good and well concealed, are nothing like as good as the Japanese positions.'[26] This comment could betray a slight bias on the part of a Second World War veteran towards the fighting abilities of his former adversary, but nevertheless, it was an observation that was backed up by other similar assessments. The comment could also reflect the very uneven quality of the North Korean troops arrayed against them. While the NKPA's Second World War veteran troops were certainly battle-hardened, there were also many more recent additions, such as Junior Lieutenant Hong Kwan To. Hong was a 20-year-old student conscripted into the North Korean army on 4 September 1950. Because of his middle school education, he was sent to officer training school, where he graduated as a junior officer just eleven days later. He was immediately sent to the front, where he joined his division on 27 September. By 11 October, he had been captured by ROK forces. Hong's total time in uniform, from conscription to capture, was just over one month, demonstrating that for all of the Soviet equipment, the NKPA nevertheless had some very significant weaknesses in terms of training and manpower.[27]

Despite the uneven qualities of their NKPA opponents, the ROK troops had a very healthy respect for their adversaries: 'The NKPA was accomplished at night fighting and at combat in mountainous terrain, and its commanders concentrated mercilessly on our vulnerabilities and shortcomings.'[28] Their political officers were also tough, using a combination of Communist rhetoric, propaganda and slogans, doused with a healthy amount of carefully applied violence to force troops to continue frontal assaults even in the face of stiff resistance.

Two months of constant fighting was having an effect on the strength of the NKPA troops. They had already taken many casualties, and in order to keep up numbers the North Koreans had started to press-gang a number of 'volunteer' civilians from the Seoul area to fill their ranks. General Paik noted that 'the breath of NKPA prisoners and wounded smelled of alcohol. The enemy was giving liquor to the youthful "volunteers" and committing them to the assault.'[29] These men were given almost no training and pushed immediately into the front line, with predictable results. Paik explained how some ROK soldiers under his command felt a certain amount of sympathy for the enemy, knowing that at least some of them were civilians pressed into service, but for the British troops, unable to tell the difference, any man holding a gun against him was the enemy.

The Inchon Landings

While 27 Bde was dealing with frustrations on its section of the Pusan perimeter, a daring and potentially war-winning event was taking place approximately 300km to the north-west at the port of Inchon.

From almost the moment he took command, MacArthur had been planning a daring seaborne landing to the north and behind enemy lines as a way of surprising the North Koreans, with the aim of cutting their overly exposed supply lines and wresting the initiative back from them. The plan was admittedly a gamble, but was exactly the sort of action that had paid off for MacArthur in the past and spoke directly of his desire for bold, 'war-winning' moves rather than the patient plodding preferred by many of his peers. As Ridgeway noted in his memoirs: 'While others thought of a way to withdraw our forces safely, MacArthur planned for victory.'[30]

The plan, dubbed Operation Chromite, called for a landing of up to 40,000 US and South Korean troops, mainly drawn from the US Marines, at the port of Inchon, a mere 20 miles from Seoul. Initially, MacArthur's top Navy and Marine planning officers strongly opposed landing at Inchon. These men, with experience gained the hard way through many amphibious landings during the Second World War, told MacArthur that a landing at Inchon was impractical and dangerous, primarily due to the narrowness of the position and the huge variation between low and high tide. The tides were critical, providing an optimum landing window of a mere two hours each day. This was wise advice from men who knew their business, but MacArthur preferred another counsel which he trusted implicitly – his own. Recognizing the gamble, MacArthur is reported to have said: 'For a five dollar ante, I have an opportunity to win $50,000, and I have decided that is what I am going to do.'[31]

In the early hours of 15 September, a massive force of UN naval and air assets proceeded to bombard NKPA positions around Inchon. These were soon followed by waves of assaulting Marines, who had to knock out several enemy gun emplacements and take the port within a restrictive timeframe imposed by the peculiarly severe tides in and around the Inchon area. The audacity of the attack took the enemy by surprise: the Marines quickly took Inchon and proceeded to move inland to assault and capture Kimpo, the main airfield serving Seoul.

The landings were an unrivalled success and have often been described as a one of MacArthur's most brilliant strategic masterstrokes. The seemingly 'impossible' landing of so many men well behind the NKPA lines completely confused the North Korean command. Their already overstretched lines of communication to the front on the Naktong were severed, and there was a real risk of the North Koreans further south being cut off and then smashed between the hammer of the Marines and the anvil of the UN forces which were just now starting to break out from their Naktong bridgehead.

With Inchon and Kimpo now secured, the Marines moved towards Seoul. A terribly vicious battle would take place over the next two weeks to liberate the capital, which would see horrendous destruction of the city and large numbers of casualties on both sides before the North Koreans were ejected and reluctantly withdrew north, back towards Pyongyang.

***

With the North Koreans now wholly occupied with the surprise thrust to their rear at Inchon, the pressure on the Pusan perimeter and 27 Bde slackened considerably. Nevertheless, despite the relative quiet, the odd enemy scouting party was still to be found during the brigade's patrols into no man's land. On 18 September, one enemy party even made its way to a forward 1 ASH platoon position and lobbed a few grenades into a Vickers machine-gun post, killing one soldier and wounding another. These were the brigade's first casualties, a sobering reminder that even a supposedly quiet sector could soon turn deadly. It also bears keeping in mind that the 27 Bde had been inordinately lucky over its first two weeks in the line. Despite the British experience, the Naktong perimeter was anything but quiet; other UN and ROK troops had been engaged in significant fighting on a daily basis as the North Koreans desperately tried to hammer home their advantage and drive their opponents into the sea. Reports in early September were that UN forces in the pocket were suffering daily casualties in the order of 1,000 men killed or wounded. While it certainly wasn't MacArthur's plan, many serious and thoughtful commanders – as well as politicians of friendly nations –

assumed that it would only be a matter of time until the UN forces were crushed and forced to evacuate to Japan.

The Inchon landings shocked the North Koreans, surprised friendly governments and gave great heart to all of the men manning the trenches and positions along the Naktong. With US forces now positioned in strength to the north, the British troops were convinced that they had a fighting chance of breaking out and pushing the invaders back over the 38th parallel.

20 September

The brigade finally moved out of its Naktong defences on 20 September. The men first moved back a short way to an assembly area, awaiting final orders from US 24th Division HQ. Orders duly arrived, but no sooner had Coad read them than they were cancelled and new ones were issued. These too were quickly cancelled and replaced yet again. To say that Coad was unimpressed with what he saw as 'sloppy staff work and indecision on the part of some American commanders'[32] is an understatement. His ire was raised, and he would continue to complain about this incident even after the war.

The final orders for 27 Bde was for them to cross the Naktong to the west of their current positions and take two prominent hill complexes which straddled the winding dirt road to the town of Songju. The 27 Bde War Diary neatly summarizes the mission as follows: 'The role of the Brigade is to cross the Naktong River and attack along the axis of the road, capture Songju and drive onto Kumchon and protect the left flank of 24 Division.'[33]

The prospect of imminent offensive action was eagerly looked forward to by many in the brigade, but less welcome was the sudden removal of their supporting artillery. The War Diary recorded: 'It was learned that our supporting artillery would not accompany the Brigade on its future operations. This was regretted as a close and friendly co-operation had sprung up between the Brigade and 77 and 82 FA [Field Artillery] during the time they had been with us.'[34]

Artillery would play a decisive role in both attack and defence for the duration of the war, and any significant action without indirect fire support was likely to result in slowness, increased casualties and, at worst, failure. The lack of organic artillery was a constant concern for Coad until he finally received a regiment of New Zealand 25-pdrs in early 1951. Coad was acutely aware that his brigade was under-gunned, and he immediately appealed to the divisional commander for additional fire support to cover his assault. He was successful. Although all UN units were likewise clamouring for scarce indirect fire resources, Coad must have been extremely persuasive as he obtained a commitment of significant artillery assets in the form of four self-propelled 105mm guns, a battalion of 155mm guns and five Sherman tanks.[35]

On 21 September, with the false starts behind them, Coad was finally able to give the order for his brigade to move out of its positions and commence the drive across the Naktong.

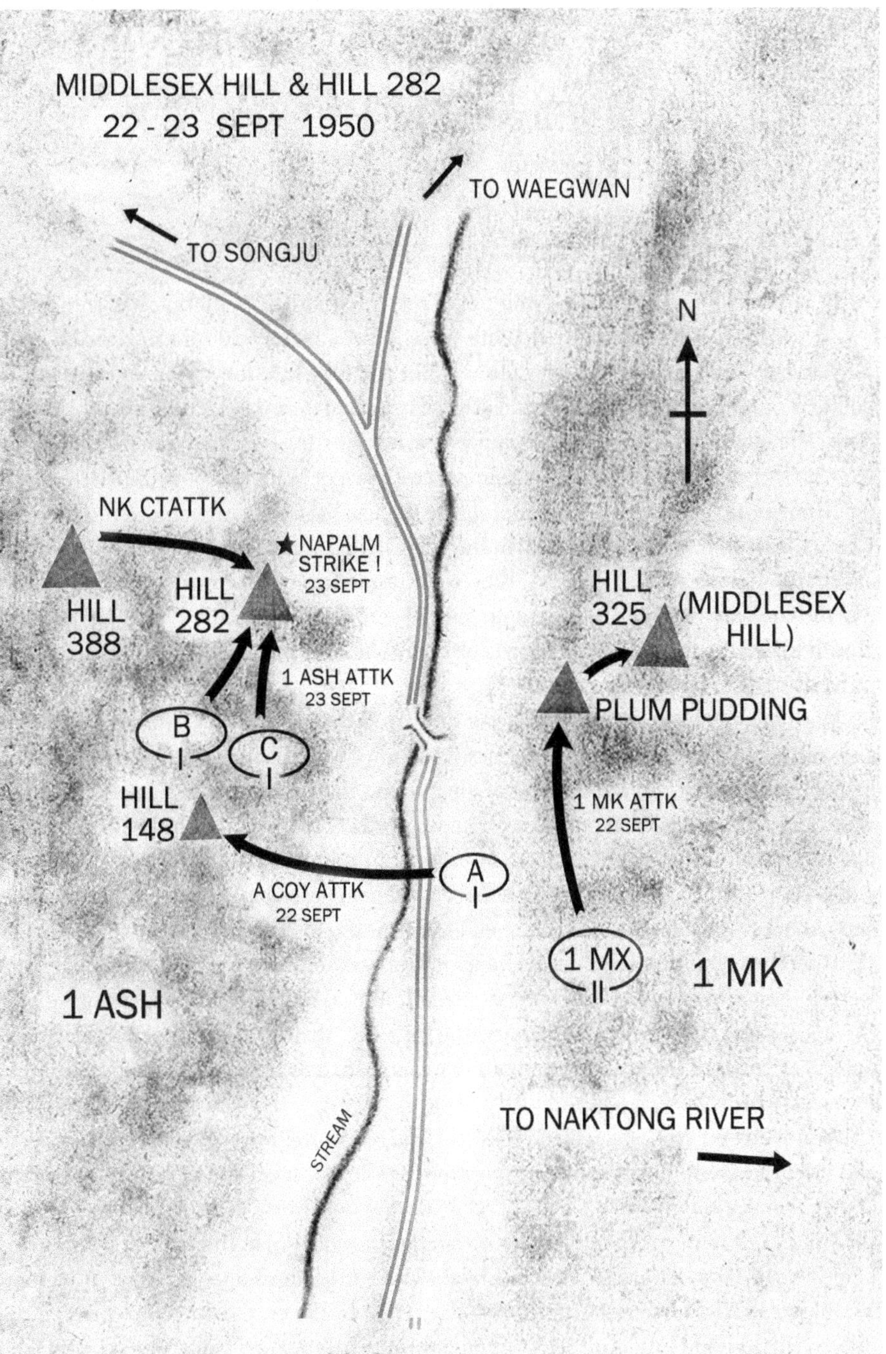

MIDDLESEX HILL & HILL 282
22 - 23 SEPT 1950
TO WAEGWAN
TO SONGJU
N
NK CTATTK
NAPALM
STRIKE !
23 SEPT
HILL
388
HILL
282
1 ASH ATTK
23 SEPT
B
C
HILL
148
A
A COY ATTK
22 SEPT
1 ASH
STREAM
HILL
325
(MIDDLESEX
HILL)
PLUM PUDDING
1 MK ATTK
22 SEPT
1 MX
II
1 MK
TO NAKTONG RIVER

Chapter 4

Fire on the Hills

Approaching the crossing point over the Naktong River, 27 Bde was confronted with a wide, languidly flowing river approximately 300 metres across at its narrowest point. The brigade was not the first UN formation to cross at this point, as significant US Army forces had already moved over the river during the past few days. The majority of these troops had now swung northwards and were paralleling the west bank of the Naktong towards the important town of Waegwan. Nevertheless, a small detachment of US troops remained in place to guard the western bank of the Naktong where the British were crossing, including, crucially, a small number of Sherman tanks.

As the British moved forward, they were immediately confronted by several dead North Koreans lying on the tracks or pushed into the surrounding scrub. This was a ghastly sight, the bodies having been repeatedly run over by trucks and tanks, each time pulverising the remains.

With most bridges over the Naktong destroyed by retreating UN forces in the early days of the war, 27 Bde's passage over the Naktong would be by a narrow 'Kapok' foot bridge. This was a precarious type of single-lane footbridge, with planks and bits of wood laid across wooden kapok floats: '…a very rickety footbridge. The [original] bridge had been demolished by the Americans earlier in the campaign. Since then it had been patched up and its 300 yard length consisted of cement slabs, sections of assault boats and rubber floats, bits of wood and metal and sandbags.'[36]

It was impossible to transport vehicles or heavy equipment over the footbridge; they were to be taken over later by way of a small, motorized ferry. After depositing only three jeeps and two tracked carriers on the far bank, the ferry's engines suddenly gave out. As a result, all ammunition and heavy weapons had to be gingerly manhandled over the rickety bridge.

At 1500hrs, 1 MX started to cross the bridge. As the men shouldered their loads and began to cross in single file, intermittent shellfire started to fall nearby, indicating clearly that the enemy were watching their every move. Most shells landed wide, either shooting geysers of water into the air or landing harmlessly in the far rice paddies and muddy banks. Nevertheless, stray bits of shrapnel did cause some casualties among the Middlesex men – fortunately nothing too serious. In the end, neither the shelling nor the casualties could hold up 1 MX's momentum, with the men being urged on by their commanders to swiftly cross the bridge and seek shelter on the far bank.

By 1930hrs, all of the battalion had crossed the river and taken up positions to the north-west of the crossing point, within easy striking distance of their objective, code named 'Apple', sitting directly ahead of them. Apple was a significant hill feature to the north (right-hand side) of the Songju road. It was a prominent feature, rising out of the otherwise flat paddy fields which flanked the river bank. Apple rose to a height of approximately 200 metres. It was relatively steep on the southern side (facing the 1 MX troops' lying-up position), with comparatively gentler slopes to the eastern and northern sides. Covering the hill, and in marked contrast to the land below, the whole of the summit of Apple was covered by scrub and the odd dwarf pine.

Even though 1 MX had crossed in good order, Lieutenant Colonel Man decided that due to the late hour, the assault on Apple should be postponed until dawn the next day. With strict orders to remain silent and not light any fires, the Middlesex men settled in for a long and cold night, waiting for the dawn.

The rickety Kapok bridge had thrown the 1 ASH timetable even further behind schedule. While originally planned to take their allotted hill features – Hill 282 and the Songsan hill which lay to the south (or left-hand side) of the Songju road – the slow crossing of 1 MX meant that the Jocks would barely be across before nightfall, meaning it was impossible to mount an attack until later the next day. Undeterred, the men of 1 ASH kept up their single-file crossing of the Naktong, carrying not only their own weapons and kit, but also the heavy weapons – 3in mortars and Vickers medium machine guns (MMGs) – ammunition and all stores necessary for their attack the following day. A dump for excess ammunition was made on the far bank and the men started the nearly 2km march up to their nighttime harbour and lying-up positions – which consisted of a slightly raised area near the road and nestled in the foothills of the objectives beyond.

Even now, the British troops were becoming very familiar with the sounds associated with enemy shelling and could easily distinguish between incoming and outgoing shells, as well as the difference between mortars and the bigger shells hurled from the self-propelled guns. But whatever the source of the fire, the general sequence of sounds at the receiving end were always the same: 'First comes the whine – a crescendo and a wicked crump, then another and another and suddenly a silence except for the patter of stones and earth raining down followed by the pick, pick, pick of everyone digging a little deeper.'[37] Even with only a few shells incoming that night, almost everyone thought it prudent to dig a slightly deeper slit trench.

Plum Pudding and Middlesex Hills

Before dawn on 22 September, 'after a perishingly cold night and no breakfast',[38] the men of 1 MX formed up at their start positions for the attack on Apple. The objective consisted of two closely connected features, originally known by the code names of Apple and Pear, but which, following the day's fighting, would forever be known by the

Middlesex men's nicknames of 'Plum Pudding Hill' (so called because its gentle rounded top resembled an English plum pudding) and the much higher 'Middlesex Hill'.

Moving out in the pre-dawn mist, A and D Companies secured a series of low ridges (Hill 148) to the south of the hill complex, which would act as their forming up points for the main attack. Scanning the hills before him, Man realized that an assault directly north towards Middlesex Hill would expose his companies to a long assault over open ground. This was unacceptable, making them intensely exposed and vulnerable to enemy fire. Accordingly, his plan called for a two-stage attack. Firstly, B Company would assault the smaller Plum Pudding Hill from the flank, supported by fire from A Company and the battalion's medium machine guns. After consolidating on Plum Pudding Hill, D Company would conduct a longer flanking attack on Middlesex Hill to take the considerably higher and more difficult summit to the east. To carry out this manoeuvre, D Company would swing around to their right and assault the hill under the relatively protected ground of the eastern slope. All the while, D Company would be supported by fire from the A and B Company men atop Plum Pudding Hill, as well as battalion mortars and medium machine guns.

It was a sound plan, and at 0630hrs, B Company's 4 Platoon, commanded by the tall, young Second Lieutenant Christopher Lawrence, led the advance towards Plum Pudding Hill. Lawrence was a relatively new and inexperienced officer. He had graduated from Sandhurst in 1949 and only joined the battalion in June 1950, a mere two months before deployment to Korea. Despite his lack of experience, he was a natural and capable leader who had already won the respect of both his men and his superiors.

The preparatory move towards the flank was unopposed, but Lawrence's platoon then suddenly started to take heavy fire from the top of the objective and an adjacent spur line. Understanding instinctively that to halt in the face of such accurate fire raining down from the high ground would lead to a loss of momentum, and likely high casualties, Lawrence immediately sought out two nearby US Sherman tanks to try to bring supporting fire. Rapping on the hatch to gain the attention of one of the tank commanders, he quickly directed their powerful fire towards the threatening enemy positions. With his fire support now in place, Lawrence raced back to his platoon to continue the assault.

With the enemy now preoccupied by incoming tank fire, Lawrence's men were able to make their way up the scree-lined scrubby slope until they crested the hill and made their way through the enemy positions.

However, 4 Platoon was alone. None of the other platoons had yet crested the ridgeline, and 4 Platoon's flanks were terribly exposed. Sensing an opportunity, the enemy continued to pour fire into Lawrence's platoon from multiple hidden locations, while the ever-present pestilence of NKPA mortar bombs started to fall around them.

The NKPA, particularly good at employing their artillery assets, continued to lob bombs at Lawrence's men on and near the crest. While the incessant bombardments were hated by the Commonwealth troops, the enemy artillerymen had gained their grudging respect. 'They were crafty', was how one Middlesex soldier described the North Korean artillery and mortar crews. They were 'not as daft as people say' and were 'spot on with the mortars and the SP guns'.[39] These compliments aside, the incessant mortaring and artillery fire continued to dog Lawrence's men, who instinctively crouched a little lower to the ground that they had just liberated.

Undeterred, Lawrence placed his men in defensive positions and continued to direct their fire at the enemy until other elements of the company finally made their way into their allotted positions. With more British troops arriving, the North Koreans had had enough; those that could do so quickly made their way down the northern slope, dodging in and out of the scrub and using the folds in the ground to escape. The remainder now lay around Lawrence's men, dead, testament to this short but fiercely fought little battle. Shortly thereafter, a signal was sent that B Company had secured Plum Pudding Hill, protecting the right flank of the road to Songju.

As the morning progressed and the sun rose higher, the work of the assaulting infantry made them hot and sweaty. A Company – tired, thirsty and hungry – soon joined B Company, adding weight to their position and readying themselves for the next phase of the plan, the attack towards Middlesex Hill.

Pleased at the success of B Company, Man soon moved up his remaining unit, D Company under Major Willoughby, for the attack on the taller and more forbidding Middlesex Hill. Moving steadily but with purpose, Willoughby pushed his men to scramble forward and up the steep eastern slopes of Middlesex hill. The wicked supporting fire from the battalion's mortars and Vickers MMGs was keeping enemy heads down and gave D Company the breathing room it needed to get to the lower slopes of Middlesex Hill. Fortuitously, the battalion fire support was augmented by a battery of American artillery, which the American Forward Air Controller decided (on his own initiative) to call up to assist in the fight. This additional firepower was very welcome, clearing a path for D Company as they strove to consolidate on top of Middlesex Hill just before last light.[40]

Despite the artillery support, D Company endured a hard, hot and difficult fight to the top of Middlesex Hill. Using the ground to their advantage, advancing up the steep slope in penny packet rushes, the D Company men finally gained the top of the hill, only to discover that there was another, previously hidden ridge ahead of them extending east–west, like the long leg of an upside-down L. Enemy machine-gun and rifle fire poured into Willoughby's precarious toe hold at the top of his false summit. This hidden enemy position made life difficult and Willoughby was worried that he might not have enough men or fire support to neutralize this threat before last light. Fortunately, he was soon joined by an American artillery observer, who calmly said 'leave this to me'. Superb shooting saw a hail of 155mm rounds hurtle down on the hapless defenders with sickening accuracy. The American gunners deeply impressed

Willoughby that day and quickly made a serious dent in the enemy, who were soon either dead or seen escaping in double-quick time. Moving forward and inspecting the slight dip where the enemy machine-gun positions had until recently been sighted, Willoughby noted the devastation, the litter of human remains, bits of field dressings, blood and mangled remains of Russian machine guns. But for the timely and accurate artillery fire, D Company would have had a very difficult job to prise the North Koreans from their hold on Middlesex Hill. Willoughby said a silent prayer in thanks for their fortuitous deliverance.

The Middlesex men's actions at Plum Pudding Hill and Middlesex Hill were textbook examples of solid infantry skills and tactics, expertly employed and with a great deal of dash and initiative. Major Rendell, commander of A Company, remarked that 'Andrew Man did a superb, staff college attack on the hill'.[41] Willoughby was less complimentary of Man's leadership (the two of them had a frosty relationship throughout their time in Korea). In contrast to Rendell, Willoughby complained that Man spent most of the battle on the other side of the river, out of contact with his companies, and left much of the fighting to Willoughby, as well as leaving the organization of ammunition, food and water to the company commanders after the attack. Water was in particularly short supply, so Willoughby had to send men to capture a small spring in order to supply his parched and thirsty unit. Willoughby was particularly displeased when, the first time he saw Man after the battle, he was overheard speaking to Coad about Willoughby's lack of grooming. Willoughby disgustedly commented: 'I was a little surprised when Brigadier Coad and Andrew Man paid their first visit to our captured hill to hear him remark that he was surprised I hadn't shaved and for Andrew Man to say that he was too. I thought it was unworthy of them both.'[42]

Griping between battalion and company commanders aside, it was clear that the Middlesex men had given a particularly good account of themselves on Plum Pudding and Middlesex hills. All of them had done well, but Lawrence had stood out. Recognizing the vital impact that Lawrence's leadership made to the battalion's success, Man recommended Lawrence for a Military Cross (MC), the first of the Korean War. The citation reads in part: 'The success of this platoon … was entirely the result of the very fine example of leadership, initiative and determination which this officer displayed over a period of several hours in the face of a superior enemy force.'[43]

This short, sharp battle came with losses. The enemy suffered an estimated fifty casualties, while 1 MX lost an officer (Second Lieutenant Geoff White) as well as five men killed. A further six men were wounded in action.

While the wounded were evacuated rearwards towards the regimental aid post for treatment, the bodies of the dead were buried in the shade of some trees and under a cairn of stones with a rough cross fashioned from what wood they could find. It was not much, but it was at least a decent burial, attended by the dead's fellow soldiers and friends. Willoughby said a few words from his small pocketbook Bible.[44] There was no time or transport available to repatriate the bodies at this time, with the Brigade still actively fighting and trying to push through the enemy defences. The dead would need to wait for reinterment at a later date.

At the time, these casualties hardly rated a mention in the contemporary records and diaries, yet by today's standards they are significant numbers. It is an indication of just how intense the fighting in Korea was that six KIA and another six WIA would be regarded as an 'unremarkable' day in Korea.

Dealing with the dead and wounded weighed on commanders at all levels throughout the conflict in Korea. Willoughby noted a few days later, after 27 Bde had finally captured Songju, that he had to face the unpleasant but wholly necessary task of penning a letter to the family of each man killed. 'It's always so hard to know what to say', Willoughby conceded to his diary in late September, 'knowing how every word of yours will be re-read for ever and the wretched inadequacy of your endeavours. God knows how they managed in 1914–18.'[45]

The fading light brought a cool evening, which was keenly felt by the Middlesex men, kitted only in their light and sweat-soaked uniforms, lying on the cold ground. They did not even have the comfort of their jumpers, blankets or other equipment, which was still in the packs they had shed prior to the attack. Most importantly, they had precious little food and water, and thus faced another cold night together with rumbling stomachs.

1 ASH – Hill 148

When the Diehards were making their assault preparations in the pre-dawn gloom, 1 ASH was being stood-to in all-round defence, ready to meet whatever the NKPA would send towards them. But the cold morning was uneventful on the Argylls' front, the men shivering in their slit trenches and fighting positions, staring out into the gloom for a glimpse of the enemy until the sun eventually rose.

Leaving B Company in possession of their overnight firm base, A and C Companies moved forward with the objective of securing a small hill approximately 2km to their front, named Hill 148. However, delays caused them to remain in position for several hours before they could commence their assault.

Seeing a small detachment of US tanks to his front (consisting of both light Chaffees and the slightly heavier Shermans), the newly arrived commander of A Company, Major David Wilson, decided to see if he could enlist their support for his attack. Making contact with the tank commander, a plan was readily devised to have three tanks form up to the left of Wilson's line of advance and provide fire support. Grabbing a US walkie-talkie from the tank troops (the British radios being unable to communicate with the American tanks), Wilson planned to talk the newly acquired armoured support forward to assist his troops.

By mid-afternoon, with the distant sounds of the 1 MX assault on Plum Pudding Hill drifting through the now hot air towards them, A Company left its assembly area. Its forward platoon was spread out in an extended line, marching steadily towards the raised ground of Hill 148. The men must have felt terribly exposed as they moved forward over the flat paddy field, with little in the way of cover between them and the slopes of the hill. The enemy responded in their usual fashion, the odd mortar round plopping with a muffled explosion into the soft paddy fields and mud to the front of the hill complex. Incredibly, no one was injured, but one or two rounds fell within a hundred metres of the advancing troops, making life uncomfortable for the Jocks and perhaps quickening the pace a step or two.

Speed was always important, but it still took the advancing troops over an hour before they had traversed the intervening land and ascended the small slope up to the top of Hill 148. As they were climbing, the men in the forward unit, 3 Platoon, spotted a party of four NKPA troops holding the crest. Wilson immediately called on the tanks to provide fire support along the crest of the hill and a small feature to its left that he guessed held more enemy troops. As Wilson had already indicated both of these features to the tank commanders prior to commencing the assault, they had no difficulty in traversing their guns onto them. They commenced to lay down a barrage of intense .50 calibre machine-gun fire into these positions. While the machine guns did their job in supressing the enemy to the front, the accurate fire from the tanks below also attracted the attention of the defending NKPA, who turned their fire towards the tanks. So intense was the return fire from the NKPA that some of the tank commanders, exposed in the turrets of their vehicles and directing fire, were wounded in the exchange.

The supporting fire of the tanks was decisive, allowing the men of A Company to surge forwards and up the last slope of the hill until they reached the crest and ejected all of the enemy soldiers holding it. In the end, this was a classic piece of infantry–armour co-operation, resulting in the taking of the important Hill 148 with no casualties suffered amongst the Jocks. Wilson was obviously very pleased with his first major action leading A Company. Later, in the battalion War Diary, he proceeded to record what he thought were the main 'lessons' from the action – namely, speed of the assault, communication with the supporting armour via walkie-talkie and providing good target indications to the tanks. Wilson noted: '[P]rovided that at least one easily recognisable point has been fixed, it is quite simple to direct the tank fire onto another. But something must be fixed on the ground first, or neither party will have any idea of what the other is talking about.'[46]

Wilson's last and most important lesson was, 'GO FOR THE HIGH GROUND', a point he emphasized by making sure that it was both written in capitals and underlined. Wilson realized the importance of this feature, which even though not the highest, was locally a dominant point, the capture of which allowed the Argylls to overlook the ground around them. This focus on dominating the high ground would be a feature of 27 Bde tactics for the remainder of the war. Again and again, Coad and his subordinate commanders would stress the absolutely vital need to clear all surrounding high points on their route of march, and to take and defend important hill features wherever possible. Many times, both during and after the war, 27 Bde commanders decried the apparent US practice of merely barrelling along a route as fast as possible (the Patton approach!) without clearing all high ground to the flanks, leaving their troops on the lower ground vulnerable to observation and fire from the high ground. It was only later in the war, after many costly mistakes had been made, that the Americans finally learned the necessity for infantry–armour co-operation and the need to secure the high ground.

***

Wilson had originally planned for Hill 148 to be a mere way point on the route to the more important Hill 282. However, his men would eventually hold Hill 148 for nearly four days. It was getting late, and while they were cheered by the news of the Middlesex men's successes to their east, insufficient daylight remained for them to continue their attack that day. The assault on Hill 282 would necessarily need to be postponed until the next morning. As darkness fell, the Jocks settled into their usual routine of digging trenches and fighting positions. While one man stayed vigilant with his weapon pointed outwards, guarding his friend, his opposite number would be busy digging and constructing the fighting position. They would then swap, this continuing for an hour or so until a narrow trench was built with the spoil spread behind. The daily chore of digging was something that was never skimped on, no matter how tired the men were, for one simple reason: digging saved lives. Woe betide a man who did not have at least a shell scrape to protect him if the enemy made a sudden assault or a stray artillery or mortar round fell around their position.

As Wilson's men were setting their defences, the battalion commander, Lieutenant Colonel Neilson, together with the B and C Company commanders, had gone forward. They conducted a reconnaissance of the objective, forming-up points and likely assault routes that they would take the next morning. Recognizing that it would be a tough climb, and almost certain that there would be a strong enemy presence at the top, Neilson made sure to obtain the assistance of whatever indirect-fire weapons he could get his hands on. Returning after last light, Neilson called his O Group (Orders Group) and gave his instructions for the attack the following day. The assault would be led by B and C Companies, with A Company maintaining its 'firm base' on Hill 148, the 'one foot on the ground' that was a fundamental tenant of infantry tactics. It was wisdom tested and verified over many years that you should never have all your men moving at the same time. Rather, you must have *one foot on the ground* providing cover while the manoeuvre elements moved forward.

Recognizing the vital assistance that armour could provide, like Wilson and Willoughby before him, Neilson now sought support from the Sherman tanks which were on the west bank of the Naktong and had already been used to such good effect that day. He also obtained artillery support in the form of a battery of 105mm guns from the US 13th Battalion Field Artillery. While the Sherman tanks would be useful in covering his men on the lower slopes, their guns were unable to rise to a high angle, leaving the Jocks wholly dependent of the 105mm field guns for support at higher elevations.[47]

Once orders were given, the Argylls settled into another cold but reasonably uneventful night. Their positions were not attacked, but they could still hear and see the thump and explosions of an intermittent but rather lacklustre artillery duel taking place between the NKPA and UN forces in the distance. Thankfully, the Jocks were unmolested, which gave the heavy weapons teams time to bring up further ammunition for the machine guns and mortars from the river bank, where it had been previously cached.

Meanwhile, efforts during the night to bring up more heavy equipment and bulk ammunition failed. With some brigade soldiers working manfully to repair the river ferry throughout the day, they were devastated when during the early evening it received a direct hit from artillery fire. This unlucky shot put paid to any hope of moving across heavy equipment or vehicles to support the infantry around their hill complexes. This left the brigade with the only option of carrying supplies and ammunition, one man at a time, over the rickety and increasingly shell-marked wooden foot bridge.

23 September – Hill 282

Although the cold, pre-dawn frost was now expected by the waiting Jocks, that did not make it any more pleasant or welcome. Those Argylls who were not on guard duty were quietly woken from a fitful and chilly sleep, quickly shaking off their slumber and readying themselves for the tasks before them.

First to leave the overnight position was 'Tac HQ', a small party comprising Neilson, his personal guard and a few signallers. It was a common procedure to split the headquarters into two elements during a battle, to ensure sufficient command of both the battle and the main body and supplies of the unit, and that a command element remained even if one was either destroyed or temporarily out of contact. The HQ would ordinarily be split into a small, mobile Tac HQ (or tactical HQ), comprising the CO and his signallers, to direct the battle, and a 'Main HQ' (often just called 'Main'), which was usually led by the 2IC and would look after the administrative and logistical tail of the unit. In highly mobile warfare, the Tac and Main would often swap as they leapfrogged each other. Splitting into two also helped ensure the survivability of the HQ elements – by splitting them up rather than having all of the HQ staff and commanders co-located in one big tempting target.

Neilson led his Tac HQ out at approximately 0445hrs and stealthily moved to a high point slightly north of the overnight harbour. From this vantage point, Neilson would be able to see the battle and direct supporting fire as needed.

A mere half an hour later, with the stars still high and dawn yet to break, the men of B and C Company shuffled up to their start line, which was a dry river bank immediately to the front of Hill 282, and snatched a brief cold breakfast from a tin. While hard to make out in the darkness, the men knew that their objective (code named Baker Ridge) lay in the high, relatively dark patch up the hill to their front. To get there, the men would need to cross an open stretch of wet paddy field, leaving them relatively exposed, before they approached the foot of the hill. They were anxious but quiet, silently checking weapons and equipment while they made their final preparations. As the men prepared to leave, they deposited their large packs in a cache, taking only their necessary fighting equipment of personal weapons, bayonets and grenades in their basic webbing pouches. But even on such a stripped-down basis, the men were still weighed down with a large quantity of fighting equipment. Each man carried several bandoliers of ammunition slung about their waist and shoulders, along with ammunition pouches stuffed with spare Bren gun magazines. Several men also carried tubes of 2in mortar ammunition in three-bomb carrying cases which resembled tubes of bamboo stacked on top of each other. Inexplicably, however, and despite the battle which they knew would come, no one wore steel helmets,[48] but rather preferred to wear the ubiquitous cap comforter, the khaki scarf-like tube, rolled in on itself and fashioned into a warm woollen cap.

They were initially very lucky. The dark shielded them from prying eyes and they were able to traverse the paddy fields unmolested. Reaching the foothills and weighed down with their loads, the men grudgingly started the climb through the rock and scree of the lower slopes, pushing their way past the scrub and odd fir tree. B Company was arranged in a rough line up to the right, with C Company to the left. No-one, not even the very fittest soldier, likes assaulting uphill, and it was hard going as the slope gradually steepened. Lance Corporal Fairhurst, near the front of the leading platoon – which was now under the command of the experienced Sergeant O'Sullivan – wondered how no one had heard them. Pushing aside these thoughts, he gripped his lightweight Sten gun tighter and dug his legs in to push further up the hill, trailing just behind his platoon sergeant.

The going was tough. The combination of the darkness, the narrowing of the ridge as the men ascended and some poor map reading soon led to the two companies becoming pushed together and intermingled. As they approached the crest, no longer were the men in their neat company groups but rather the two companies had nearly changed sides – B now on the left and C on the right.

Despite this minor hiccup, the Jocks' climb up Hill 282 went unnoticed by the NKPA troops who everyone suspected had to be somewhere nearby. Suspicion was soon satisfied; as they crested the hill, some of the Argylls saw a large group of not less than fifty NKPA soldiers over the ridge. They were sitting in a bowl-shaped clearing just down from the crest, apparently preparing their breakfast. Incredibly, no guards had been posted, which was incomprehensible to the Argylls given the noisy attacks by

1 MX the day before and 1 ASH's own assault on Hill 148. But for whatever reason, the North Korean troops were caught unawares, breakfast in hand.

The Argylls immediately started firing at the North Koreans, killing a number of the hapless diners outright. But the others quickly flung away their breakfasts and started returning fire at the Jocks. A furious firefight ensued, O'Sullivan being one of the first to be hit, closely followed by Lieutenant McKeller.

With his command team wounded and now out of the fight, Fairhurst rallied his section and prepared to charge the closest group of enemy. 'Then I heard a "pphhhhtt",' Fairhurst recalled, 'something kicked me in the stomach. [I guess] someone came up and fired a burp gun at me. I fell down, tried to get up but my legs wouldn't move.'[49] Fairhurst had received a slug from a burp gun in his stomach and went down hard. Luckily his mates, Richard (Dicky) Peet and Corporal Bob Sweeny, soon found him and dragged him under the cover of a nearby tree before they went off to rejoin the fight. Fairhurst quickly passed out as a result of blood loss and remembered little more of the upcoming battle as he passed in and out of consciousness.

With the disturbed breakfast party now returning a large amount of fire from their personal weapons, two platoons of Jocks formed up and prepared to charge down the hill. Corporal Bob Sweeny immediately took charge of one of the two intermingled platoons near the summit and led a bayonet charge directly at the startled North Koreans. His initiative and aggressiveness was instrumental in routing the enemy troops; for this action and the rest of his leadership during the day, he would later be awarded the Military Medal (the equivalent of the Military Cross for other ranks).[50] Of the initial fifty enemy troops, about fifteen now lay dead around their pots and pans, while the others had managed to scarper away. It was now about 0700hrs and the hill was firmly in the hands of the Argylls.

The Argylls had, however, taken casualties too. One man was killed and there were six wounded men near the top, including Fairhurst. With the remainder of C Company now reaching their comrades, the combined companies were put into all-round defence and were ordered to dig in and make what defensive positions they could. Yet the hasty defences would prove of marginal assistance as enemy artillery fire started to pound the position. The accurate shelling severely tested the newly arrived Jocks, and a further five men were soon wounded from red-hot shrapnel raining down on them from the skies.

***

Surprise and aggression had won the breakfast fight, but the battle for Hill 282 was far from over. In their somewhat confused scramble up the slope, the Argylls had somehow missed a group of enemy soldiers to their rear, who were now laying down machine-gun fire into the Scotsmen. The Argylls also started to become aware that although they had crested Hill 282, it was in fact overshadowed by a second and higher peak, slightly to the west. And this feature was crawling with alerted and angry North Korean soldiers, who started to lay down aggressive fire in the direction of the attackers as well as artillery fire. The Argylls were thus now being caught in a crossfire, the majority of fire coming from the new feature but also some from the bypassed groups to their rear, as well as some harassing fire from the remnants of the breakfast party.

***

Down in the flatland, the early-morning gloom had prevented Neilson at his Tac HQ from seeing clearly what was happening on the hill. All he saw was brief flashes of fire as a Sten or Bren gun opened up, and all he heard was the muffled thump of mortar and artillery rounds. It would not be until about 0600hrs and the first light of day that events on the top of Hill 282 unfolded to those waiting on the slopes and hills below. But even with the coming of the narrow dawn, it was not clear to Neilson exactly what was happening, nor crucially who was winning.

The US Forward Observation Officer (FOO) attached to the battalion tried in vain to locate the enemy artillery positions in order to bring in counter battery fire. The enemy guns were just too well camouflaged. None could be found, despite their obvious presence, clearly indicated by the slow but methodical artillery fire that continued to rain on the Argyll position. At the same time, the NKPA had now reorganized themselves and were attempting to infiltrate the position, using the cover of the thick vegetation and scrub to stealthily move back to the hill crest. Out on the flank, 7 Platoon discovered the infiltration and brought fire to bear on the sneaking enemy troops, scattering them back to their start lines. Nevertheless, the short encounter had resulted in both the platoon commander and platoon sergeant being wounded. Seeing the shrinking size of 7 Platoon, a decision was made to pull them back towards the main defensive position.

Despite the aggression shown by the Argylls, the NKPA were not going to leave these superb defensive positions easily. After reorganizing, the North Koreans tried to force their way back onto the hilltop, having first infiltrated stealthily from the left (southern) slope of the hill. Their attack was supported by mortar and SP artillery fire, yet again proving to be deadly accurate. But having just taken the position, the Argylls were not going to give it back so easily. Despite the NKPA reaching their forward positions, the Jocks were able to beat them back and retain control of their newly acquired territory.

Still unable to clearly see his men near the crest, Neilson moved his small Tac HQ again, this time to a point just to the rear of A Company on Hill 148. From here, he ordered C Company to be prepared to move off towards the higher Hill 388 (Songsan) as soon as they had finished their 'Reorg' (reorganization) on Hill 282. Reorg is a process conducted after every battle, in which a unit takes time to replenish ammunition, clear enemy dead and prisoners and see to their own casualties. All of this was conducted while the men were on high alert, ready for a possible counter-attack.

But the enemy did not give the Jocks time to reorg and get themselves in order. Leading with the hated pestilence of mortar fire, the NKPA troops started to move towards them from Hill 388. At the same time, a group of North Korean soldiers had got round to the left flank of Hill 148 and were threatening the men of A Company in their firm base. This development severely limited Neilson's freedom of action, since his battalion only had three companies and he now had to deploy his only reserve troops to meet this new threat. He would have no men spare to reinforce those on the crest of Hill 288.

It was now around 1100hrs and the Jocks had been moving and fighting for several hours. All were tired, but the adrenaline was still pumping and the men were fighting staunchly to retain their hard-won hill. Their manpower was, however, slowly diminishing, either through wounds or from the men detached from the battle to carry the wounded men back to the regimental aid post. When a unit is already operating on a light scale, such as the Argylls were here, every man absent from the fight represented a serious depletion of the battalion strength.

But just when the men were getting the upper hand, the first of a string of disasters struck, which would ultimately prove fatal to 1 ASH's continued occupation of the hill. With the battle still in full swing and with no prior warning to anyone at 27 Bde HQ, the American artillery support, won by Coad after so much persuasion, was suddenly and without warning withdrawn and allocated to another sector. The US FOO co-located with C Company on the hill received his orders over the radio to withdraw, and then immediately packed up his observation post, collected his small party of observers and set off downhill and away from the battle.

The loss of the supporting artillery was critical and could not have come at a worse time. With resistance mounting, only the 105mm guns of the American artillery could reach high enough and far enough to fall on the North Koreans attacking from Hill 388. The battalion mortars did not have enough range to do so, and due to the height of the hills, the guns of the Sherman tanks in the lowland below could not angle their barrels high enough to assist. The result was that suddenly the Jocks found themselves without any support whatsoever. To make matters worse, this was just as a major counter-attack was brewing, friendly casualties were mounting and ammunition stocks were dwindling. As can be imagined, both Coad and Neilson were livid at this unexpected setback, but were unable to do much about it.

***

While commanders fretted about the loss of their fire support, the battalion sergeant-majors and the Regimental Aid Post were busily trying to arrange evacuation of the casualties. Movement of the wounded was proving difficult as the steep, scree-lined slopes that the Jocks had just clambered up were even more dangerous on the return journey when encumbered by stretchers and wounded men. Stretchers being difficult to manage on the slope, it was found that the best method of casualty evacuation was often to place the wounded man on a ground sheet, with each of its four corners being grasped by one man. However, this was tough going on both the casualties and the bearers. By this time, the Argylles had around forty men wounded from both the original assault and the follow-on artillery fire and infiltrations. The difficulties in evacuation meant that it took four men approximately one hour to get a single wounded man all the way from the hill crest back to the casualty collection point near Hill 148.

While casualties rose, ammunition was starting to get low. It had been a furious two-hour fight and the men had expended a large quantity of ammunition. Clearly, they would need resupply if they were to retain the hill, let alone attempt the further assault towards the higher position on Songsan. Seeing the need of the forward companies, stretcher bearers with medical supplies (including morphine) and parties carrying ammunition had been dispatched from HQ to resupply the hill. However, the shelling and fire from the NKPA troops had slowed them down and pushed some parties back. Without ammunition, the men on the crest would be unable to hold on.

As the day progressed and the sun rose higher, it was clear that while not yet desperate, the Argylls' position was deteriorating. Without decisive action at the front, it was possible that the hard-won gains of the morning could be squandered. Accordingly, Major Kenny Muir, the battalion 2IC, asked Nielson for permission to go forward and take charge of the two companies on Hill 282.

The battalion 2IC was a curious position. On the one hand, they were an experienced and senior officer, ready to take command of the battalion at an instant should anything happen to the CO. On the other hand, for much of the time, the 2IC appeared to be a little superfluous, looking after mainly administrative matters despite the acknowledged skills and experience which had landed him the second-in-command job in the first place.

Muir was not one for shrinking from the action; when he saw a chance to do something useful, he took it. Despite being of only average height and somewhat slight of build, Major Muir was an extremely experienced and talented officer. He had seen service with the Argylls in India prior to the Second World War, and then in Africa, Italy and Europe. Seeing the situation on the hill, Neilson was grateful for such a forward-leaning officer and immediately gave Muir permission to press on and take command.

Accompanying a party of stretcher bearers, Muir soon reached the crest and started to take charge of the now-intermingled B and C Companies. With fire still being traded by the steadily advancing NKPA soldiers on Hill 388, Muir organized for some of the more badly wounded men to be loaded onto the stretchers for the arduous and steep descent to the battalion base and its aid station.

As Muir started to take command of the men spread around the crest of Hill 282, the NKPA on 388 continued to cause difficulties for the Jocks due to their elevated position. The enemy, determined to regain the ground that had been lost, were now pouring streams of machine-gun fire downwards onto the Argylls. Furthermore, parties of the enemy, skilfully using the cover of the terrain and the trees, were able to infiltrate right up to the forward edge of the Argyll positions. Well camouflaged by the scrub, they got almost up to the leading edge of Second Lieutenant Edington's 7 Platoon, before commencing a furious assault, heralded by the staccato ripping sound of the burp guns and the thump of exploding grenades. Edington's men coolly fought back the unwelcome guests, but the assault nevertheless took its toll, 7 Platoon took casualties and gaps started to form in their perimeter. With the numbers of wounded mounting and the supply of ammunition almost critical, it was clear that their position was deteriorating.

Muir, however, remained undaunted. Exuding confidence – that quality so needed of officers to inspire hard-pressed men – he reported back to Neilson via radio that 'the situation was still well in hand'.[51] It was reported that Muir had taken charge of the remaining men on the crest and amalgamated the two companies into a single unit to provide all-round defence – 'wherever the need lay, there was the short, square shouldered figure in a Balmoral ... encouraging the men by voice and example, helping the wounded and distributing the ammunition and directing the fire'.[52]

But it was clear that the Jocks were only just holding on. The lack of fit men, ammunition and fire support would, in time, likely turn decisive. Still fuming at the sudden loss of his artillery fire support, Neilson decided to request an airstrike on the Hill 388 position as a way of evening the odds and disrupting the flow of enemy from there towards his men on Hill 282. Muir agreed with Nielson's plans and ordered his men to place the correct air recognition panels near their position to act as a warning to the incoming aircraft as to the location of his troops.

Air recognition panels were large pieces of brightly coloured fabric which were laid out on the ground to alert friendly aircraft to the position of their own forces. The panels could be laid in different configurations, with the correct sequence changed frequently to prevent the enemy copying them to confuse UN aircraft. There have been many conflicting accounts as to exactly what panels were laid out that afternoon – orange ones, red ones, panels laid out 'like St Andrews Cross'[53] – but whatever the configuration, there is unanimity in the recollections that the correct panels were laid out. This was even confirmed by General Partridge, commander of the Fifth Air Force, who 'was by coincidence in the air in another aircraft at the time and [said] he clearly saw our ground strips displayed on the hill crest just before the start of the air strike'.[54]

At around 1215hrs, the beleaguered men on Hill 282 watched in anticipation as three US Air Force Mustangs flew towards them and circled over the position. The Mustangs were a fast, propeller-driven fighter-bomber, deadly efficient and a mainstay of the US Air Force in the Second World War. The men on the ground could clearly see the heavy load of silver napalm canisters under the belly of the sicraft, together with the rows of rockets attached under the wings, and were looking forward expectantly to the damage that they would inflict on their foes high up on Hill 388.

But expectation soon turned to dread as the first Mustang, finishing its reconnaissance of the position, started to dive straight towards the men of B and C Company and dropped its load of napalm directly on their fighting position. The men below saw the fat canister fall, as if in slow motion, and then explode almost directly on them. A huge *whuump*, then there was fire everywhere on top of the hill as the sticky liquid ignited, coating both the hill and the defending Argylls. A surging ball of flame, wreathed in an outer layer of black smoke as the petroleum ignited, continued to burn for several minutes, accompanied by a rich, choking smell of gasoline.

The attack killed a number of troops outright. Others, covered by the fire and the burning liquid, screamed in agony as they desperately tried to get away from the flames, while those further down the hill at the A Company position could only look on in horror.

Willoughby, over on Middlesex Hill, saw the strike but initially was not aware that it had landed on the Argylls, later writing: '[Napalm] is a frightful weapon and it was a hideous sight: First there is a dull orange ball of fire and at once rivulets of yellow flame cascade down and fill every fold in the ground and a column of black smoke pillars into the sky.'[55]

While the sight was horrific from a distance, it was truly horrendous to the Jocks caught up in the attack. Frantic attempts were made to call off the fighters, but as there was no direct radio link with the circling Mustangs, the aircraft continued to circle the position menacingly. Private Cochrane of C Company recalled desperately searching through the pack of a dead signaller, trying to find the Very pistol so as to shoot a Very light to warn the pilots. But someone in B Company had beaten him to the punch and was firing the brightly coloured flare up into the sky.[56] It was to no avail, and the horror continued as a second Mustang, close of the tail of the first, dropped another load of napalm over the Jocks' position. Then all three fighters dove towards the stricken Argylls and fired salvoes of rockets and machine guns at the men below, who were now desperately trying to clamber off the crest and away from the fearsome aerial forces.

As the planes departed Hill 282, they decided to expend what was left of their ordinance on the men of A Company, way down the hill and on the ridge at Hill 148 below. The A Company soldiers endured a light strafing as the Mustangs screeched over their heads before banking and making their way back to base. Fortunately, this afterthought of an attack did not result in any further casualties.

It is estimated that this attack took less than two minutes. The fatal error had caused approximately between thirty and forty casualties, some of whom had already been wounded in the initial assaults during the attack on the hill. When the first napalm canister was dropped, men were seen diving for cover and several even threw themselves down sheer slopes to get away from the 'veritable sea of fire'.[57] While some managed to escape, for many of them – even if only splashed by droplets of the burning liquid – the agonizing pain from their burns would mean that their fight was over and they would take no further part in the battle.

When the fires eventually subsided, Hill 282, still smouldering and enveloped with a sickly gasoline smell, was virtually undefended. Only the dead and wounded remained on the crest of Baker Ridge; all except for a single rifleman, Private Watts, who was still bravely firing towards the enemy with his .303 rifle in an attempt to keep them at bay.

Apart from Watts, most of the men still alive on Baker Ridge had been terribly wounded. Corporal Dicky Peet recalled that the napalm 'just decimated the two platoons ... The hill was on fire, lads lying everywhere on fire ... there was one man, sitting in an overhang. The skin on his face had come off. He was terrified.'[58]

Nearby, on the relatively unscathed Charlie Ridge, Muir and a very small band of about nine survivors (including Gordon-Ingram) surveyed the carnage before them. This small band was extremely lucky to have avoided the effects of the airstrike. However, as the flames died down, they also spotted a band of enemy troops quickly moving towards Watts' position in an attempt to capitalize on the chaos brought about by the errant airstrike.

Watts' courage in fighting off the enemy, at this point almost single-handed, was later recognized by the award of the US Bronze Star. The citation reads in part: 'Private Watts displayed tenacious valour ... he fought conspicuously and continuously throughout the day until he was wounded in the late afternoon when the position was overrun by overwhelming enemy forces. His inspiration, bravery, superb fight[ing] qualities, and sustained courage reflect great credit on him and the military service.'[59] It is certain that without Watts' dogged determination to hold Baker Ridge single-handedly, that the Argylls would have immediately lost control of the crest.

Muir, determined not to let the beleaguered Watts fight them off alone, arranged a Bren gun to provide covering fire while he led his small band in an attack along the ridge and back towards Baker Ridge. Speed and aggression proved decisive, and Muir was able to throw back the enemy and retake the ridge. But the little victory was unlikely to last, as Gordon-Ingram described:

> 'Although Baker ridge was retaken, the defenders were not more than 14 all ranks and the ammunition situation was desperate. The fire had destroyed what little reserve was left, and a service burst [i.e. a 2–3 round burst] from the Brens became a luxury that could be ill-afforded. A few men began to return from the valley but the enemy was closing in with determination, firing from trees overlooking the position, and coming close on three sides.'[60]

Reunited with Watts, the rapidly shrinking band of Argylls tried to hold off the advancing NKPA troops. At this stage, Muir was said to be 'everywhere', trying to arrange the defence, encourage the men, evacuate the casualties and all the while actively fighting back against the enemy. With ammunition now almost exhausted, the men were described as 'literally picking up loose rounds from the ground in order to be able to fire at the enemy'.[61] Muir was reduced to firing the 2in mortar in almost a direct-fire role. Muir and his men were using every last weapon available to fight back and hold off the enemy. Muir's last words were reported to be 'Neither the Gooks or the US Air Force will get the Argylls off this ridge!'[62] Just as he finished shouting these words, he was hit by a burst of machine-gun fire across his stomach and thigh. Mortally wounded, Muir collapsed to the ground; despite being evacuated as soon as possible off the crest, he died shortly thereafter.

The loss of Major Muir was a terrible blow to the little band on Baker Ridge. With only ten men still alive, many of whom were also wounded, and no more than a single magazine of ammunition left for the Bren guns, Major Gordon-Ingram assumed command. He ordered the remaining men to withdraw to the lower Charlie Ridge and reunite with C Company. Moving back down the hill, Gordon-Ingram found that the remaining men in C Company were in little better shape, having sustained equally high casualties and possessing minimal ammunition.

Surveying the situation, Gordon-Ingram knew that despite the gallant fight to take it and the Argylls' stubborn resistance to hold it, there was little prospect of retaining Hill 282. His priority now was to evacuate the wounded and get his remaining men back down the hill to safety. He duly radioed Neilson for permission to withdraw from the hill.

Despite the lack of fit fighting men, the withdrawal was organized by Gordon-Ingram in a planned and methodical manner. The men moved down the hill one step at a time, first setting up a temporary fighting position in order to provide covering fire for the casualties to pass through before establishing a new position a little further down. This leapfrog manoeuvre was a slow and exhausting process, but one which provided maximum protection for the withdrawing troops. At the same time, fire from 1 MX Vickers machine guns and the mortars of A Company, 1 ASH, gave some covering fire in an attempt to dissuade the enemy from following up the withdrawal. In this manner, the evacuation succeeded in getting all of the wounded off the hill. As Gordon-Ingram escorted the wounded down the slopes, he caught up with several victims of the napalm bombing who were still struggling to withdraw. Some were being carried by men from A Company and a few by some members of 1 MX who had come to help as soon as they witnessed the napalm strike. As the stretcher bearers struggled downhill with their loads, the enemy inexplicably let up their fire. Only the ever-present enemy artillery fire pursued them as they carried their wounded downhill.

At approximately 1500hrs, nearly ten hours after they had set off that morning, all the Argylls were finally off Hill 282. The many casualties were being treated or transported to field hospitals, while the relatively few fit men found themselves slightly dazed and back at their start positions. Seeing the large pile of packs and personal equipment that had been stashed at the line of departure just a few hours before, these exhausted survivors were likely somewhat shocked and stunned. While thankful that they had somehow made it through the day unscathed, at the same time they were distressed that so many of their comrades had been killed or injured in the ultimately futile assault.

The Casualties

A constant consideration and strain for commanders during the whole of 23 September was the issue of how to evacuate and then care for their growing number of casualties. From the first attack on the summit, 1 ASH took heavy casualties, and this initial flow grew throughout the day into a veritable torrent, especially following the 'friendly fire' napalm attack.

The treatment of any wounded man started on the hill itself and then passed through several stages until, if they were fortunate, they made it back to a field hospital, generally located many miles behind the front lines.

All of the 27 Bde soldiers knew that during an assault, a wounded man could expect little to no help from his fellows, as the others could ill afford to stop in the middle of a battle. At best, a man might be dragged under cover by a nearby comrade and then would need to administer self-aid. This is exactly what happened to Lance Corporal Fairhurst when he was shot by the burp gun near the summit.

When the immediate assault was over, fellow soldiers or stretcher parties comprised of bandsmen/medics would find the injured man and administer immediate first aid – usually being little more than bandages to staunch the flow of blood. They would then need to be carried, either on a precariously balanced stretcher or a sagging ground sheet, back down the hill to the Regimental Medical Officer (RMO) at Battalion HQ. The RMO could do little more but assess a wound, administer morphine to dull the pain and prepare the wounded man for further transport rearwards.

Many a wounded Jock owed his life to the efforts of the indefatigable Company Sergeant Major Tom Collett. After the summit had first been gained and casualties were being taken due to shell and mortar fire, Company Sergeant Major Collett started the vital work of supervising the evacuation of the wounded men back down the hill, often moving about in the open, without regard to his own safety, intent on saving the wounded men of his battalion. 'Finally, handing over his rifle to another man whose weapon was out of action, he continued his work, unarmed, in an area in which considerable enemy infiltration had taken place. Even after the airstrike, CSM Collett immediately returned to the hill to help care for and evacuate the wounded.' Following the final counter-attack and the loss of Muir, 'despite the fact that he [Collett] was without a weapon, enemy fire was intense and the enemy themselves very close, he was among the last to leave the position … He gave no thought for his own personal safety and his example was a an inspiration to all who saw him.'[63] For his tireless actions in caring for the wounded, Collett would later be awarded the Military Medal.

***

Fairhurst, being injured early on in the assault, was lucky to have a stretcher party of two men to carry him down the hill. It was a tough descent, and the stretcher bearers must have had painfully aching arms and shoulders as they tried to gingerly walk down the scree-covered slope, trying hard not to further bump or injure their wounded comrade. With the hill descended, the stretcher team continued to plod on to the water's edge and stepped up to the swaying kapok bridge, eager to get their charge to the RMO on the other side.

However, not more than halfway across the bridge, the stretcher bearers must have heard or sensed the incoming shells and, as gently as they could, put Fairhurst's stretcher down onto the rough planks of the bridge. Unfortunately, it was the last thing they did as both men were felled by glowing hot pieces of shrapnel from the incoming fire. Miraculously, Fairhurst was unscathed and would later be retrieved by other men and taken across the river to the relative safety of Brigade Headquarters.

As the day progressed, evacuation of the wounded men tied up a great deal of the brigade's resources. All spare men from Brigade HQ rushed forward to assist in carrying the wounded on stretchers to waiting transport. Even men from 1 MX over near Middlesex Hill made their way back to 1 ASH to help.

While most men were evacuated from the Regimental Aid Post by either jeep or ambulance, some of the most seriously wounded were taken by a new addition to the battlefield, the helicopter. The H-13 Sioux light helicopter had started to be introduced into the US Army in 1948, and it would prove to be both a godsend to wounded soldiers on the battlefield and an iconic symbol of the Korean War. It was a small, three-man helicopter, characterized by a distinctive bubble canopy and a long, skeletal steel tail assembly. The Sioux was used extensively for reconnaissance, but its most famous role would soon be that of a medevac helicopter. In this configuration, a stretcher for wounded men would be affixed on each side of the helicopter on the skids. The wounded man would be strapped into the stretcher and an acrylic glass cover was used to protect the patient from the wind. While this could prove a scary, semi-exposed ride for the wounded soldier, it had the advantage of bringing a badly wounded man to a hospital in a fraction of the time that it would take using conventional road transport – if available. Given the rough terrain of Korea, a helicopter was often the only way to get a badly wounded man down from a ridgeline quickly and safely. Undoubtedly, the helicopter could be credited with saving many lives. At the time, however, the number of helicopters available for medical evacuation was small. Since use of the helicopter was still in its infancy, they could only be used in ideal flying conditions – which precluded night flying, long-distance flying, flying in rain or mist or even when too hot. In all, only a very few of the most critically injured Argylls would be ferried away by air that day, with the vast majority transported by road to safety.

Fairhurst was not among the lucky few to be flown to safety. Rather, his journey started with his stretcher being laid sideways across a jeep until, a little over mile or so back from the front line, he was transferred from the jeep and loaded onto the floor of an ambulance. Another badly wounded man was strapped into the bunk above him before the ambulance set off. Fate would yet again strike Fairhurst when either a mine or a stray shell went off near the vehicle, killing all the other crew and passengers. Fairhurst was merely knocked unconscious, being rescued later by friendly troops who found him and transported him rearwards.

Fairhurst woke up days later, finding himself in a clean hospital bed in Japan, with tubes down his nose and stuck into his leg. Thick straps tied him to the bed in order to restrain him and prevent any further damage to his seriously injured body. Amazingly, and despite the apparent seriousness of his wounds, after several months of convalescence in both Japan and Hong Kong, the now Corporal Fairhurst returned to the Argylls just as they returned to Hong Kong in April 1951. He then also learned that he had been awarded the US Bronze Star for his actions on Hill 282.[64] Near the end of his tour and the end of his service contract, his answer to whether he would like to re-enlist was an immediate 'no way' – his experiences in Korea being more than enough to last him his entire life.

***

While the medical system and the rest of the brigade struggled manfully to assist the casualties, the butcher's bill for the fighting on and around Hill 282 was calculated - and it was high.

It took some time to calculate the total number of casualties suffered by 1 ASH on 23 September. This was in part because 27 Bde was still engaged in action (albeit at a slower tempo) for some time after the withdrawal from Hill 282 as well as the tragic fact that many of those who were responsible for recording and reporting battalion casualties were casualties themselves.[65] Nevertheless, it was finally recorded that the total casualties for the day amounted to ninety-four killed, wounded and missing, including the battalion 2IC, Major Muir.[66] This was a huge number of casualties sustained in a single action, representing the loss of the best part of an entire company. With 1 ASH starting the war on a very light scale anyway, these losses almost rendered the battalion temporarily ineffective. In an attempt to pull together at least two effective fighting companies, B and C Companies were amalgamated under the command of Major Gordon-Ingram and pulled back to the location of the CO's first Tac HQ at Point 779. A Company remained where it was at Hill 148 and the battalion spent an uneasy night trying to sort itself out and make some sense of the day's events.

One peculiar feature of the day's action was how to officially characterize the loss of those men killed or wounded in the 'friendly fire' incident. As the War Diary succinctly put it, 'It is impossible to separate those killed and wounded by the air attack from those killed and wounded by enemy action.'[67] Indeed, this was to be an issue of particular sensitivity for Air Vice Marshal Cecil Bouchier, the Ministry of Defence's liaison to MacArthur's headquarters. Over the following days, as he investigated the matter further, Bouchier felt very strongly that there should be no distinction between those killed or wounded by enemy fire and those killed or hurt during the accidental bombing in any subsequent reporting – particularly to the press: 'I strongly suggest that casualties resulting from the bombing should be classified as having been caused in action with the enemy ... It is invidious and unnecessary and unkind, I suggest, to publish in any form, the names of those who died or went missing and were wounded solely as a result of accidental bombing. All the Highlanders casualties on 23rd September should, I suggest, be given without any repeat any differentiation.'[68] Bouchier's views were readily acceded to by London, and henceforth no official distinction was made between those killed or wounded due to enemy fire and those from accidental bombing.

Assessment and Aftermath

The bravery and gallantry of the Argylls in taking the hill and pushing back the NKPA despite the reverse caused by the air strike is not in question. All of the officers and men of the battalion displayed the highest levels of professional skill, determination and grit in attacking and clearing the hill in spite of significant odds. In recognition of these efforts, a number of medals for bravery were issued for the actions on Hill 282.

Most conspicuous was the posthumous award of a Victoria Cross (VC) for Major Kenny Muir. The VC is the highest order for gallantry that can be awarded to a soldier or officer in a Commonwealth army. It is awarded for conspicuous valour in the face of the enemy. Unlike most Commonwealth awards issued at this time, the VC can be awarded posthumously. It is also necessary that at least two witnesses are available to attest to the gallant act.

Neilson recommended Muir for the VC shortly after the battle, and his recommendation was supported by the two majors who were on the hill with Muir (Gordon-Ingram and Gillies), as well as CSM Tom Murray. All paid tribute to Muir's personal inspiration and leadership in the face of the enemy. Muir's VC citation recounting his actions on Hill 282 includes the following:

> 'Muir's actions were beyond all possible praise ... The effect of his splendid leadership on the men was nothing short of amazing, and it was entirely due to his magnificent courage and example and the spirit which he imbued in those about him that all wounded were evacuated from the hill, and, as was subsequently discovered, very heavy casualties inflicted on the enemy in the defence of the crest.'[69]

The Victoria Cross was gazetted in January 1951. The medal was a fitting recognition for Muir's actions as well as a source of tragedy-tinged pride for the battalion. In purely military terms, the attack on Hill 282 was not a success, but the award of the VC would later provide the battalion with some small acknowledgement and honour from what was otherwise a terrible day for the Argyll and Sutherland Highlanders.

By nightfall, the battalion was in shock after the day's events, but even at this early stage it tried to claw some comfort from the disaster. The Argylls' War Diary noted:

> "It was later ascertained that the force of the enemy which counter-attacked us was in the region of 400 strong, and there is no doubt that a large number of casualties was inflicted on this force. The proof of this is, that while we were driven off our objective because of various factors, of which the air attack must play a large part, the enemy evacuated the position within 12 hours of taking it, and before a further attack could be mounted against them.'[70]

***

Hill 282 was a significant battle for 27 Bde, representing one of the first major engagements it had fought since arriving in Korea. Yet it can also be argued that the events on Middlesex Hill and Hill 282 were perfectly 'normal' or 'ordinary' battles, mere replications of the hundreds of major and minor actions occurring up and down the line as the UN forces tried to bludgeon their way out of the Pusan pocket.

But the action on Hill 282 had the advantage (or disadvantage) of being closely watched by a number of the international press corps, who were at that time accompanying the brigade and were hungry for stories about the newly arrived British forces. A number of them were with Coad and his Brigade HQ on the east bank of the river, including members of the Associated Press. When information about the airstrikes on the Argyll position started to filter back to the headquarters, newspapermen rushed forward to get over the bridge and report on what was happening. Because of their eagerness to move towards the action, there are now photographs available taken by the Associated Press which clearly show Argyll stretcher bearers bringing down wounded comrades from the hill shortly after the attack.

The airstrike on Hill 282 quickly became a major news story; by the next day, the events there were on the front pages of several international newspapers. The front page of the *New York Times* led with the headline 'US Planes Strafe British in Error; 60 Are Casualties',"[71] whereas *The Times* (of London) noted 'Accidental Attack on British' as part of a multi-page feature describing recent developments in the Korean War.[72] It is curious that such a significant loss of British life, so early in the war, did not make the front page in the British paper, but perhaps there was a desire to downplay the tragedy so as not to stoke any anti-American feeling that might otherwise have ensued.

Of more immediate concern to Coad and his fellow commanders was that the speed with which the photographs and stories hit the front pages did not even allow them time to first inform the next-of-kin about their dead and wounded relatives. Fortunately, names were not mentioned in the articles, but nevertheless, the stories would likely have caused some anxiety amongst the families of the Middlesex and Argyll soldiers.

It is interesting to note the slant of the press coverage that developed almost immediately after the accident. While all of the articles noted the tragedy of the airstrikes, none of them attributed blame directly towards the US Air Force. For example, the article in *The Times* was at pains to report that the pilots were not blamed for the loss of life:

> **'Pilots not held at fault – Taegu, Sept 25** – The pilots of the American Mustang aircraft who carried out the accidental attack on British troops near Songju are not being held at fault, a spokesman stated here today. They bombed troops on the position after ground controllers were said to have stated over the radio that there were no British troops west of the Songju road at this point. In fact, The Argyll and Sutherland Highlanders were there, having dislodged the Communists from the hill during the morning. An observation aircraft got the green light for attack from American ground control in the British sector. There also was confusion about the colour of the identification panels. The attack was launched, but the airborne controller stopped it when it became doubtful whether the troops being attacked were North Koreas – Reuter.'[73]

But despite the rather gentle coverage of the incident, the fact was that this was a significant military blunder that had the potential to develop into a political crisis. How willing would Commonwealth governments be to continue supporting the war when the greatest danger appeared to come not from the Communists but from their US allies?

Investigations were launched immediately into the causes of the accident, and to date there have been a number of different theories as to the cause of the 'friendly' bombing.

The Argylls' Major David Wilson appeared convinced that the mistake arose from within Battalion HQ. He believed that the pilots saw the panels and didn't want to attack, but nevertheless they were given orders to proceed. Wilson said that 'sadly the order had emanated from our Brigade HQ but they couldn't see what was happening'.[74]

Wilson's comment that the order came from their Battalion HQ appears on the face of it credible, and there is no evidence to suggest that the pilots simply disregarded the panels and put in the attack anyway. On the other hand, it appears more likely that the order to attack did not emanate from British officers in the HQ but rather from the attached American US Air Liaison troops stationed with them.

Investigating the matter within days of the accident, Air Vice Marshal Bouchier sent a cable to the British Chiefs of Staff on 26 September which noted the following:

'Spoke to General Partridge [commander US Fifth Air Force] in Tagu yesterday about accident. He is conducting investigations. From his remarks, it appears to me, firstly, that American Fighter Calculation Control Team were not close enough up to battalion on the hill crest because they could not get across a small river … secondly, some confusion, possibly caused by the fact that spotter aircraft had different scale of map to that used by Ground Control team; thirdly, accident appears to have been caused mainly by officer of Ground Control Team making a mistake in hill crest which was required to be attacked in spite of the fact that spotter pilot in the air reported back that the hill crest ordered by Ground Control to be attacked was clearly showing the right ground recognition signals and that friendly troops appeared to be in occupation of it. After the aircraft in the air had been told by Ground Control that enemy often copied our ground signals and hill crest in question was the one to be attacked, it appeared that the aircraft finally attacked our positions. American officer-in-charge of Ground Control was immediately replaced and I assume appropriate action will be taken after completion of American investigation.'[75]

The US investigation report has not been located and thus it appears that the truth of the matter will never be known. Nevertheless, whatever the details, all agreed that it was a tragic mistake, the type of which unfortunately happens in all wars. While the Argylls (and indeed all of the British troops) were 'hopping mad'[76] at the time, after a relatively short period both the British government and the troops on the ground accepted that this was just one of the deeply regrettable realities of a deadly war.

For their part, the Americans were mortified by the mistake. The US Fifth Air Force quickly started an impromptu raising of funds for the victims of the Hill 282 accident. General Stratemayer, commander of all East Asian Air Forces during the war, recorded in his diary:

'[W]e were met by General Partridge [and] he explained to me the catastrophic error made in our strafing of the British troops. He said it was terrible and it showed in his eyes filling with tears when talking with me; however, he informed me that both General Robertson and Air Vice Marshal Bouchier had absolutely cleared the Air Force, stating that it was one of those errors that take place in war.'[77]

Apologies were also received from numerous US generals as well as the US Embassy in Britain, copies of which were quickly obtained by and circulated in the press. Even the official history of the Argylls in Korea stated:

'I can assure you that we all understand all too well how liable such mistakes as that of the 23rd September 1950 to occur under the stress and hazards of war

> ... [the battalion] has spoken in glowing terms of the wonderful co-operation afforded to them by the United States Air Force, and no hard feelings have arisen as a result of this accident.'[78]

But was such Anglo-American solidarity and remarkable forgiveness just a front? Was there a conspiracy at the highest levels to conceal the truth, lest it fracture the very tender bonds of US–UK co-operation, so vital in maintaining a united front against the Communist enemy?

The answer appears to be 'no'. There is simply no evidence of any sort of conspiracy, either then or now. What is more likely is that all parties realized that these sort of accidents, appallingly tragic as they were, just happen in war. Also, context is important, with many of the participants having seen such accidents (or worse) during the Second World War. While infuriated by thc attack, most of the experienced commanders and men knew that they would likely happen again; it was just one of the many terrible events that accompanied modern warfare.

While sticking to his theory of how the accident happened, David Wilson, in an interview in the late 1990s, provided a glimpse of attitudes to such accidents in 1950:

> 'And the airstrike? All who took part are dead now, and the whys and wherefores are best forgotten. One thing we do know: the pilots could clearly see the recognition strips, and refused to attack them, but someone told them they had been overrun by the NKPA ... At least in those days we did not have hordes of counsellors and the press around, with their satellite links and their instant communications throughout the world – and threats of lawsuits and damages for casualties from what we now call "friendly fire" or in even more modern parlance "blue on blue" ... For the first time the world realized that we, the British (or the Scots if you prefer), were involved to the hilt in Korea.'[79]

Yet despite all the high-level understanding that such things 'just happen', for the Jocks on the ground this was an awful day. 'We didn't think much of the US aircrews that did this,' said Private Richard 'Dicky' Peet, adding that 'it was disgusting'.[80] Peet, recalling the event forty years later, said that it was the worst day of his life and one that continued to haunt him.

***

With the casualties now evacuated, 27 Bde continued to reorganize itself in the early evening. The Argylls amalgamated companies, distributed ammunition and supplies, and the men were at last able to get some food. But the darkness did not dissuade the enemy gunners and the hidden SP guns, which continued to lob the odd shell lazily towards the British, as if to just remind them that the North Koreans were still there. The kapok bridge, which had already taken a few hits throughout the day, was cut three times during the night by shellfire. Each time, however, it was rapidly repaired with whatever supplies were available in order to keep the precious lifeline to the east bank open.

With enemy guns continuing to make life miserable, Coad called in friendly air assets the following day. Estimating that the guns were located somewhere to the south of the brigade position, an airstrike was put into a small village several kilometres to the south. It is not known if the SP guns were in this location at the time, but the guns soon fell silent. That was almost the last the brigade heard of the North Koreans, who now withdrew from their positions, which they had defended so doggedly, as they made their way northwards, away from the advancing UN forces.

Two days later, on 26 September, the first units of a much-reduced 27 Bde marched into Songju. The brigade was now ready for further action, but there was no mistaking that the loss of so many men over the past few days had seriously weakened it.

Fortunately, the brigade was just about to get a much-needed boost to their morale, one that would transform it from an understrength two-battalion brigade into a fully manned Commonwealth brigade.

The Australians were coming.

The Australians

3rd Battalion, Royal Australian Regiment

Chapter 5

Raising 3 RAR

Australian politicians would in later years boast that they had committed Australian ground troops to the cause in Korea even before the British had announced their participation. While the claim was technically true – mainly due to time zone differences – in reality, Australia's support to the UN cause was not quite as full-throated as the politicians' boast would suggest.

When news of the North Korean invasion of the South broke, the Australian government almost immediately offered the services of two warships, HMAS *Shoalhaven* and HMAS *Bataan*, for service with UN forces. Australia was an enthusiastic supporter of the United Nations, and the early commitment of naval forces was a clear demonstration of that support. This was soon followed on 2 July by the provision of the squadron of Royal Australian Air Force Mustang fighters that were based in Japan.

These two early offers of military units demonstrated support to the two emerging pillars of Australia's post-war security architecture – the United Nations and the United States. In relation to the United Nations, Australia was an early signatory to the UN Charter, having high hopes that it would be a better guarantor of peace and security than its ill-fated predecessor, the League of Nations. While support for the United Nations was based on hope for the future, support for the United States was based on the realization, demonstrated so forcefully during the Second World War, that Australia's future security now lay in closer ties to Washington rather than London. The United Kingdom still had an important role to play in Australia's 'backyard' (i.e. Asia), but it was no longer the power it once had been, whereas the United States was clearly now the dominant player in the Asian theatre.

It was against this backdrop, as well as the public's spontaneous desire that Australia be seen to be 'doing something' in Korea, that Australia became one of the first countries to commit military forces to the fight in Korea. However, approval to send ground forces was another thing entirely. The Australian Prime Minister, Robert Menzies, was at this stage extremely reluctant to offer army units for service in Korea.

Several factors militated against the provision of ground forces. Most critically, the Australian Army was a mere shadow of what it had been at the end of the Second World War. From a total strength of several hundred thousand troops at the end of the global conflict, by June 1950 the size of the Australian Army had fallen to a paltry 14,651.[81]

Demobilization at the end of the war, financial constraints and a reduced appetite for serving after a world war had significantly reduced the Australian Army's manpower reserves. Similar to the UK, labour shortages across Australia found Army wages much less competitive than those of other industries. Thus, in early 1950, the Australian Army was very small indeed.

Future plans for Australia's Defence Force had focussed on building up the Royal Australian Navy, and there were neither funds nor available manpower left over for the Army. Nevertheless, a certain minimum number of soldiers were required, and in early 1950 the government had planned to introduce a National Service scheme which would see young men serve a short period in the regular army before spending three years in the Reserves (then known as the CMF, the Citizens' Military Forces). The plan called for the small regular army to act as a cadre, focussed on administering the National Service scheme. In relation to overseas commitments, it was envisaged that any such deployment of Australian troops would likely be to support UK efforts in either Malaya or the Middle East. These were the considerations that drove most politicians, and senior Army officers to recommend against the provision of Australian ground forces for Korea. Quite simply, there were insufficient men to be found.

Nonetheless, Australia still had one significant, but rapidly dwindling, overseas commitment in 1950. Since the end of the war, Australia had taken an active part in the occupation of Japan, and it was still a major contributor to the British Commonwealth Occupation Forces (BCOF) in Japan. At its height immediately after the war, nearly10,000 Australians were deployed to Japan to assist in supervising the disarmament of Japan, administer the occupied country and assist in the hunt for suspected war criminals. So successful was the occupation and so rapid the demilitarization of Japan that by 1950 there was little left for the BCOF, or any of the occupation forces, to do besides carry out simple garrison duties. By 1950, the BCOF was being dismantled and most troops were in the process of being shipped home. In June 1950, the remaining Australian commitment consisted of a single understrength infantry battalion – the 3rd Battalion of the Royal Australian Regiment (3 RAR), together with its constituent administrative units.

Even this modest commitment was being wound down, with plans afoot to withdraw 3 RAR over the next year. When the war in Korea broke out, 3 RAR consisted of a mere two companies of riflemen, mainly preoccupied with packing up for their return to Australia. This was clearly not an aggressive fighting force ready for the unexpected war which had just broken out next-door in Korea.

Life for the Australian occupying forces in Japan was very good. The work was not too hard, conditions were good, entertainment plentiful and the pay went a lot further than in Australia. Also, despite a 'no fraternization' policy, a good number of the Australian contingent had also found themselves long-term Japanese girlfriends, with more than a few now having wives and children.

A sergeant in the occupation forces noted:

> '[S]o far as the Australian soldier was concerned, the Occupation could go on for another thirty years. This was a far better life than just training in Australia – he was part of a formation doing a specific job in an interesting country, it was an easy life, it was economical to live, he wanted for nothing, and he took the utmost pride in his unit and formation.'[82]

The War Diary of 3 RAR for the early part of July 1950 showed clearly that the men had no inkling that they would be bound for Korea within a few short months. For example, as late as 21 July, the highlight of the day was to announce the following: 'The inter-company swimming sports for the Canberra Cup commenced at the BCOF Signals regiment swimming pool. The preliminary events were highlighted by the remarkable stamina of Pte Eyre, A Company who came second in the 800 metres event.'[83]

Unbeknownst to everyone in the battalion, from Commanding Officer to lowly private, such carefree sporting and leisure activities were about to come to a sudden halt, soon to be replaced by frantic preparations for war.

***

For most of July, no pressure was placed on the Australians to assist with ground forces. MacArthur himself had discussions with the Australian commander of the BCOF, General Horace Robertson, and was made aware that 3 RAR was not in a fit state to assist materially on the ground. However, this all changed in late July, as the ground situation in Korea had become critical.

On 25 July, the CO of 3 RAR, Lieutenant Colonel Floyd Walsh, attended a briefing with Robertson, who informed him that that MacArthur had formally requested that BCOF troops be available for use in Korea. The request signal had already been sent to Australia asking for approval, which was granted the next day.

Following the briefing with Robertson, and even before formal approval from Australia was obtained, Walsh immediately started the ball rolling to get his battalion ready. Appreciating that his men could be committed to combat at any time, Walsh issued a warning order to them to start preparations. This was the first that any man in the battalion had heard of a potential deployment to Korea, but the warning order proved to be a prudent step.

This sort of careful planning was indicative of the type of soldier Walsh was. Having joined the army and obtained his commission prior to the war, Walsh had a great deal of experience in the Second World War. However, this experience tended to be in planning, organizational, staff and liaison roles rather than command in combat of fighting troops. As this was to be his first serious command in battle, Walsh knew that concerted training of both the men and himself would need to take place before they were ready.

While training would be one concern, a more immediate problem was the pitifully small number of men available to the battalion – partially due to the drawdown of the BCOF in Japan and partly to an extant policy which prevented 3 RAR men from being deployed anywhere outside of Japan. Unlike the understrength British battalions that had been sent so hastily from Hong Kong, Australia decided that it would send a fully staffed battalion of 960 men. This meant that the strength of 3 RAR would need to more than double before it was ready for action.

As a first step, and in order to get around the current restrictions on deploying the men outside of Japan, all current 3 RAR soldiers were asked if they wished to volunteer for service in Korea. Almost to a man, each member volunteered. This still only amounted to a scant two companies of soldiers; more men would need to be found.

The upshot was that the Australian Army as it stood in June 1950 was unable to field a single battalion of infantry for Korea. So Australia resorted to what it had done in previous wars, putting out a call for volunteers.

Advertisements were put out in all of the major cities in Australia, asking for volunteers to serve in Korea. The response was overwhelming, and in a few short days the Army was spoiled for choice with several thousand applicants clamouring for the few hundred positions currently on offer. The volunteers mainly fell into two types of men: older Second World War veterans who had specifically enlisted to fight in Korea and a smaller proportion of younger regular army men. Most of the older 'K Force' volunteers were at this time in their late 20s or even early 30s, whereas the regulars were generally only 18–20 years old.

The non-commissioned officers were without exception veterans of the last war, and all officers at company level and above had likewise served in the Second World War. Given the number of applicants, only the very best were selected, generally being those with extensive combat experience. Such was the overwhelming response to the call for men that many experienced officers and NCOs accepted a position at a lower rank to their previous position just to ensure that they were selected.

Motivations to volunteer for Korea were varied. Most appeared to be interested in adventure or to do something different from their everyday civilian lives. For many veterans of the last conflict, post-war civilian life lacked the adventure and camaraderie of active service, and the chance of combat in Korea offered an opportunity to regain both. For the younger men, who had grown up on the stories of their relatives and friends during the war, Korea seemed to offer an opportunity for them to show their mettle and engage in adventures of their own.

Almost none of the volunteers had much knowledge about Korea, much less the issues of Communism and the beginnings of the Cold War. An exception was Lieutenant Harold Mulry, the 33-year-old commander of 3 Platoon, A Company. Mulry was considered a 'bit old' to be a platoon commander, yet he proved to be an extremely tough and able officer. He was also, unusually for an Australian, a non-drinker, frowned on bad language and was very, very religious. When asked why he was going to Korea, he replied: 'Communism is an evil thing and we have a duty to fight it.'[84]

But Mulry was very much in the minority. The chance of seeing the world and taking on something new seemed to drive more of the young men signing up at the recruitment stations than any concern about the global spread of Communism. Whatever their motivations, all of the volunteers were soon kitted out and received an abbreviated period of basic training in Australia before being flown directly to Japan for final pre-deployment training.

In terms of equipment, the Diggers (as Australian soldiers have been known since the First World War) being sent to Korea were almost indistinguishable from those who had been demobilized following the end of the war just five years ago. Like their British counterparts, the primary infantry weapons carried by the Australian soldier were the .303 Lee Enfield rifle and the Bren gun. One point of difference was that while British troops used the No 4 'spike' bayonet – essentially an 8in-long steel pin mounted to the front of the rifle – the Australians continued to use the old style 18in sword bayonet. This vicious-looking weapon had first been introduced into service in Australia prior to the Great War, and despite ceasing service in other Commonwealth countries, continued to be manufactured and used in Australia up to the end of the Second World War. The length and weight of this bayonet was designed to elicit fear into the hearts of even the stoutest enemy, and as such it was a favourite tool of the Australian soldiers.

Rounding out the section weapons was the uniquely Australian Owen sub-machine gun. A domestically designed weapon, it was extremely popular with Australian troops due to its rugged and reliable design. Unlike the British Sten gun, the Owen would keep on working even after being subjected to mud, dirt and the harshest environments. One reason for its reliability was the position of the top-mounted magazine, housing a full magazine of thirty-two 9mm rounds. The top loading allowed gravity to assist in feeding the weapon so that even when dirty or fouled it continued to function. Despite weighing nearly 5kg, the Owen was used by section commanders and scouts and was the preferred weapon of both.

As with section weapons, the personal equipment that the Diggers would carry to Korea was largely unchanged from the last war. Dressed in an Australian version of serge battledress, which was essentially the British one but with a longer jacket featuring pockets over the front waist, nail-shod boots and 37-pattern web equipment, they were virtually indistinguishable from their Second World War forebears.

Besides the Owen, the other uniquely Australian item carried – or rather worn – by the Diggers was the ubiquitous slouch hat. This broad-brimmed felt hat had been the trademark headdress of the Australian soldier since the Boer War. It would be worn proudly by the Diggers throughout the Korean conflict, and at all times except in the very depths of a frozen winter. Steel helmets were packed for Korea, but rarely worn in preference to the slouch hat.

***

Training in Japan during August was compressed but hard. Live fire training, overnight exercises and instruction on signals equipment was interwoven with long, toughening marches. One such march was dubbed by the Diggers as the '2 I/C death march'. As the tired and sweating men started to relax as they neared the end of a day's marching, the transport that was meant to take them back to base was suddenly and without warning withdrawn. The men now really had something to complain about, with a further 10-mile return journey on sore and blistered feet.

Despite their initial reluctance, the Australian government by now appeared firmly behind the scheme to send ground troops. On 15 August, in a show of support, the battalion received a visit from Robert Menzies, the newly elected Prime Minister of Australia. The recruitment programme was also going very well, and new recruits were soon arriving in Japan. A total of twenty-nine new K-Force volunteers arrived at the end of August, and more would continue to arrive in packets of thirty to forty men each day over the next week or so until the final group arrived on 11 September, finally bringing the complement of men up to its wartime strength of 960. These numbers meant that 3 RAR would be the largest of the battalions in 27 Bde, being almost 50 per cent larger than either of the two British battalions.

In addition to the newly arrived men, more equipment started to pour into the BCOF camp. New jeeps and trucks were acquired and a full complement of tracked Universal Carriers was found. These small, tracked and lightly armoured vehicles could be very useful in moving heavy weapons, stores and ammunition over the rugged terrain of Korea. However, as later events would prove, many of the carriers were starting to show their age; more than a few would soon be found wanting when it came to combat. But that was in the future, and at this stage the battalion was grateful to receive 'new' equipment and increasing numbers of men.

In many ways, the Australian battalion was very fortunate. Unlike the two British battalions that had sailed a mere week after orders were given, the Australians would arrive in Korea with a full complement of personnel, all of their mandated equipment and with time to conduct a limited but very important period of pre-deployment training.

Training was kept at a high tempo, and Walsh continued to push his men and prepare them as best he could. Lectures from US soldiers recently returned from Korea were particularly welcome, as was instruction on how to use bazookas and other weapons. In an ominous portent of the future, lectures were also given by US staff on US Army winter clothing; it was anticipated, even at this early stage, that it was highly likely the Australians would be operating in Korea during the harsh winter and that all winter stores would, of necessity, need to be sourced from the Americans.

***

While Lieutenant Colonel Walsh was working hard to bring his battalion up to speed, unknown to him, plans had been set in motion to replace him with a new commander. As already stated, Walsh was an experienced staff officer but had very little combat experience leading a battalion. Accordingly, senior command in both Australia and Japan believed that they needed to bring in an officer with more direct combat experience.

Walsh was completely unaware that moves were afoot to replace him. Nevertheless, on 8 September, having spent the past five weeks furiously training his men, he assembled them on parade to declare that 'his term as Commanding Officer had expired'[85] and that he would be replaced by a new commander from Australia, Lieutenant Colonel Charles (Charlie) Hercules Green, DSO. It would have been deeply disappointing and not a little embarrassing for Walsh to hand over command at this late stage, but he apparently accepted the decision with good grace, perhaps realizing that for Australia's first combat deployment to Korea it was essential that the battalion be led by a much more experienced combat officer. So Walsh stepped sideways into a headquarters role with BCOF, a position that more appropriately fitted his temperament and experience.

Green arrived in Japan two days later to take command of the battalion. At 30 years old, Green was relatively young to hold a battalion command, but was already acknowledged as an extremely accomplished combat soldier. He joined the militia in 1936 and then the regular army as a lieutenant in 1939. He saw active service in the Middle East and Greece before returning to the Pacific, where he was involved in extremely heavy fighting during the New Guinea campaign. When promoted to lieutenant colonel and CO of 2/11 Battalion, he was the youngest battalion commander in Australian history, being only 25 years old. For his able handling of 2/11 Battalion through some of the toughest fighting in New Guinea, Green was awarded the Distinguished Service Order (DSO).

With the war over, and following a very brief stint as a civilian upon demobilization, Green rejoined the regular Australian Army. Unlike many veterans who had to settle for a more junior post-war rank, Green was again given battalion command before being sent to Staff College. This was a great honour for the young lieutenant colonel, recognition that Green was likely destined for service in the most senior ranks of the Australian Army. When the Korean War broke out, he was still in the middle of his studies at Staff College.

It is a very rare thing to replace a battalion commander who had served with and trained his men almost up to their embarkation for war. It is rarer still to select someone who was currently a student at Staff College, particularly when there were at that time so many other capable officers available with recent combat experience. But such was Green's reputation as a skilful combat commander that he was actively sought out for the role, withdrawn from Staff College and piled on the next plane for Japan.

Green knew that he had precious little time left to get his new battalion ready for Korea. As soon as he arrived, he proceeded to put his stamp on the battalion by throwing them into a series of hard and realistic training exercises. 'The credit for transforming a heterogeneous assembly of strangers into a strong, cohesive fighting unit belonged to

LTCOL Charles Hercules Green DSO' was how 3 RAR Signals Sergeant Jack Gallaway described Green's effect upon taking command of the battalion.[86]

***

On the afternoon of 27 September, under gently falling rain, the entire battalion of just under 1,000 troops embarked on the troopship *Aiken Victory*.

It was a mere two weeks prior to the Australians' departure that the first news of the Inchon landings and the initial successes of the UN forces in rolling back the North Koreans started to come in. While undoubtedly good news, to many of the Australians furiously training in Japan, it appeared as though they might be arriving too late and that the war was effectively over. Had all of the intense training been for nothing and would they once again be relegated to simple garrison duties? Such thoughts went through many of the Diggers' minds as they pulled into a dishevelled-looking Pusan harbour on the afternoon of 28 September, met by the now ubiquitous US Army band and well-wishing Korean civilians, who presented Green and his 2IC, Major Ferguson, with flowers.

Like their British comrades before them, the Australians were greeted by the overpowering sights and smells of Pusan before being quickly allocated a train towards the Naktong. UN forces, having already commenced their breakout, had pushed back the remnants of the North Korean Army and were already moving northwards. Green's job was to follow his new brigade and get his men up to the front as soon as possible. Trucks were found and the entire battalion moved first to Teagu and then to a field near Waegwan, where 3 RAR finally caught up with its two British sister battalions.

For his part, Coad was both delighted and relieved to have the Australians join his command. Not only did the addition of nearly 1,000 well-armed and well-trained troops significantly boost his brigade's numbers, but the Australians also had a reputation for being tough and determined fighters, which was exactly what Coad would need in the months ahead.

Coad addressed the assembled Australians and told them that the immediate task of the brigade was to mop up remnants of the enemy who had been left behind during the US advance towards Seoul. He also informed the men that with the arrival of the Australians, the brigade's name would change from 27 Infantry Brigade to the new, and more accurately descriptive, 27 British Commonwealth Brigade (27 BCB).

While Coad was impressed with his new troops, the feeling was reciprocated by the Australians. Major Ben O'Dowd of 3 RAR noted that when the Australians joined the brigade, 'Coad caught the imagination of the Diggers instantly. Being a large man with a pronounced, ruddy nose, the nicknames of Plonky or Penfolds [the name of a well-known Australian red wine] were respectfully appended.'[87] Far from being disrespectful, the affectionate monikers showed that 3 RAR were happy to have Coad command them. It would be the start of a mutually appreciative and respectful relationship between Coad and the Australian troops.

Chapter 6

The Broken Bridge

The arrival of the Australians at the brigade lines around Songju in late September coincided with a generally upbeat assessment of the strategic situation on the part of UN Command. Seoul had been liberated on 29 September, and UN forces now seemed to be in the ascendency. A secret cable from Air Vice Marshal Bouchier to the British Chiefs of Staff reported: 'The 13 divisions of North Korean Army in the south have been cracked wide open and are attempting to beat a hasty retreat on all escape roads leading to the north. It is safe to say that 90% of the North Korean Army is a beaten force but not yet destroyed.'[88]

This was not to say that the enemy had simply disappeared and was no longer a threat. Quite the contrary, as many tens of thousands of enemy troops were still embedded throughout the South and were maintaining the defence of key locations. Bouchier noted that 27 BCB was still involved in mopping up large numbers of enemy forces bypassed on the UN's march north, particularly in the Songju area. Despite the ongoing operations and the recent calamity on Hill 282, Bouchier was at pains to reassure the Chiefs back in London that the troops 'are in great heart in spite of the rather heavy losses by Argyll and Sutherland Highlanders on 23 September'.[89]

The last few days of September saw the brigade occupy Songju, their original objective before the attacks on Plum Pudding Hill and Hill 282. The brigade then spent its time patrolling and clearing out parties of North Koreans who had been left behind during their hurried withdrawal. Time was also spent refitting and reorganizing the brigade.

With the rapid withdrawal of the enemy and the liberation of Seoul, Coad was now under great pressure to move the brigade quickly north towards the front. Instead of an agonizing 260-mile road move, the troops were to be loaded onto US Air Force planes at Kimpo airfield and then flown north. Giving credit where it was due, Coad noted the extreme efficiency in the planning and execution of this move: 'All went very smoothly, one American staff officer and my [staff] organized the emplaning and one American staff officer organized the deplaning. No bumf was written by anyone. I think the whole thing was a great credit to the American staff.'[90] High praise indeed from Coad, who was often scathing of US staff work.

***

With the earlier prospect of imminent defeat now being rapidly replaced by optimism of a likely military success, the issue of the 38th parallel started to excite much discussion and a good deal of handwringing in world capitals and in the United Nations itself. Some, concerned about triggering a wider war with the Soviet Union or Communist China, cautioned against any move into North Korea itself. On the other hand, most realized that it made no military sense to let the North Koreans off the hook and be allowed to simply scamper back to safe havens in the North, to rearm and re-equip. As the UN forces had only just managed to stave off defeat through the expenditure of much blood and treasure since the shocking July invasion, few were feeling charitable towards the North Koreans; no one wanted them to be in a position to launch a refreshed strike after a period of reorganization.

In the United States, most voices in the Truman administration acknowledged the need for some form of limited pursuit into North Korea 'to finish the job'. Nevertheless, almost all expressed the firm view that UN forces, and US troops in particular, should not approach anywhere near the Chinese and Soviet borders, for fear of provoking a wider war. If any troops needed to move near to the Chinese border, it was felt that task must be undertaken by South Korean forces alone.

This debate and dithering did not extend to MacArthur. Supremely confident in his own abilities and bolstered by the evidence of his overwhelming success in planning and executing the Inchon landings, he was convinced of imminent victory and the absolute necessity of pursuing the North Koreans past the 38th parallel.

On 1 October, in typical MacArthur style, he issued a demand to the North Koreans to lay down their arms. 'The early and total defeat and complete destruction of your armed forced and war-making potential is now inevitable,' MacArthur said, in a confident but ultimately premature message to the Commander-in-Chief of the North Korean forces. He then called on the North Koreans 'to lay down your arms and cease hostilities under such military supervision as I may direct'.[91]

Even as MacArthur's demand was sent over the airwaves, South Korean troops had already started to cross the parallel. US forces of the Eighth Army would follow about a week later, eager to conclude the war as quickly as possible. What ensued was a spate of tough fighting lasting about a week, after which the North Koreans broke and the UN forces started a speedy, headlong drive north towards the Manchurian border and what many had concluded would be victory by Christmas.

***

Back at 27 British Commonwealth Brigade, 3 RAR was to find that its honeymoon and settling-in period was unexpectedly cut short. On 3 October, the 2IC of C Company, Captain Hummerston, and his driver, Private Sketchley, were travelling in a Bren gun carrier a few miles south of Waegwan when they drove over an unmarked minefield, setting off a series of Russian, wooden box-type anti-tank mines. The mines exploded one after another until the carrier was overturned, killing both occupants. This was a tragic beginning to Australia's campaign but helped to remind everyone in the battalion that Korea was a dangerous place, even when operating in a supposedly quiet sector.

The battalion had no time to dwell on this loss as the whole brigade soon received orders to move north. On 12 October, lead elements of the brigade crossed the 38th parallel. Curiously, and despite the symbolism of crossing the parallel, it was hardly remarked upon by the men of 27 BCB. The Brigade War Diary says little about the event. Even the 3 RAR War Diary, which gave the most fulsome account of the crossing, merely noted that on 13 October, the battalion moved about 100 yards north of the parallel.[92]

More important than the line on a map were the orders for UN troops to move northwards at all speed in order to crush the fleeing North Koreans and finish the war. For most American and South Korean troops, these orders were interpreted literally, resulting in a fast advance northwards, with speed and aggression prized over caution and patience. Part of the rapid advance can be put down to the American desire to capitalize on the North Korean collapse. But part can also be attributed to the character of the overall commander, Douglas MacArthur, as well as divisional commanders such as General Hobart Gay, who had been on General Patton's staff during the Second World War and had inherited much of his former chief's hard driving approach to combat.

The result was an extremely fast advance of UN forces deep into North Korea. The advance was, however, concentrated on major roads, which allowed the highly mechanized Americans to move forward at great speed. The NKPA troops appeared to melt into the landscape, apparently fleeing before the all-conquering Americans.

Coad, however, had a different conception as to how he would advance his brigade. Rather than the impulsive dash along the roads, which he frequently criticized US forces for adopting, he preferred to use a methodical 'one foot on the ground' approach to keep momentum while ensuring the security of his forces. He was insistent on clearing flanks and hills overlooking the main line of march, and at all times tried to ensure that his brigade was covered by some form of indirect fire support. These hallmarks of the Coad approach helped to ensure the safety and security of his forces as well as placing it in the best possible position to fight should that become necessary.

Sariwon

The brigade continued in its northern advance, even when torrential rain struck on 15 October, turning tracks to thick mud. Even the most enthusiastic soldier can become downbeat when they are cold and wet, and to a man, the riflemen were wrapped in their individual thoughts as they huddled together, shoulder to shoulder and soaking wet in the open-top backs of their US Army trucks. At least the Aussies received a modicum of protection from their broad-brimmed slouch hats, whereas both the Argylls and the

Middlesex men just removed their sodden caps and berets, useless in warding off the incessant rain.

Fortunately, the rain receded the next day and spirits consequently rose slightly. On 16 October, Coad received orders that his brigade was to capture the town of Sariwon the next day. Sariwon was an important military base and town, just to the north-east of the brigade's current position near Kaesong and south of the North Korean capital of Pyongyang.

Sariwon was taken on the 17th by 1 ASH following a stiff fight on the outskirts of the town against some remnant NKPA troops. Thereafter, 3 RAR entered the town and moved through the Jocks before taking up defensive positions to the north of Sariwon.

What happened next could almost be considered comical were it not for the deadly serious consequences if things had gone differently. After clearing the outskirts of the town, elements of 1 ASH were patrolling into and through Sariwon, unaware that North Korean troops were at the same time entering the town from the other direction. Both parties then met each other at various places inside Sariwon, but luck was on the side of the Scotsmen as neither side opened fire. Somehow, the NKPA troops thought that the strangely clad British troops, wearing their soft comforter hats, were Russians sent to assist them rather than British troops sent to fight them. The Argylls were able to deduce this from the frequent cries of '*Ruski, Ruski*!' made by the North Koreans as they moved past. The Argylls, terribly exposed, did little to dissuade them, and both sides waved to each other as they went by.

The fact was that UN forces and North Korean troops were hopelessly intermingled, which but for the confusion on the part of the Koreans could have turned into a vicious close-quarter fight. The Australian War Diary described this mixing of Korean and Commonwealth troops as follows:

> 'The confusion caused by the rapid advance of Allied units can be imagined when it is realised that between 24th US Division's advance north and 7th US Cavalry Regiment moving south, the following troops were located in a 20 mile road: reading from south to north, 24th Inf Div, North Koreans, Two Companies of 1 ASH, North Koreans, remainder of 1 ASH, North Koreans, 3 RAR, North Koreans, 7th Cavalry Regiment.'[93]

The fortunate misunderstanding did not last, however, and shortly thereafter a firefight broke out, which quickly shattered the bewildered North Koreans. At the end of the day, over 200 North Korean troops had been killed and a staggering 1,200 were captured in and around Sariwon. On the British side, only a single soldier was killed.

One can be forgiven for doubting that the North Koreans could have been so gullible and believe that this incident was perhaps invented by imaginative British soldiers after the fact. However, these events were reported in numerous first-hand sources, which strongly suggests that the incident did indeed take place in the manner outlined above.

Race to Pyongyang

Following their overwhelming success at Sariwon, Coad and all the men of 27 British Commonwealth Brigade had hoped that they would have the honour of marching into Pyongyang ahead of other UN forces. But it was not to be. Despite being one of the closest UN units to the North Korean capital, it was perhaps inevitable that Coad was instructed to halt his men and not to enter the city. Rather than British forces, the first UN units to enter Pyongyang were South Korean, elements of the 1st ROK Division under the command of the experienced and capable General Paik Sun Yup, supported by a large compliment of American armour.

With the prize of the enemy capital denied to them, Coad received orders to move his brigade to the west of Pyongyang. Just what the brigade was to do when it got there was unclear, and despite his best efforts (including personally visiting the nearby divisional headquarters), Coad never received any clear orders as to his task beyond, 'go to grid XXX and wait for further orders'. Coad, unhappy about such vague directions, would later officially report: 'From 18 to 20 October there literally ensued a race as to whom was to get to Pyongyang first and there seemed to be no form of co-ordination by the higher command. 27 Bde was put out to the west on what turned out to be an atrocious axis, as usual, and told to get there as soon as we could.'[94]

Pakchon, 25–26 October – Broken Bridge

As the brigade vehicles wound their way to the west of Pyongyang, they moved into an area criss-crossed by many wide, fast-flowing rivers. These major rivers, together with their minor tributaries and streams, proved to be significant obstacles and slowed down the brigade's forward movement significantly. The rivers were hard to cross, and the delay in doing so was exacerbated by the fact that the brigade had no assault boats or any integral engineering resources. As with many things, the brigade had to rely solely on external US engineering assistance – which was at this time in precious short supply – in order to cross these significant water obstacles. To make matters worse, most of the bridges that had existed in this area had already been destroyed, either by the US Air Force earlier in the war or more recently by the retreating North Koreans, desperate to slow down the rapidly advancing UN forces. The result was that the brigade was often forced to take lengthy detours to find a suitable ford or to use hastily constructed sandbag bridges as a makeshift expedient to cross.

Otherwise, the men had no choice but to wait for the precious few available assault boats delivered by overworked US engineers. This was not a preferred option, however, as the far banks of the river were often held by groups of enemy soldiers, making even the shortest crossing hazardous for the Commonwealth troops, exposed to machine-gun fire.

One of the more famous river crossings was that made by the Australians across an already demolished bridge south of Pakchon on 25/26 October. Coad succinctly described the action, with enormous understatement, as follows:

> 'One section managed to cross the broken bridge, when a number of Koreans dressed in white clothing came down the hills waving South Korean flags. They suddenly went to ground and opened fire. The section was withdrawn and a proper attack launched with a fire plan and by dark two companies were across the river on the high ground. The 3 RAR had a sticky night with their two companies across the river as two enemy tanks got behind their forward defended localities.'[95]

Describing it as 'a sticky night' is probably not how the men of 3 RAR would have characterized the battle, which took place at the soon-to-be-nicknamed 'Broken Bridge'. The full story was much more complicated and resulted in one of the Australians' most significant actions of late 1950.

***

On 25 October, the Australians moved through the muddy tidal flats and banks of the Taeryong River near the village of Kujin. From Kujin, the main road towards the north (and ultimately the border with China) turns west across the Taeryong River and on towards the towns of Chongju and Sinuiji. The Taeryong at this point was not much more than 100 yards across at low tide. However, due to the river experiencing a large variation between high and low tide, the width of the river swelled appreciably at high tide. Furthermore, the waters in late October were bone-chillingly cold and it was almost impossible for anyone to attempt to swim the river. To cross the Taeryong, the Australians needed a bridge.

Sadly for the Australians, the bridge they did have – a large, two-lane concrete and steel structure outside the town of Kujin – had been partially demolished and was now lying in pieces with a number of its spans demolished, broken and hanging down into the river below. A contemporary photograph, taken on 26 October at low tide, shows the eastern end of the bridge (i.e. the bank closest to the Australians) abruptly shorn off and hanging perpendicularly down over 20ft to the river surface. With difficulty, it was possible for individual soldiers to climb the perpendicular section and up onto the flat portion of the bridge, which remained intact above them. They could then gingerly make their way across the wreckage to the other shore. While this would prove a difficult trip for a lone rifleman, it was plain that it would be impossible for any of the battalion vehicles to cross at this point until a more significant repair was effected or an alternate crossing located.

Owing to the condition of the destroyed bridge, it was from this point onwards dubbed by the Aussies – uncreatively – as the 'Broken Bridge'.

At around 1630hrs, with daylight fading but wanting to ensure that he had control of the far bank, Green sent two sections from 4 Platoon, B Company, under the command of Lieutenant Alby Morrison to cross the bridge and take up positions on the high ground immediately to the forward left on the west bank. With no enemy in sight, Morrison led his men carefully over the broken concrete and steel spans to the far bank. After crossing the bridge and making their way up the steep western bank, the men took up temporary defensive positions. The Australians then saw some fifty or so enemy soldiers approaching them from the right (i.e. north), with their arms held high and without any visible weapons. Evidently, the North Koreans had been observing the Australians moving forward and were looking to surrender.

As the enemy got closer to the wary 3 RAR troops, small-arms fire suddenly erupted from the high ground to the left (south), with rounds splashing around both the B Company troops and the surrendering North Koreans alike. Fortunately, the enemy fire 'was not very accurate', explained Morrison. 'I mean, they must have been as scared as anybody else was.'[96] The Aussies returned fire and the prisoners either went to ground or scattered, desperately trying to find some cover.

The enemy troops, however, soon found their targets and both the weight and accuracy of fire increased markedly. This rise in tempo convinced Morrison that the attackers were unlikely to be some isolated listening post but rather a sizeable group of North Koreans intent on holding the far bank and repulsing the Diggers. This supposition was confirmed by a Mosquito reconnaissance aircraft patrolling nearby, which soon spotted what looked to be up to two companies (approximately 200 men) of enemy troops hidden nearby. The discovery made it clear to the forward soldiers of 3 RAR that their foothold on the west bank was untenable.

Assessing the situation, Green immediately requested an air strike to give cover to the forward platoons while they withdrew back over the bridge towards the rest of the battalion. At 1715hrs, a pair of F-80 Shooting Star jet aircraft appeared and put in a strike with guns and rockets on the high ground to the south of the bridge where the enemy were sheltering. The Shooting Stars were among the first type of fighter jets employed by the US Air Force at the tail end of the Second World War. While their distinctive straight-wing design would soon prove to be inferior to Russian MiGs in air-to-air combat, they were nevertheless formidable ground-attack aircraft. Their quick presence over the battlefield and accurate rocket fire would have been very welcome to the withdrawing Australians. Further pressure was put on the North Koreans with 3in mortar and artillery fire, quickly and accurately called in by Green.

Morrison was full of praise for the US Air Force and the support they gave on that occasion: '[T]hey brought in air and blasted [them] to get me out. Now … I could still get down the pillars [of the bridge], they were still there, and they [the Air Force] really blasted the hills around. My twenty soldiers got out ... and ten prisoners – and that was due to the Air Force.'[97] Under the cover of the US Air Force, Morrison withdrew to the bridge, taking ten prisoners with them (the remainder having either escaped or fallen to 'friendly fire'), before once again making the slow and perilous crossing of the bridge back to the battalion on the east bank.

With all of his men back on the west bank, Green now faced a choice. He could withdraw and move his battalion north towards Pakchon and try to cross the river there the next day, or alternatively attempt to move a larger force across the river, eliminate the enemy troops on the other side and secure the bridgehead for further operations. Green chose the bolder move and immediately made plans to move two full companies, approximately half of his force, across the river after nightfall.

As preparations were being made to re-cross the Broken Bridge in force and assault the enemy, D Company, commanded by Major Wally Brown, was ordered to move a mile-and-a-half to the north to clear the village of Pakchon. Brown was accompanied by a platoon of engineers from the 72nd Engineer Combat Battalion, who were planning to make a ford on the river in the vicinity of Pakchon which eventually would allow the vehicles and tanks to cross. Major Brown's men made short work of their task and in less than an hour had cleared the town and were on the way back to Battalion HQ, leaving behind a platoon to provide security for the engineers. Brown's company also brought back a staggering 225 prisoners to add to the ten that Morrison's men had captured on the far bank. It appeared that the North Koreans in Pakchon were so demoralized that it took little more than a bold show of force on the part of Brown's men to persuade the enemy to give up. This was despite the North Koreans having a numerical advantage nearly double that of Brown's force.

While Brown was herding his prisoners back towards Battalion HQ, Green had arranged preparatory artillery fire to pound the far bank of the river opposite them. At 1900hrs, the battlefield was already covered in darkness, only to be punctured by the rhythmic bright flashes and explosions of the falling HE shells, quickly followed by the crumping sound of the shells reaching the 3 RAR HQ from the far bank. With this deadly but comforting light and sound show ahead of them, lead elements of A and B Companies started to silently slip back across the bridge. One by one, the soldiers climbed back onto the intact spans of the bridge and made their way over to the other side, whereupon they took up positions, scanning the darkness for signs of the enemy. Amazingly, both companies got across without incident; B Company was allocated positions to the right of the road and A Company to the left. C and D Companies remained on the eastern bank of the river, supported by a small number of US Army tanks.

The calm was short-lived. As soon as B Company had assembled on the far shore, small groups of enemy soldiers could be seen forming up for an attack. A quick call for mortar support resulted in a short crumping barrage of flame and shrapnel, which quickly dispersed the disorganized North Koreans and disrupted their attack. While this small action was taking place, the final few men of A and B Companies continued to thread their way through the broken spans of the bridge, and upon reaching the muddy bank beyond they clambered onto the higher ground on the west bank.

It had been an hour since Green's preparatory artillery barrage, but now, around 2000hrs, enemy artillery shells from a camouflaged North Korean SP gun started to fall among Battalion HQ and C Company back on the far shore. While the falling shot caused a deal of anxiety among the headquarters troops, fortunately very little damage was done since most of the shells failed to explode. The cause was likely the fact that they were armour-piercing shells rather than the standard High Explosive ordinance.

With A and B Company now safely across the river and having prepared what defensive positions they could in the dark, the men strained their eyes looking for signs of an enemy that they knew to be close by. They did not have to wait long. At around 2230 hrs, more enemy activity was detected near the forward platoons, which the company commanders surmised was likely some form of preliminary reconnaissance prior to an attack. In hushed voices, they alerted their men, telling them to get ready. Accompanying the reports of enemy scouting parties was a lazy barrage of mortar fire, sent down by some nearby but hidden North Korean mortar crew.

Sure that the enemy was fully aware of their presence, there was now no point in keeping silent. B Company responded to the North Korean reconnaissance with short, controlled shots from the riflemen's .303s, together with bursts from their Bren guns. The forward companies called for reinforcements, whereupon Green quickly ordered C Company to detach one of its platoons to cross the bridge and bolster the B Company position.

Having determined the location and distribution of the 3 RAR men, the North Korean commander increased the pressure on them. Enemy small-arms and machine-gun fire increased markedly, soon starting to take its toll. By midnight, the combination of the increased fire and the regular barrages of enemy mortars resulted in B Company having two of its number killed and a further three wounded. A Company was also starting to take casualties, and the long night was only halfway over.

While the battle continued on the far bank, Sergeant Tom Murray, leading the stretcher bearer teams, took charge to try to evacuate the wounded men and provide what first aid they could. His efforts were hampered by the Broken Bridge, which was proving a formidable obstacle to smooth casualty evacuation. Adding to the challenge, the rapidly rising tide soon made the journey across the bridge extremely difficult for even a fit and unencumbered man. For those carrying a stretcher and a wounded man, the journey was now impossible.

Undeterred, and fully aware that the chances of a wounded man surviving decreased sharply with the passage of time, Murray was desperate to find a way to move his wounded men back across the river. He initially borrowed a small foldable boat from the American engineers and attempted to use it to cross the river, but the boat was in bad shape and it quickly sank. Taking another boat, Murray had a wounded man loaded on board while he attempted to guide it across by means of a series of ropes while he stood on top of the bridge. While attempting this difficult and delicate manoeuvre, he was continually exposed to enemy sniper fire; rounds kept on pinging and ricocheting off the spans near the intensely focussed sergeant. Despite Murray's efforts, the strong tide proved too much for the rickety craft. When the boat grazed a damaged pylon, it immediately began to sink in the 7ft of icy water, threatening to drag down and drown the wounded passenger strapped onto his stretcher.

With no time to arrange a rescue, Murray immediately raced along the bridge to the spot of the stricken vessel, flinging off his clothes as he went. He then dove into the frigid waters, the cold knocking the air out of his lungs as he surfaced. Undeterred, he managed to get to the boat and was able to guide it safely back to shore and the assistance of waiting bystanders, saving the wounded man from what otherwise threatened to be the battalion's first death by drowning.

Murray, now suffering from exposure and cold, was taken to the Regimental Aid Post and was soon warmed up. He did not dither, soon returning to lead his stretcher bearers and assist the wounded. This painstakingly slow task would continue into the daylight hours until, by means of a series of ropes, pulleys and makeshift wooden ladders, all of the wounded men were transported safely across the broken bridge, lowered to the river bank and ultimately taken to an aid post on the east bank.

Murray's actions earned him one of the rarest of medals bestowed during the Korean War, the George Medal. The George Medal is ordinarily awarded to civilians for 'acts of great bravery', but can, very rarely, be awarded to military personnel 'for gallant conduct that is not in the face of the enemy' and for 'actions for which purely military Honours are not normally granted'.[98]

Murray's superiors clearly recognized that he deserved some form of award for his actions, but were at a loss regarding what to recommend him for. Technically, his rescue efforts were not involved in the fighting (although he was clearly in immediately danger from nearby snipers and enemy fire). The original citation prepared by 3 RAR's commander merely recommended him for a Mentioned in Despatches, the very lowest award possible. This was also recommended by both Coad and Robertson in Tokyo.

Nevertheless, this parsimonious and wholly inappropriate recommendation was overturned by the Australian Chief of the General Staff, Lieutenant General S.F. Rowell, who believed that Murray deserved much more than a mere MiD. Rather, he recommended Murray for a British Empire Medal, a significantly higher award, which can be awarded to both civilians and military personnel. Finally, however, Murray was awarded the George Medal, which was gazetted in 1951. According to Jack Gallaway, the battalion's Signal Sergeant: 'The award of the George Medal to Tom Murray was one of the more popular ones of the campaign. The drum major's performance, and that of his men on the broken bridge, was a forerunner of the consistently gallant endeavours to help their comrades in the battles to come.'[99] Many wounded men of 3 RAR would ultimately owe their lives to the tireless actions of Murray and his stretcher parties, men who in peacetime would ordinarily be members of the battalion's band.[100]

While Murray was performing his singular act of bravery at the bridge, the battle on the far bank continued, both sides trading fire, manoeuvring and taking casualties. At about 0400hrs on 26 October, the North Koreans mounted an attack involving some sixty troops in Russian-made jeeps and on a motorbike. More worryingly, the attack was supported by two of their formidable T-34 tanks. The tanks and jeeps deposited the infantry at their start lines, then the tanks started to slowly clatter forward. As they did so, they trained both their main guns and machine guns on the men of B Company on the high ground on the right side of the road. It was fortunate for the Aussies that it was still dark and the tankers were poor shots. Nevertheless, large-calibre machine-gun rounds from the tanks intermittently splashed near the B Company men, while high-velocity rounds from the main guns were fired ineffectually towards Battalion HQ over the far side of the river.

To provide some support to their B Company comrades, the men of A Company poured everything they had at the newly arrived North Korean infantry. Muzzle flashes lit the night as the A Company Bren gunners fired their distinctive, growling four to five-round bursts. They were trying desperately to break up the North Korean attack and buy time for B Company to get out of the killing zone. At the same time, the stranded B Company soldiers were attempting to hide from the lumbering T-34s, lying flat in any fold in the ground or hiding behind anything that might offer some protection from the tanks' machine guns. The advancing T-34s were fearsome, even from a distance. Private Geoff Butler of A Company, over on the left side of the road, is reported to have said afterwards that the tanks 'looked about the size of the Taxation Building and equally fearsome'.[101]

The tanks continued to move up to the B Company men, at one stage getting as close as 10ft from their headquarters. This spurred the men to try out their new 3.5in bazookas on the temptingly close flanks of the T-34s. Spotting the nearest tank, the bazooka crew momentarily popped up to take a shot. At this range they couldn't miss, and yet something went wrong. The team depressed the bazooka's trigger, but all they heard was a 'click' as it failed to fire. Swearing, the bazooka team dove back behind cover before the rotating turret and machine guns could fix on them.

After the battle, the cause of the fault was revealed, much to the embarrassment of the bazooka crew. Far from being a mechanical fault, the failure was wholly crew-related. 'In the excitement of the moment,' said the 3 RAR War Diary, 'the safety catch had not been released by the operator.'[102]

The infantry fire from A Company was having considerably more success, tearing into the North Korean infantry. By about 0630hrs, once the sun had made its way above the horizon, the remnants of the enemy troops fled the scene, leaving behind many bodies of their fallen comrades, together with a number of destroyed jeeps and motorcycles that had brought them forward a scant two hours before.

Many of the vehicles were bullet-riddled, with smashed windshields, damaged engines and shredded tyres, making them completely unusable. However, one or two were somewhat serviceable, and with a bit of work and some new paint, the commandeered vehicles were swiftly absorbed into the battalion's transport pool.

Of more significance was the discovery of a pile of maps and documents on the body of a North Korean colonel, which would yield valuable intelligence to UN forces when they were quickly passed up the chain of command.

The documents consisted of a series of notebooks and maps belonging to a Lieutenant Colonel Kim In Sik, the Reconnaissance Section chief of 17 Tank Brigade. Kim also appears to have been the 'cultural officer' of 17 Tank Brigade, a position peculiar to Communist armies. In the North Korean Army (and also both the Soviet and Chinese armies) there existed a parallel command structure which saw all major units having both a military commander and a political (or cultural) commander. Technically, the military commander was senior in all military matters, but in reality the political officer had great sway and could at times overrule a military commander or even have him removed. Kim's notebooks gave a good insight into the work of a political officer. They detailed military matters such as the numbers of North Korean troops and comments on their enemy. They also contained candid descriptions of the challenges facing the North Koreans at this stage of the war, with the heady days of victory in July and August now long behind them.

One entry, made on 25 October 1950, a mere day before the Australians attacked the Broken Bridge and where Kim would meet his end, is illustrative:

> '[I]t seems that our Infantry and tank preparations were late before the enemy. The demands of the front line troops were ammunition … Since morning, members of the Culture Section were sent out to recruit local farmers and retreating soldiers for our transportation purposes. The problem of clothing for our troops has not been settled … the enemy's air attacks have increased. It seems they are supporting the ground troops who will probably cross the river and advance. We are in a bad position.'[103]

These notes were a frank admission that the North Koreans were not doing well. They also suggest that at least some of the men whom A Company fought, who had arrived by jeep on the morning of the 26th, were likely either newly recruited farmers or retreating soldiers, press-ganged into service. They were unlikely to have included many of the crack troops who had spearheaded the North Korean victorious advance several months before.

Kim's notes then take an interesting turn, describing how the men of 17 Tank Brigade planned to address their shortcomings: '[T]he time for overall counterplan is here … a new culture propaganda plan was established to change the tide of battle from defence to attack … former staff members were replaced … yesterday I, the Corp chief of staff and the Brigade commander conferred about the education of the men.'[104]

Admittedly, the focus on propaganda or 'cultural' matters was likely to feature more prominently in the notebooks of the political commander than in those of the military commander. Nevertheless, it shows that significant time and energy was being directed at political matters, even when the North Korean soldiers were very clearly on the backfoot. Indeed, the fact that they were on the defensive may have caused the leadership to double down on political and cultural 'education'. It can be imagined that when ammunition and suitable clothing were in short supply, it may have been tempting to turn to the remaining inexhaustible resources at the Koreans' fingertips – political slogans and cultural lessons. Unfortunately for the North Koreans at the Broken Bridge, including Colonel Kim, no amount of cultural indoctrination could compensate for lack of ammunition and weapons against an extremely well trained and equipped band of fighting soldiers such as 3 RAR.

***

C Company could now thread their way across the Broken Bridge unopposed and they too soon took up defensive positions on the far bank. By 1100hrs, the bridge and the ridges to the west of the river were firmly in 3 RAR's hands. The remainder of 3 RAR, its HQ and transport then moved off to cross the river 2 miles north near Pakchong. It would take the best part of twenty-four hours before the entire battalion was reunited on the west bank of the Taeryong River.

The clash at Broken Bridge was a bloody one and set the standard for much of the fighting that 3 RAR would encounter over the coming months. It was estimated that around 100 enemy had been killed during this action, including the North Korean colonel. A further thirty-eight prisoners were also in custody, keeping the battalion Company Sergeant Majors busy working out a plan to send them to a divisional holding facility. While undoubtedly an Australian victory, the fighting at the Broken Bridge had come at a cost. Eight men had been killed and another twenty were wounded, depleting the fighting companies and providing yet another headache for the overworked stretcher bearers and medical teams.

Having succeeded in a tough fight against a determined enemy and over such a difficult obstacle, they could be forgiven for congratulating themselves on their well-earned success. However, the unrelenting war in Korea did not allow the luxury of celebrations and the men were soon on the move again.

The constant movement across atrocious roads and terrain, travelling in vehicles that often broke down under the harsh conditions, also led to a slow drip feed of casualties from vehicle-related accidents. For example, on 27 October alone, the Brigade Major was killed in a traffic accident and the commander of A Company, Major Gordon, suffered serious injuries when his jeep had an unfortunate scrape with a Sherman tank. Gordon's jeep inevitably came off second-best from that encounter, and he was quickly evacuated, Captain Chitts, his 2IC, assuming command of the company.

These accidents were not isolated. The entire brigade suffered a slow but constant loss of key personnel, usually company and staff officers, to vehicle accidents throughout the campaign. Korea was a deadly and dangerous place for the Commonwealth Brigade, even when not directly in the line of fire.

***

Despite the casualties and setbacks, spirits in 3 RAR remained high. Following the actions at Pakchon, the battalion was content to fall back to supporting roles, acting as brigade reserve as the Argylls and then the Middlesex Battalion in turn assumed the lead. Both of the British battalions had several sharp encounters, including with more T-34s and self-propelled guns. Fortunately, the Middlesex men had learned the lesson of their hapless Australian cousins, and when the lumbering tanks came close enough they were sure to disengage the safety catch before firing their potent bazookas. Together with deadly accurate airstrikes, a total of ten T-34s were knocked out, together with a number of SP guns, showing that the Commonwealth Brigade appeared to be immune from 'T-34 sickness'.

This significant loss of enemy armour would have delighted the 1 MX soldiers, who would have engaged in some light-hearted ribbing of their Australian counterparts over their recent safety catch failure. The actions during October had proven that the Australians were extremely capable soldiers – possibly the best battalion in the brigade at this stage, owing to a combination of being significantly larger than the British battalions, relatively fresh, well equipped and extremely well led. Nevertheless, the Australians' pride, satisfaction and enthusiasm borne out of their recent successes would suffer a significant setback during the very last days of October.

Chapter 7

Chongju

On 29 October, 3 RAR was once more back in the lead of the 27 Bde. The brigade's new objective was Chongju, an important town located some 40 miles south of the border with China. Chongju was also a critical road and rail junction, so the brigade needed to capture it to secure the lines of communication for further UN operations in the area and the expected advance to the frontier with China.

With Green's battalion now in the van, the brigade was making good progress despite almost continual contact with the enemy. Several miles short of Chongju, 3 RAR entered a valley filled with paddy fields interspaced by several pine and scrub-topped hillocks. Intelligence from an overhead Mosquito reconnaissance aircraft had alerted Green to the presence of enemy forces up ahead, who had set up defensive positions among the hills straddling the east–west road to Chongju. Worryingly, the Mosquito also reported that there were a number of well-hidden T-34 tanks and self-propelled guns to the battalion's front.

Quickly realizing that the tanks would be the most serious obstacle to his advance, Green put in a request for immediate air support. Co-operation from the Americans was outstanding and the Australian commander was soon given a ringside seat to a masterful display of American firepower. US Air Force F-80s and F-51 fighter-bombers were quickly on station, the morning air punctuated by the sounds and explosions of the aircraft knocking out several of the tanks and SP artillery guns. Reports at this time of critically low fuel and ammunition supplies on the part of the NKPA armoured units may explain the rapidly mounting losses of enemy armoured vehicles and their inability to use those assets to full effect. That said, even overflowing supplies to the NKPA would have done little to counter the overwhelming air superiority enjoyed by the UN forces and the deadly accuracy of the US Air Force.

Green, for one, was delighted with the US air support. With the armoured threat to his front now reduced (but not eliminated), he ordered his forward companies to advance and assault the remaining enemy defending the hills either side of the east–west road. As the Diggers moved forward, they found that the NKPA infantry were still very much in evidence, continuing to fight and harass the advancing 3 RAR men from ridge lines and concealed positions among the dense vegetation. Small-arms fire and the odd mortar round harassed and peppered the Aussies as they continued their steady advance. Fortunately, most of the incoming fire was reported as being both light and inaccurate

– more of an annoyance than a serious threat. Nevertheless, by early afternoon, North Korean resistance was stiffening and the Australians started to encounter much tougher pockets of enemy that could not be easily silenced.

The battalion was advancing in a formation with three companies forward and one company in reserve, using a rough road as the axis of advance. This formation gave the battalion a wide frontage, allowing maximum firepower to be brought forward as needed. D Company, under Major Brown, was advancing on the south side of the road, with B Company in the centre along the axis and A Company on the northern side of the road.

At approximately 1430hrs, D Company started taking accurate fire from a small hill to its front. This was a well dug-in position which necessitated Brown putting in a full company attack supported by a number of attached US Army Sherman tanks. Shortly thereafter, Brown's lead platoon moved forward to the objective, riding on the backs of the Shermans to a point as far forward as they could before accurate rifle fire forced them to dismount, seek cover and then carry on the attack by foot. The Shermans moved to a flank and provided covering fire, spraying the enemy position with deadly machine-gun bursts while the dismounted infantry quickly moved up in bounds. As the Diggers closed on the enemy trenches, a vicious fight ensued which lasted over two hours. The NKPA troops would not be easily dislodged, employing both small arms and a quantity of anti-tank weapons to keep the attackers at bay. Firing several armour-piercing anti-tank rounds at the Shermans, one of them hit home, blowing off the turret from the lead tank and destroying it. Nonetheless, by late afternoon the combination of excellent infantry skills, dash and aggression succeeded in giving victory to the relentlessly advancing D Company.

With resistance on the southern side of the road neutralized, the focus of the battle swung over to A Company, advancing to the north of the road. They too started to meet stiff resistance from a knot of enemy soldiers dug-in on a small pine-studded hill. This stubborn enemy position necessitated another company attack, again supported by two platoons of Shermans. This fight, however, only lasted an hour before all the North Koreans had either been killed or fled.

As night started to creep over the battleground, the enemy used the coming darkness as an opportunity to counter-attack. Directly to the front of D Company, the NKPA assembled troops, determined to regain control of the hill they had just been ejected from. D Company, hearing NKPA soldiers massing at the foot of the feature for an attack, readied themselves for the assault they knew would soon follow. With eyes straining to spot the advancing enemy, and anxiety growing, it would have been all too easy to start firing down the hill towards suspected enemy forming-up points, but Brown told his men to hold their fire. He wanted them to wait until the enemy was directly to their front, where he knew his men could not fail to hit their targets. Finally, when the Koreans came into view, the order was given and the whole company opened up with all their weapons, cutting a terrible swathe through the attackers and pushing them back.

During the fighting, a lone T-34 briefly provided covering fire to the attacking NKPA troops before it was set on fire by D Company's Private Jack Stafford. When the fighting began, Stafford had crawled forward with his Bren gun to get a good view of the tank. Lucky to remain unseen by the crew of the hulking metal monster, he unleashed a concerted stream of rounds towards the tank; he was luckier still when tracer rounds hit the T-34's external fuel tanks, causing them to explode and quickly set the entire tank on fire. As the tank started to burn, Stafford calmly killed all of the crew as they tried to escape from their hatches.

With the attack on D Company failing and desperate to regain lost ground, the previously dispersed enemy to the front of A Company had re-formed themselves. Spurred on by their commanders, the North Koreans were urged to make a spirited frontal attack, described in the 3 RAR War Diary as a 'banzai charge' – a reference to the fanatical frontal charges often adopted by the Japanese in the Second World War. Despite the undoubted bravery of the attacking troops, it was ultimately a foolhardy attempt, quickly broken up by accurate 3in mortar and artillery fire. As the bombs and shells fell among the Koreans, their momentum was soon destroyed, leaving them vulnerable to steady fire by the A Company men. Near midnight, all attacks petered out and finally stopped: 3RAR had succeeded in both taking and holding the position.

The fighting around Chongju demonstrated once again the cool and lethal professionalism of the 3 RAR commanders and men. Over the course of some twelve hours, they had inflicted over 150 casualties on the enemy. They had also knocked out several well camouflaged T-34s with their new 3.5in bazookas and called in successful air strikes against several others. On the debit side, nine Australians were killed that day and a further thirty wounded. While a fraction of the enemy dead, these were nevertheless serious casualties – in effect an entire rifle section was killed and a platoon made ineffective from wounds. While the Australian battalion was a relatively large force (compared to the British battalions), these were heavy losses for a single afternoon's work. Unfortunately, such casualty rates would continue in the months that followed.

Green

As dawn broke on the morning of 30 October, 27 Bde's relentless advance continued. Resistance had slowed appreciably, and while there were still some isolated exchanges of gunfire, they were much lighter than those endured by 3 RAR over the preceding few days. Several prisoners were also taken throughout the day, suggesting that the fight had temporarily gone out of the North Koreans. By late afternoon, the battalion came to a halt and started to make preparations for their evening camp. As the men executed their by now well-drilled evening routine, Green had every reason to be pleased with the men whom he had only led for a mere six weeks. They had shown themselves to be capable, professional and tough, and Green was rightly proud to lead such a battalion.

At approximately 1810hrs, and with shadows lengthening, Green was in his tent, resting and preparing orders for the next day. Battalion HQ was situated in a relatively safe position, inside a gully and surrounded by the four fighting companies located on the higher ground around it. Although Green had been on the move for the past two days, he still went to visit each of his company commanders and issued orders before returning to rest in his tent in the gully.

Men moved all around the headquarters, completing the hundreds of small jobs necessary to establish a HQ in the field. Signallers ran communications line to the forward companies, the RAP was set up and the Company Sergeant Majors were busily tallying up ammunition expenditure and arranging resupply. Meanwhile, jeeps came in and out of the HQ position with supplies of food and ammunition. The well-rehearsed and automatic activity of the headquarters was pleasing to the commander, indicating a battalion that despite having just fought several hard battles over the past few days was still a thoroughly efficient and well-oiled fighting machine.

Then suddenly, and without any warning, a volley of six artillery shells fell on the Battalion HQ. The volley was likely fired at random rather than being carefully directed by forward observers. With more than fifty men working around the site, amazingly no one was hit – no one, that is, apart from the battalion commander resting in his tent. 'The CO's copped it!" someone yelled, and men rushed to help. Unfortunately, when they got to the remains of Green's tent, they immediately saw that a large piece of hot shrapnel was lodged in Green's abdomen. Apparently, the piece of jagged metal had hit a nearby tree and was deflected before slicing into Green.

It was a terrible wound, necessitating immediate evacuation to a hospital. Captain Gandevia, the Battalion Medical Officer, could do little more than patch him up, administer morphine for the pain and then load Green onto the ambulance jeep to take him back to Pakchon. In Pakchon, Green was loaded into a larger vehicle, which set off for the 8063 Mobile Army Surgical Hospital (MASH) at Anju. The roads to Anju were rough, pitted and pockmarked, and the journey would have been tough for a well man, let alone the seriously wounded Green. Arriving at the MASH, the surgeons did all that they could but by midday the next day, Green was pronounced dead.

Given the speed of the UN advance, there was no time to remove Green's body, so he was interred at Pakchon, with a service attended by members of 3 RAR, Brigadier Coad[105] and Major General Church, commanding officer of the US 24th Division. Eventually, when the battlefront allowed, Green's body was moved to the permanent UN Memorial Cemetery in Pusan, where he still lies. Fittingly, when his wife, Olwyn Green (who published a well-regarded biography of Green and was a keen researcher of the Korean War), passed away in 2023, she was buried alongside her husband in Pusan.[106]

***

The loss of Green was felt hard across the battalion and all of 27 British Commonwealth Brigade. Despite having been with 3 RAR for less than two months, Green had quickly welded the old Japan occupation force men and the newly arrived K Force reinforcements into a superb fighting unit. Green did not have the luxury of time to gradually get to know his officers and men, but he had a clear vision of what he wanted. This vision, clearly articulated and implemented by way of his forceful character, quickly turned the newly reinforced 3 RAR into an extremely effective fighting force, one which Coad was able to rely upon time and again.

Gallaway commented: 'Green's ability to size up a given situation in a trice, and then devise and execute a plan for its resolution, almost on the run, earned him the admiration of all who served with him.'[107]

Chapter 8

China Enters the War

'There can be no excuse for looking idly on when a neighbour's house is imperilled'

– Mao Tse-Tung

China's spectacular and massive entry into the war in October 1950 changed the entire course and indeed final outcome of the conflict. It is no exaggeration to say that without China's assistance, North Korea would have lost the war and UN forces would have occupied the entire peninsula. But with China totally committed to the fight, the UN troops could no longer achieve an overwhelming victory – at least not without incurring costs that no democratic country was willing to bear – and were instead thrown onto the defensive.

With hindsight it seems incredible that no senior commander on the UN side seriously envisaged that the Chinese would enter the war to assist their Communist brethren. Even as UN troops got closer and closer to the Chinese border in October 1950, and even as US intelligence had by now belatedly recognized that China *might* intervene, MacArthur – in command of UN forces in Korea – remained stubbornly convinced that China would not enter the conflict.

The Chinese decision to enter the war had been telegraphed long before they finally crossed the Yalu into Korea. A mere look at the map should have alerted MacArthur to the fact that the Chinese were unlikely to sit idlily by while a large anti-Communist force was barrelling its way towards its border. From the Chinese perspective, not only were UN forces attacking a fellow Communist country, but there was a very real fear that it might take the fight across the border into the newly 'liberated' Communist China. Furthermore, the demeanour and aggressiveness of MacArthur likely did little to reassure the new Chinese Communist leaders that his intentions towards China were wholly peaceful. As early as August, China had started making secret preparations and was actively sending troops from southern China into North Korea, just in case they were needed.

By 5 October, Mao had already decided to deploy Chinese troops to Korea.[108] Following the collapse of the North Korean forces, the stunning drive north by the UN and Kim Il Sung's plea for help, Mao decided that he needed to act. He appointed General Peng Dehuai, China's second-highest commander, as overall commander of the

Chinese forces that would be sent to Korea. Peng quickly set up a headquarters near the Korean border, directed troops towards the frontier and then, on 18 October, secretly started to move his soldiers across the Yalu River and into Korea. It is quite amazing that Peng was able to organize and deploy such a large number of troops in less than three weeks, all the while keeping this deployment hidden from the UN and MacArthur.

Both the name given to the Chinese forces deployed to Korea and their initial deployment tell much about China's state of preparedness. Whilst most of the units initially deployed to Korea were currently serving Chinese People's Liberation Army (PLA) soldiers, when serving in Korea they would be renamed as the 'Chinese People's Volunteer Army' (CPVA, *zhongguo renmin zhiyuan jun*). This was an attempt to distinguish them from the Chinese PLA, and as such served to provide a wafer-thin layer of deniability that China was in fact going to war with the US. Likewise, the CPVA troops were told to remove the red star emblem from their caps and use a plain red banner as their flag rather than the red banner with yellow stars of the People's Republic of China.

In terms of deployment, the CPVA was not yet fully ready to face the UN forces. Despite the huge numbers of men who were being sent south during early October, CPVA logistics at this time was haphazard and a great deal of essential equipment was in very short supply. Accordingly, the Chinese forces were initially deployed to mountainous regions, out of sight of UN troops, and remained hidden for several weeks until their initial preparations were complete.

Chinese troops, equipment and tactics

When the Chinese eventually attacked UN forces in late October, the shock of hundreds of thousands of highly motivated Chinese troops apparently springing from nowhere had an immediate, serious and morale-sapping effect on all of the UN soldiers. This appeared to be even more pronounced among the South Korean contingent, perhaps because they also bore the brunt of many of the initial surprise attacks. As one ROK general noted, 'my men have heard that the Chinese are in the war, and the bottom has dropped out of their morale'.[109]

ROK units were the first UN troops to encounter the Chinese. Having targeted several ROK units, the Chinese sprang a series of large-scale ambushes, attacking the ROK 1st Division from three sides. The South Koreans were able to hold on, but were badly shaken. When the first Chinese prisoner was captured, he was immediately brought to General Paik for questioning, eager as he was to find out anything about this new enemy, its organization and intentions.

Having served in China with the Japanese fighting the Communist armies in the Second World War, General Paik was fluent in Chinese and was able to question the man himself. He found that the prisoner was 'about thirty-five and wore a thick, quilted winter uniform that was khaki on the outside and white on the inside and manufactured in such a fashion that a soldier could wear it with either colour showing, a simple but effective method to facilitate camouflage in snowy terrain. The prisoner's thick winter cap was equipped with integrated ear muffs, and he wore rubber sneakers.'[110]

Paik's POW was typical of most of the CPVA soldiers who entered Korea in October. Most of the rank-and-file Chinese were illiterate farmers, since any man with even a primary or high school education was usually selected to be an officer or a political officer. Many of the initial contingent of troops deployed to Korea were experienced soldiers and had fought against either the Japanese in the Second World War or the Chinese Nationalists during the Chinese Civil War – which had only finished several months previously. Chinese soldiers were on the whole very hardy, being used to long marches and hard living. They were largely unmechanized, had limited artillery or armour and were used to existing on a fraction of the supplies considered to be of 'subsistence' level by US and UN forces. Most of their armament was a hodgepodge of captured Japanese weapons, although some were of US or UK provenance, supplied to the Nationalists during the civil war. Many Chinese soldiers were impressed by the relatively modern Soviet weapons carried by the North Koreans and looked forward to being equipped with the same in due course.

In relation to logistics and food, the Chinese rations were usually very simple affairs indeed. Most carried *shaobing*, a hard, breadlike food made of various grains. They sometimes carried some other cold foods, including cooked rice or a tin of canned meat. There was little opportunity to eat hot food due to the restrictions on lighting fires. This precaution was essential because of the ever-present threat posed by US reconnaissance and fighter aircraft. Many commentators have theorized that while it was amazing that the Chinese were able to exist on so little, such poor and unvarying food likely had a negative effect on the capability of Chinese troops. In particular, as the war dragged on into the winter months, poor food and unpredictable supplies would affect the Chinese soldier's performance and his morale.

Nevertheless, Paik was impressed with the Chinese ingenuity in the face of material inferiority. He noted that 'the Chinese forces … were so lightly equipped that a single cavalry unit of some one hundred Mongolian ponies could transport its equipment. Yet this same unit had so many organic infantrymen that it was able to maul a US Army Regiment armed with tanks and heavy artillery.'[111]

While Chinese troops were at a significant material disadvantage to the UN forces, they compensated with mass, nearly 300,000 soldiers entering Korea in October, most of whom were combat soldiers. Likewise, many senior Chinese commanders had fought throughout the Chinese Civil War and many also had experience fighting the Japanese in the Second World War. While this experience was not the same as fighting the better-equipped Americans, it cannot be said that the Chinese commanders did not know what they were doing. To the contrary, the Chinese were well aware of their strengths and weaknesses, as well as having a good sense of the enemy they faced. Consequently, Chinese commanders were able to adapt their way of fighting to the strengths of their army and the weaknesses of their enemy. A bulletin released by the Chinese Army to their troops following the initial fighting in November 1950 summarized their American foes as follows:

> '[T]he US Army relies for its main power in combat on the shock effect of coordinated armour and artillery ... and their air-to-ground attack capability is exceptional. But their infantry is weak. Their men are afraid to die, and will neither press home a bold attack nor defend to the death ... They are very weak at attacking or approaching an enemy at night ... If their source of supply is cut, their fighting spirit suffers, and if you interdict their rear, they withdraw on their own.'[112]

While Coad would likely have disagreed with this assessment, at least in respect of 27 Bde, it was otherwise a remarkably accurate summary of certain elements of the UN forces at this stage of the war. The oft-quoted maxim 'If you know the enemy and know yourself, you need not fear the result of a hundred battles'[113] certainly applied to the Chinese commanders, who were well aware of both their own strengths and weaknesses and those of their opponents.

Unfortunately, the same did not apply in reverse. When General Peng finally let his men off the leash to spring from their mountain hideouts in late October, the UN troops were initially so stunned they were at a complete loss as to what they should do. Overnight, the war had entered a new and even more deadly phase, one which Paik summarized thus: 'Our enemy was now the Chinese Army. An enemy dozens of divisions in size had waited patiently as our own momentum carried us deep into its mountain ambush, had cut off our routes of retreat, and had sought to annihilate us. We were in a completely new war.'[114]

Chapter 9

The First Offensive

November 1950 would prove to be a confused, freezing and ultimately disastrous month for UN forces in North Korea. The true scale of the ferocious Chinese attacks launched in late October was now clear to all. This was no mere raid or demonstration. It was a full-throated major offensive, consisting of hundreds of thousands of highly motivated troops, determined to eject the UN from their borders – and the entirety of Korea. With several major units, mainly ROK forces, already having been shattered by the initial assault, and with many US front-line troops having suffered a bloody nose, morale quickly fell and in several places unit cohesion buckled. By early November, it appeared that everyone on the UN side had only one thought in mind – to bug out.

Faced with a reality on the ground that even his own magnificent self-confidence could not ignore, MacArthur reluctantly ordered a withdrawal.

The 27 Bde War Diary for 1 November 1950 summarised the situation with its customary British understatement:

> 'A general withdrawal was ordered today. Chinese forces have appeared in strength on the central front and had attacked and driven back the II ROK Corp in the general area of Tokchon. The right flank of I US Corp had thus been exposed and the Chinese, taking advantage of the situation had encircled elements of I ROK Division and later 8 CAV Regt and had inflicted considerable losses and damage on both these forces.'[115]

The words of the War Diary wholly failed to capture the utter chaos and destruction that the Chinese were inflicting on the surprised UN troops on the ground. 'Stunned' is an accurate word to describe UN forces in early November, since many of them, in particular the hapless ROK forces, seemed temporarily paralyzed by the sudden appearance of hundreds of thousands of determined Chinese troops attacking them as part of their so called 'First Offensive', almost as if they were vengeful ghosts emerging from thin air.

The Chinese First Offensive launched between 25 October and 7 November is something of a misnomer, since it was not really a carefully planned general offensive. Initially, Mao had wanted to infiltrate 300,000-plus soldiers down the spine of Korea and then fan out in a defensive line along the 40th parallel. The plan envisaged that only after the Chinese had established a strong defensive base in the mountainous regions would the Chinese and NKPA troops move south to attack the UN forces. Unfortunately, the rapid speed of the UN advance in late October had made these plans moot and forced the Chinese hand. With some ROK units a bare 20km from the Manchurian border, the more careful and conservative initial plan had to be abandoned. Instead, the Chinese found themselves forced to conduct a number of large-scale encounter battles, ambushes and night operations – all tactics that they had perfected during their long war with Japan and during the following Chinese Civil War.

The offensive commenced on 25 October, when CPVA troops emerged from their secret hiding places in the mountains to attack UN forces. Chinese commanders initially focussed their attention on several major ROK divisions, with the aim of not merely inflicting casualties but rather to annihilate these units. The Chinese stratagem was to utterly destroy such formations, causing a general panic amongst UN forces which would lead to wholesale alarm, terror and disintegration. This plan achieved a great deal of success, at least initially.

Several ROK units located on the far northern edge of the UN advance were surrounded by Chinese forces, which outnumbered them by more than three to one. Capitalizing on the element of surprise and bolstered by overwhelming numbers, the Chinese soon caused several ROK regiments to disintegrate. The hapless ROK units suffered significant casualties during these surprise attacks, and several hundred soldiers immediately surrendered and were taken into captivity.

Seeing the destruction of their brother units and fearing that they would be next, other ROK formations lost their nerve and started to pull out of the line and move southwards. This was in spite of the flurry of orders coming from higher headquarters ordering them to stay put and fight on. This destruction of morale was like a highly communicable disease, spreading quickly among the UN forces along the Chinese border. As more and more ROK units buckled and started to flee, the disease metastasized and even started to spread to US forces. Although US troops had not borne the brunt of the First Offensive, they too caught the 'bug out' fever and started to pull back as fast as their snow-covered trucks and tanks could carry them.

Within a week of launching the First Offensive, the whole character and direction of the Korean War was completely changed. The UN Command, slow at first to acknowledge the threat, was now under no illusion as to what was really happening – the Chinese were committed to the Korean War, and in full force.

***

The Commonwealth Brigade was very fortunate in not being an immediate target of this first Chinese annihilation campaign. Located on the western edge of UN forces, they were relatively far from the main Chinese thrusts, which fanned out from their hiding places along the mountains of central North Korea. Nevertheless, as the Chinese offensive gathered steam and spread out from the centre, Coad's brigade was becoming increasingly isolated and exposed. While it seemed as though every US and ROK unit which could do so was already driving south as fast as they could, the brigade's lack of transport hampered the ability of the Commonwealth troops to move south – or anywhere – with any great speed.

The lack of sufficient integral transport was no longer merely an issue of inconvenience; it was now potentially detrimental to the very survival of 27 Bde. The initial rushed orders in Hong Kong to leave all transport behind, only to have the order rescinded a day before embarkation, continued to have major negative repercussions for the brigade. Even now, having been in theatre for several months, 27 Bde still didn't have a sufficient number of vehicles for the type of fast, mobile warfare that had characterized the initial breakout and advance up the Korean peninsula into the North. Even the few vehicles that the brigade did have were in very poor shape and frequently broke down. None more so than the Bren gun carriers that were old and decrepit even before they arrived in Korea. After several months of constant punishment in the region's harsh weather and terrain, most of them were on their last legs and many had already been abandoned after repeated mechanical failures.

The result of this dearth of transport was that Coad was frequently in the position of a supplicant, having of necessity to almost beg US forces to assist him and allocate trucks and drivers to move his battalions. This was something he hated doing, it not being in his nature to always have to ask for assistance, but he had little choice. The US Army for its part was unfailingly generous and gave assistance to the Commonwealth forces wherever possible. But inevitably, when vehicles were in short supply and US troops needed them for their own withdrawal, Coad's men were often last in line. It didn't help that Coad's men were ordered to act as the rearguard of the division, covering the withdrawal of US and ROK forces as they sped past in their trucks and jeeps. This was deeply ironic, the Commonwealth men being the last men out, watching others speed by while they themselves would soon have to withdraw – on foot.

The order for 27 Bde to withdraw would come only several days later, and for now the brigade still had work to do in the Pakchon area. From the start of November, the brigade moved by bounds southwards, until on the 4th it was back at Pakchon. Likewise, 3 RAR once more took up defensive positions around the site of its old battleground, the Broken Bridge. The three-day move of around 70km had been accomplished in an orderly and disciplined manner, with only minor skirmishes and encounters with the enemy. However, owing to the lack of vehicles, some units were forced to withdraw south on foot, only being picked up when the forward battalions, mounted on trucks, had already been deposited at their destination. This shuttling to-and-fro was a rhythm that was to be repeated many times over the next month as the brigade made its way south.

It was also frequently accompanied by grumbling from the foot-sore troops, who had to trudge through the snow while waiting for their turn to be picked up and sit in the back of a freezing, open-topped truck. As General Robertson laconically informed the War Office in one of his reports, 'where withdrawals are concerned it is not pleasant to be in a British Brigade which has to rely on its feet'.[116]

Fortunately for the brigade, few enemy troops were sighted during this withdrawal to Pakchon. They had been incredibly lucky thus far. Yet luck is a precious commodity, often in short supply, and that of 27 Bde was soon to run out.

Pakchon

Unit War Diaries are remarkable records, one of the chief resources used by historians to understand the details of a formation's actions during combat. But they do not reveal everything. Much information is omitted, and that is as it should be; otherwise the records would become overly long and unwieldy. Nevertheless, sometimes details are omitted on purpose, sometimes to protect reputations or to obscure the failings of certain participants. The 27 Bde War Diaries are on the whole remarkably accurate records. However, the diaries for 5 November 1950, and in particular those of the Brigade HQ and 3 RAR, suffer from some glaring omissions in their recounting of the second Battle of Pakchon which took place on that day and evening.

If the 27 Bde War Diary was the only document consulted, you would find the record showing a day of serious fighting south of Pakchon. The brigade had been tasked to relieve a US artillery battalion which had been cut off and surrounded by Chinese forces, who had managed to hook around far to the east of the brigade and were now operating approximately 2km to the rear of the brigade's rearmost battalion, the Argylls. In the diary you would also discover the many letters of congratulations sent to the Argylls from the US command thanking them for their splendid relief of the artillery unit. Likewise, you would read about the exploits of 3 RAR to relieve the Argylls and clear the Chinese from the hills to the east of the artillery position.

What one wouldn't discover from the War Diaries, or even Coad's secret post-war report, is a story of confusion, order and counter-order, disobedience of command and ultimately the removal of a battalion commander.

***

It is perhaps fitting that the events which unfolded around Pakchon took place on 5 November, more popularly known as Guy Fawkes' or Bonfire Night in England. Guy Fawkes was traditionally a patriotic day to commemorate the foiling of the Gunpowder Plot of 1605, when King James I survived an attempt to kill him by blowing up Parliament. While much of its original meaning has now been lost, it is still commemorated in

England by the lighting of bonfires, setting off fireworks and singing the well-known verse:

'Don't you Remember,
The Fifth of November,
'Twas Gunpowder Treason Day,
I let off my gun,
And made 'em all run.
And Stole all their Bonfire away.'

Guy Fawkes' Night 1950 would see certain similarities in Korea, with 27 Bde being exposed to prodigious amounts of gunpowder, explosions and all-round confusion and mayhem, in the now familiar surrounds of Pakchon.

The day commenced with the brigade securing the bridge and crossings over the river. For November in North Korea, the day was unexpectedly clear and relatively sunny. It was still cold, however. Coad had placed the Middlesex in the surrounds of Pakchon itself, defending to the north, whereas both 3 RAR and the Argylls were held on the west bank of the Taeryong River, defending to the north and west, the likely directions of enemy advance towards them.

For several kilometres to the south of the Broken Bridge, frozen paddy fields lined the banks of the river for a distance of about 500 metres before the land suddenly rose up to a series of low hills and ridges. Neatly running along the boundary between where the paddy ended and the hills began was a single-lane road leading from Pakchon to the vital road and rail crossing at Maenju-dong, about 10km to the south.

Approximately 2km south of the brigade, located astride the road and the paddy fields, were six US 105mm guns of C Battery, 61st Field Artillery Battalion, harbouring for the night and positioned to provide fire support to the brigade.

Prudent as always, Coad was also alive to the possibility of enemy attacks to his rear. Accordingly, he sent a company of Argylls under Major Wilson several miles south of the US artillery position to secure the roads and bridgeheads towards Maenju-dong and thus keep open his line of withdrawal south. In Wilson's words, his company was to act as the 'longstop' of the brigade, a cricketing term used where a fielder is placed as the last line of defence between the wicket keeper and the boundary.

Wilson was typical of the company commanders deployed in both of the British battalions, having served extensively in the Second World War. Notably, Wilson had fought at the pivotal Battle of Kohima in 1944, where Japan had attempted an ambitious and vicious overland attack of north-east India from Burma. A very capable soldier, Wilson was not easily flappable, having already seen his fair share of brutal and close combat. Yet despite it all, Wilson retained a somewhat sunny disposition and as a result was known as 'chuckles' to his friends.

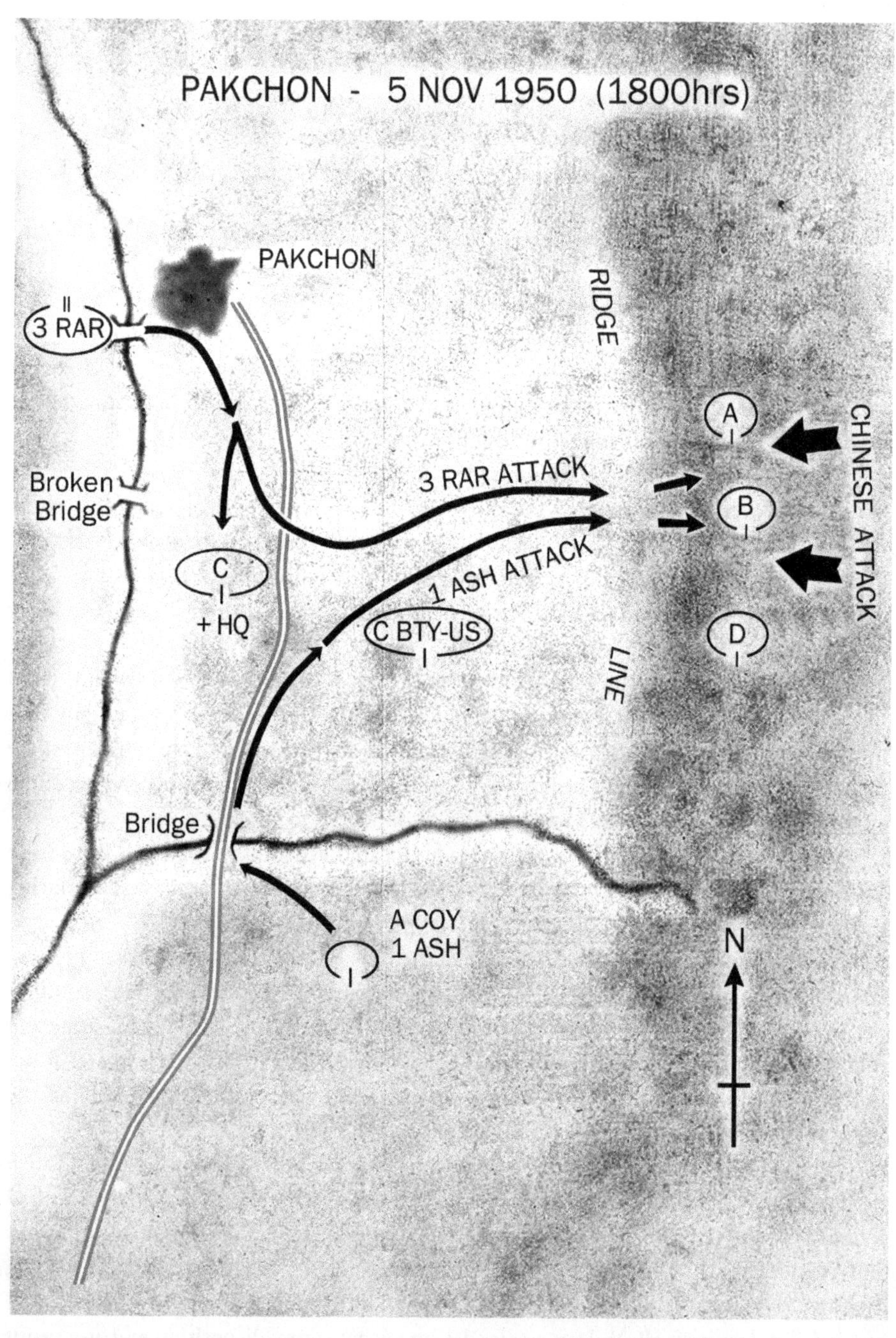

PAKCHON - 5 NOV 1950 (1800hrs)
PAKCHON
3 RAR
Broken Bridge
C
+ HQ
3 RAR ATTACK
1 ASH ATTACK
C BTY-US
RIDGE
LINE
A
B
D
CHINESE ATTACK
Bridge
A COY
1 ASH
N

Perhaps Wilson's previous experience at war had sharpened his senses, but whatever the reason, Wilson felt that along with the chill winds of November, a definite change had blown into the brigade. 'The war had changed in the preceding seventy-two hours,' said Wilson. '[U]ntil then, we had been pursuing a defeated North Korean Army, which could man a few rear-guard positions, but was gradually disintegrating. Now a strange new menace had appeared from Manchuria: the Chinese ... There was a smell of uncertainty in the air.'[117]

While all was relatively quiet within the 27 Bde perimeter in the early morning of the 5th, the general premonition of unease was soon found to be backed up by reality. Unbeknownst to the brigade, large concentrations of Chinese soldiers had already bypassed the Commonwealth troops to the east of Pakchon and were moving south through the hills and ridges to the east of the river. At approximately 0800hrs, a large force of Chinese, estimated to be approximately 400 strong, broke cover from the high ground to the east of the 61st Field Artillery guns. This was a perilous situation for the isolated American gunners, sitting vulnerable in the middle of a frozen paddy. The Chinese held the high ground and looked down at the guns spread out over the road and paddy. For their part, the Americans had their guns facing north and west towards what they thought would be the probable direction of enemy advance. As it happened, the guns were facing the wrong way. In any event, artillery units, while wielding powerful indirect fire, have limited ability to defend themselves from a close infantry assault, usually requiring support from infantry.

Faced with a large force of enemy suddenly appearing to their rear, many gunners would have decided that discretion was the better part of valour and tried to escape. But the men of the 61st Field Artillery stood firm. Seeing what looked to be an easy target, the Chinese made their way off the hills in bounds to start an attack on the gunners. As the Chinese were moving forward, the gunners of C Battery, those closest to the enemy, lifted the trails of their guns and manhandled the heavy weapons around until the barrels were facing to the east and at the rapidly advancing Chinese. Quickly bringing the guns into action, they depressed the barrels of their guns to almost horizontal so that they could fire directly at the enemy over open sights. While Chinese small-arms rounds pinged off the front shields of the guns, the gunners started to fire high explosive rounds directly at the Chinese. These rounds were not designed for this role and there were report of some of them skipping over the frozen ground before exploding harmlessly in the hills beyond. This was reminiscent of artillery fire during the Napoleonic Wars, where cannonballs would sometimes bounce their way towards the enemy, skipping over the ground before either breaking up concentrations of enemy forces or continuing into the rear.

Nevertheless, so stout and determined was the defence by the US gunners that Captain Howard Moore, commander of C Battery, would ultimately be recommended by Coad for the award of a British Military Cross. Moore's citation read in part:

> '61st Field Artillery, under the command of CAPT Howard Moore, had put up a most gallant defence. The trails of the guns had been lifted to enable the guns to point east instead of north and west, and were being fired at point blank range at the advancing infantry. Enemy dead were lying within 30 yards of the guns and as gun numbers were wounded and killed, others immediately took their place. In addition, every type of small arms weapon were being used. When the Argylls reached the guns, they were practically out of gun and small arms ammunition.'[118]

But it was a very close run thing; for the best part of an hour, the gunners had no choice but to fight on alone. Despite putting in a call to the brigade for urgent infantry support, it took what seemed to the artillerymen an age before Wilson and his A Company could get to the scene of the battle, by which time the situation was getting desperate.

***

When the Chinese first broke cover and C Battery radioed through to Brigade HQ, Wilson and his men were just starting to eat a lukewarm breakfast, hoping to get some warmth back into their bodies after a night of teeth-chattering cold. Wilson had somehow managed to scrounge breakfast from a nearby US tank unit and was just starting to eat a mouthful of hot cakes and syrup when one of the supporting American tanks drove up to his Company HQ and told him they had a message from his battalion commander. Lieutenant Colonel Nielson told Wilson that the 61st's battery was at risk of being overrun and that the Chinese were likely trying to block the road between his position and the gunners. If successful, the Chinese would be able to prevent any rearward movement of the brigade, which would then be isolated and easy pickings for the enemy. Nielson stressed that it was imperative that Wilson take whatever transport he could find and move to relieve the beleaguered C Battery men as soon as he could. Further support from the brigade would follow in due course, but for now Wilson was on his own.

Unfortunately, Wilson had precious few troops to spare. He needed to leave a platoon in its current longstop position, so could only afford to take two platoons of less than thirty men each, two of his 3in mortars and two Vickers machine guns. It was a very small band for what could prove to be a nasty fight. Fortunately, he was also able to get assistance from the four nearby US Army tanks, whose breakfast he had so recently shared. Boarding the tanks and two commandeered US Army trucks, Wilson's little band set off north to the gunners' aid and to clear the Chinese roadblock.

With the help of their armoured steeds, the Jocks arrived at the gunners' position just in time. The guns were almost out of ammunition and they had suffered several casualties. Without the fortuitous arrival of Wilson's men and the four tanks, it is very likely that they would have been overrun as the enemy were now within 30 metres of the battery perimeter.

The Chinese attack was now hopeless in the face of the steadily advancing US armour. A stream of .50 calibre rounds from the tanks' machine guns made quick work of any enemy still in the open paddy between the gun position and the ridge line. Those Chinese soldiers who managed to find some minor cover were soon feeling the pinch from Wilson's men. Whenever a Chinese soldier tried to make a dash for better cover, he was instantly met by well-aimed shots from the Argylls' .303 rifles or a quick burst of Bren-gun fire. Wilson recorded: 'Hardly had we started to move forward when gooks started up like quail or partridges in all directions. I can honestly swear that this was no exaggeration.'[119] Indeed, several men told a similar story of how this stage of the action resembled a 'snipe shoot'.

With the gun line now secure and resistance in the open ground and along the ridge almost neutralized, Wilson decided to turn his attention towards the remaining Chinese on the ridgeline. With enemy fire slackening, he sent his platoons to clear the nearby ridge, all the while covered by fire from the tanks and his pair of 3in mortars.

Initially, the advance to the ridge line was fairly easy and met little resistance. The hill directly to the east of the gun position was low by Korean standards, and the Jocks were able to quickly clamber up its lower slopes with little difficulty while mortar rounds were lobbed ahead of them to suppress any curious enemy left on the hill.

The two platoons of A Company managed to clamber up to the top of the hill and take up positions, whereupon to their surprise they were counter-attacked by a large force of enemy soldiers from the far (eastern) side. Several of the Jocks, including the mortar section sergeant, were hit and killed almost immediately by the weight of fire pouring down from the rapidly advancing Chinese.

It was by now about 1100hrs and the Jocks were in a precarious position. They held – just – the west side of the hill opposite the US battery, while the Chinese held the far, eastern, side. The gun position was now secure, with the tanks having received a much-needed resupply of ammunition. However, due to the elevation of the hill, there was little that they could do to support those still stranded on top of the ridgeline. The Chinese were also moving additional forces up onto the ridge to the south of the hill where the Argylls were fighting. Wilson, desperate to assist his men, did what he could by calling in airstrikes from circling Mustangs in order to keep the Chinese at bay.

Regular runs were made by the aircraft, which launched salvoes of rockets and machine-gun fire towards the Chinese attackers, punctuated at intervals by the 'whoosh' and black curling flames of napalm strikes. The air cover proved critical in stabilizing the situation, but was insufficient by itself to turn the tide. The few survivors left on the hill were now alone, mostly wounded and just holding onto the western side of the ridgeline.

***

While A Company was tied up in its own private war on the slopes facing the gun battery, Coad was working desperately to both bring in support for Wilson's men as well as considering the implication of the Chinese roadblock to his rear for the whole of 27 Bde.

'It was now obvious that the Chinese were in strength behind us, the air reported a whole Division,' Coad reported. This was clearly a significant threat to the brigade. There was a distinct possibility that if it remained in place, the brigade was in danger of being cut off, surrounded and then destroyed by the rapidly increasing numbers of Chinese. Coad tried to get some clarity and firm orders from 24th Division HQ, but as had happened on several occasions, he received no assistance whatsoever: 'He [the task Force Commander] had no idea at all and eventually left it to me to do the best I thought.'[120]

With no assistance or guidance coming from Division HQ, Coad was once again forced to rely on the old maxim 'The Gods help those who help themselves', and proceeded to quickly develop his own plan to relieve his brigade. The plan had two parts. Firstly he would have the entire Australian battalion cross back onto the east bank of the river and then move south to relieve Wilson's men and the gun battery. At the same time, the Middlesex battalion and those Argylls who still remained at Pakchon would move south to secure positions just north of Anju. When these units reached their new position, Brigade HQ would follow. Such an approach would secure the guns and Wilson's men as well as ensuring that the brigade could not be cut off by the Chinese behind them and to the south.

***

It was about 1400hrs when the forward companies of 3 RAR made their way to the defensive position of the US gunners 3km south of Pakchon. Walsh quickly deployed his two forward companies, with A Company to the left and B to the right, and ordered them to assault the hill complex to relieve the Jocks who were still fighting on up on the ridgeline. Walsh decided to hold back his other companies to act as a firm base and ensure the security of the gun position.

As the two forward companies advanced over the open ground of the paddy fields, the Chinese called in mortar fire on the extended lines of Australians. Initially, most of these rounds exploded harmlessly on the frozen fields, but as they found their range, the Australians started taking casualties. The unlucky men, mainly hit by shrapnel in the legs, were left where they were in the fields, to be collected later by stretcher parties.

In return, Walsh ordered his own mortars to fire on the Chinese. The advance was also accompanied by a steady stream of machine-gun rounds from the Vickers section, which had a plentiful supply of ammunition and was helping keep enemy heads down.

As the Australians started climbing the hill, they found that the slope was working to their advantage. Whilst standard military doctrine declares that he who holds the high ground holds the advantage, in this case it would prove fatal to many of the inexperienced

Chinese soldiers. 'All the Chinese up the top of the hill fired at us, but they made a fatal mistake,' recalled George Harris, a platoon sergeant taking part in the assault. '[A]s we were going up the hill, they had to get out of their weapon pits to fire down at us. They exposed themselves and we were able to shoot them.'[121] The Australians were thus able to clamber up the hill in relative safety and push any remaining enemy troops back to the far side.

As they moved forward, they passed several wounded Argylls, still there since the initial assault in the morning. Among them was Private Gurr, who had had been lying unconscious on the side of the hill, wounded by a number of shots to his legs and shoulder. Unfortunately Gurr's slumber was broken by yet another bullet, this one hitting him square in the chest. He recalled: 'I was hit again, this time in the chest with the force of the impact moving me a couple of inches and I was stunned and passed out … when I regained consciousness, the light was fading and the Australians had retaken the hill.'[122]

Amazingly, after taking at least five rounds in the legs, hand, shoulder and chest, Gurr managed to survive. He would eventually be evacuated to a field hospital before being sent to Japan for surgery and recovery. While almost unthinkable today, after a period of recuperation, Gurr returned to Korea to see out his period of service guarding POWs near Pusan.

By 1600hrs, after suffering several casualties, 3 RAR was in possession of the ridge. However, the men were not yet safe. While the Chinese infantry had been cleared off the ridgeline, the Aussies still had to deal with the ever-present danger of mortar rounds, which continued to land among the newly arrived Diggers with murderous regularity. One round landed with a sharp bang of whizzing shrapnel almost directly on top of A Company's command group. Two men were killed outright, while several more signallers and Company HQ staff were wounded. This included the company commander, Captain Bill Chits, who copped several pieces of shrapnel to his legs and had to be evacuated. With a single stray mortar round, A Company had lost almost its entire command team. Following the usual chain of command, leadership of the company devolved down the line to 22-year-old platoon commander Lieutenant Lawrence 'Algy' Clark.

With A Company now in possession of the main ridge, Walsh proceeded to deploy his B and D Company along the line of hills running south from the new A Company position. Walsh held C Company in reserve at the road and then placed his Battalion HQ about 500 metres to the south, also astride the road. By 1700hrs, 3 RAR was in a commanding position along the ridgelines. The rest of the brigade could now move south in relative safety, knowing that their rear was well protected.

Standing in his Battalion HQ, Walsh was immediately recognizable as he was dressed somewhat differently to the rest of the men. He was sporting a long white Arctic coat and a metal helmet. As a new arrival, he hadn't yet had time to acquire the nearly ubiquitous American field jacket which most of his men wore on top of their battledress in order to keep warm. But Walsh didn't mind being recognized and was quietly satisfied with his battalion, which had performed well that day to relieve the Argylls and clear all Chinese forces from the ridgeline.

Just as the battalion position was being consolidated and its HQ dug in, a small convoy of twenty reinforcements made its way into the headquarters position. They were a very welcome addition and would in time help to reconstitute some of the platoons who had suffered casualties over the last month. But for now they were immediately put to work digging slit trenches and helping to bed in the Battalion HQ area. Shortly thereafter, the well-oiled HQ machine had established a fully functioning command area, with communication wires linked to all relevant sub-units, defences dug in and weapons sighted. They were thus in a good position to face any challenges that the Chinese might throw at them with the coming of the night.

Casualties for the day's fighting had been high. While it was estimated that up to 200 Chinese soldiers had been killed, ten Commonwealth troops had also died, with a further seventy wounded, many of them – like Private Gurr from the Argylls – seriously hurt.[123]

***

To this point, both the 27 Bde and 3 RAR War Diaries paint a relatively consistent and detailed picture of the day's fighting. The night of 5 November, however, would see one of the strangest episodes in the Australian battalion's history. It is one which is completely absent from the War Diary accounts, or indeed any of the official contemporaneous reports. It is an episode that would not receive much attention until many years later, when veterans started to publish their own personal accounts of the matter.

The official 27 Bde War Diary merely notes: '[C]ertain adjustments of position were made during the night … 3 RAR, which was holding an isolated position and had been receiving enemy attacks, was withdrawn to WEST of the road … During the withdrawal, this company brushed an enemy force and some confused fighting broke out.'[124]

This entry is suffused with understatement, making no mention of a night characterized by failure of command, disobedience of orders, confused fighting and movement, and ultimately the sacking of a commander who had only been in command for five days.

The first sign of trouble came sometime between 1900 and 2000hrs, when the ever-present enemy mortars started ranging in on both the reserve company – C Company – and Battalion HQ. Walsh was rightly concerned about taking further casualties and radioed Coad for permission to move his battalion. While the shelling was of concern, Coad was more anxious to ensure that the northern flank of his brigade, which faced the most likely threat from advancing enemy forces, was secure. Since he knew that Walsh's men held the dominating ridgeline in force, he told Walsh: 'If your headquarters is being mortared it may be wise to move it, but the rifle companies must remain in present localities.'[125] Further, Walsh was ordered to detach one company, likely C Company, and move it south to secure the important bridge to the south of the gun position.

Despite the clear orders from Coad, Walsh continued to focus on the immediate threats from the mortars and thus took a series of actions which failed to take into account the 'big picture' and the overall security of 27 Bde. Firstly, Walsh ignored Coad's instructions to secure the bridge. He made no moves to secure it, leaving it to chance as to whether the Chinese might take it.

While Walsh did nothing about the bridge, his first active command was to order Battalion HQ to move about a thousand metres to the south, just down the road from its present position. This order was apparently met with incredulity and some disbelief by the officers and men, who had spent the last few hours developing a perfectly functioning headquarters. This was no mere grumbling of soldiers who wished to avoid further work, but rather a complaint as to the wisdom of moving during the night to a location that had not been reconnoitred and offered no appreciable tactical advantage over their current one.

The medical officer was the most vociferous in his objections. He was still in the process of working on the many casualties still in his care, trying to dress their wounds and stabilize them before they could be evacuated to a field hospital. Unnecessary movement was certain to disrupt his critical work and could potentially affect the chances of survival of several of the wounded men.

But Walsh was not to be dissuaded. He repeated his order, which set in motion a largely disorderly and confused movement of men, equipment and vehicles over the next few hours. When the still-grumbling men arrived at the new location, they found that there was no clear plan as to where they should go or how they should be set up. Instead, troops and equipment were just dropped wherever they found themselves, which was more or less just strung out along the road in a long and disorderly line. It was complete chaos.

If the disorderly move of Battalion HQ was not bad enough, Walsh's next command was completely inexplicable; he ordered the complete withdrawal of all of the rifle companies off the ridgeline and for them to pull back to the Battalion HQ position. This was contrary to Coad's clear instruction that the rifle companies were not to move from their present locations.

Walsh's decisions have been damned ever since, with almost no one able to find any excuse to defend his actions. Ben O'Dowd, who would soon receive command of A Company, gave a highly emotional description of what he thought about the tactical blunders resulting from Walsh's orders:

> 'It is inscribed in letters of fire on any commander's heart that it is fatal to withdraw, retreat, bug out or whatever whilst under attack; to do so is to invite disaster. But in the dark, the rule is doubled and redoubled in spades. Withdrawal of a group from prepared defences is only on when more suitable ground has been selected. Where in hell were the companies supposed to go? How were

> the platoons and sections to be sited in the dark? It was not on. If Walsh was concerned about gaps requiring rearrangement of the companies, he should not have left it until after dark. I can see nothing in defence of Walsh's decision to move the companies when he did.'[126]

The sentiment was endorsed by almost everyone in 3 RAR.

When the orders were received by the company commanders on the ridge, each of them acted in a different way. At the extreme south of the ridgeline on Hill 63, Major Brown, in command of D Company, was heard to reply to Walsh: 'I won't be moving, and I'll see you about this in the morning.'[127] Despite this gross insubordination on the part of Brown, it ended up being a good call; D Company made it through the night with little disturbance from the Chinese, who were once again moving up to the edges of the 3 RAR positions. Brown did, however, have a small wobble in his convictions and at one stage started making preparations for a withdrawal. However, just as the first of his platoons began to move down the hill, he changed his mind and immediately ordered them back into their original positions. There was quite a bit of understandable grumbling from the platoon that had been ordered to change positions, at both the unnecessary move as well as the risk that the Chinese could have filed into the abandoned pits during their brief absence. Nevertheless, D Company was ultimately fortunate and spent a relatively uneventful night continuing to occupy Hill 63.

B Company, the middle unit on the ridgeline, followed Walsh's orders and moved off the ridge at about 2300hrs. With platoons leapfrogging each other to provide firm bases and cover for the next withdrawing platoon, the company moved easily down to the road and railway line and by dawn was already near the new 3 RAR assembly area. They too were lucky and did not face much trouble from the enemy.

A Company, however, now led by Lieutenant Algy Clark, would have a terrible time during its withdrawal. Newly appointed to command, Clark acted immediately upon receiving Walsh's order and told his forward platoon to withdraw back down the ridgeline towards the road. This was despite the fact that this platoon, which had been in reserve during the fight up the ridge in the afternoon and was therefore the freshest and with almost full stocks of ammunition, could hear noises to its front which were likely the enemy.

The platoon members left their fighting positions and moved off in single file. As they did so, one nominated soldier counted each member of the platoon out of the position. This was a usual procedure to ensure that no man was accidentally left behind in the dark. The somewhat tired soldier counted mechanically, not really paying too much attention until he started to get into the high 30s – 36, 37, 38… This number was much higher than the thirty-odd men the platoon was supposed to have, and it suddenly dawned on him that the Chinese had silently tagged on to the end of the platoon and were now among them!

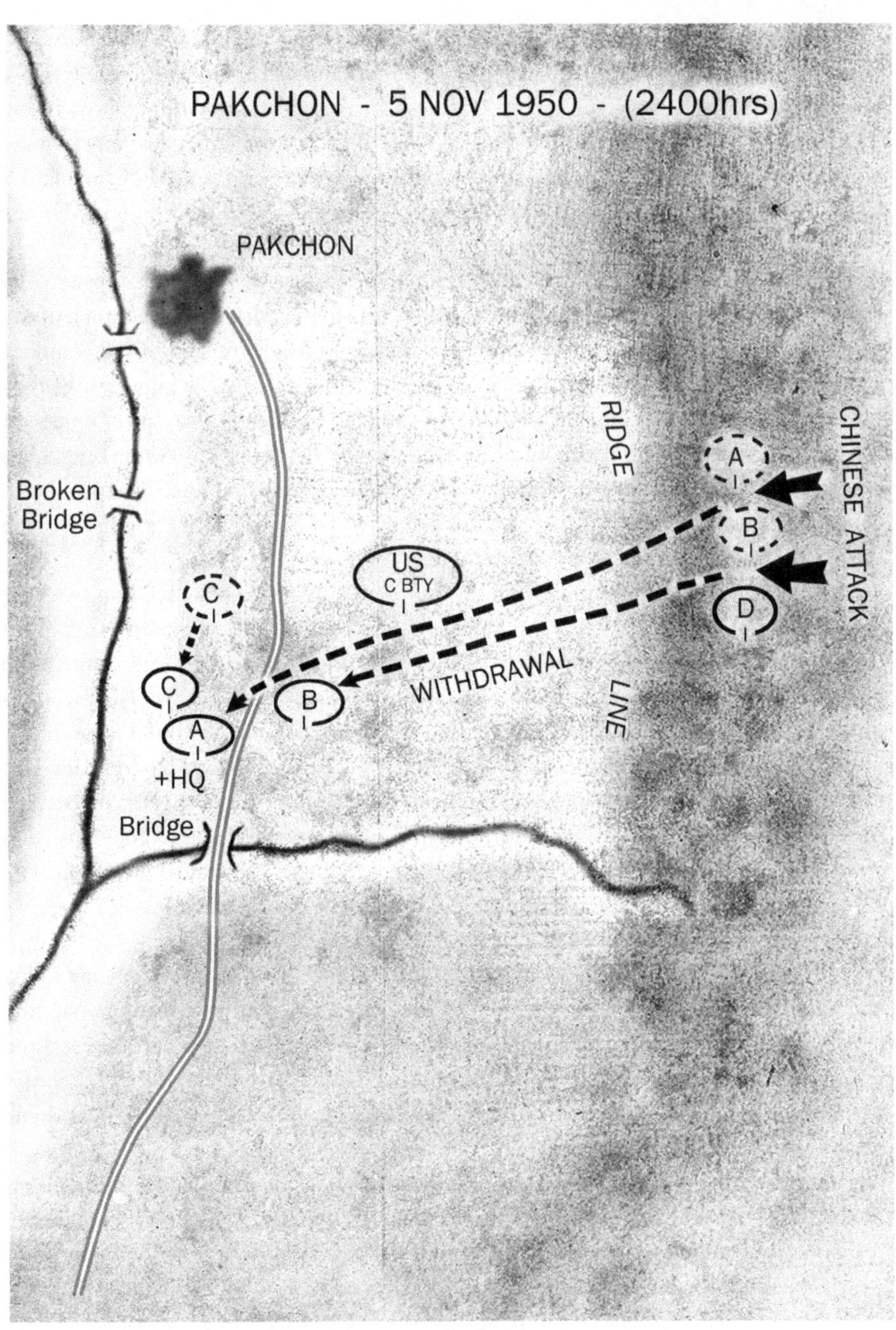
PAKCHON - 5 NOV 1950 - (2400hrs)
PAKCHON
Broken Bridge
RIDGE
LINE
CHINESE ATTACK
A
B
D
US C BTY
C
C
A
+HQ
B
WITHDRAWAL
Bridge

As other members of A Company also started to realize that the Chinese were now hopelessly intermingled with them, a ferocious firefight erupted at extremely close quarters, both the Australians and the Chinese struggling to make out who was who. The newly reconstituted Company HQ that Clark had put together just a few hours before bore the brunt of the attack, with both the Company Sergeant Major and Clark's batman being killed immediately. Other men were also quickly killed or wounded in the close-contact combat.

Fortunately for Clark, one of his platoons had swung to the south through the B Company position, and was from there able to form a hasty defensive position halfway down the ridge. This platoon then provided covering fire for the rest of the company as it sought to extract itself from the melee with the Chinese. More importantly, they formed a refuge that escaping members of A Company could move to over the course of the next few hours. The escapees came into the platoon defensive position in ones, twos and other small groups, demonstrating how the fighting had completely destroyed unit cohesion. Apart from this isolated platoon defensive position, the fighting had broken down to a series of small actions and individual combats.

As dawn broke, the fighting died away and both sides pulled back. Upon reaching the platoon defensive line, Clark was able to count just over sixty men remaining in his company, a significantly smaller group than the 100 or so who had set off to launch the attack on the ridge the previous afternoon. Many of the survivors were sporting wounds of various types, including Clark. Luckily, his was a relatively minor wound so he simply bound it up and remained at his post, determined to continue to lead his company.

As the exhausted Clark looked around the remnants of his company, he became furious and started to berate himself for what he thought were his failings. For many years afterwards, he believed that he had been at fault – 'being a very young, inexperienced (aged 22) and I now believe a stupid officer temporarily in command of A Company, I did exactly as I was told'.[128]

Clark regretted his actions, which had resulted in so many of his men being killed and wounded. But was he really to blame? He was given a clear order by his commanding officer and had immediately carried it out. It can be argued that the order was executed inexpertly, and perhaps a more experienced officer could have exercised more control over his troops during the withdrawal. Be that as it may, Clark was clearly just doing what he was told.

Of course a company commander – indeed all levels of command – must follow orders. But they are not mere puppets and must always exercise their own judgment. A distinctive feature of Commonwealth forces was the concept of 'mission command', which at its simplest means that a commander tells you *what* he wants achieved and then the subordinate decides *how* he will achieve it. While Clark was obliged to follow Walsh's order to withdraw, he was well within his rights to decide how he was to do so. Clark could not be faulted for following the order, and if he is to accept any blame it can only be for the way he moved his men off the ridgeline, especially when it was clear that the enemy was close to his forward platoon.

In any event, the night withdrawal and the disorder that ensued would exact a terrible toll on 3 RAR. Sixteen men would succumb to their wounds and be dead by the next day as a direct result of the chaotic movement off the ridgeline, almost as many as the battalion had suffered in total to this point in the war.

***

As the battalion started to reorganize itself in the early-morning gloom, Coad was furious, calling for Walsh to see him immediately at his headquarters. Upon arrival, Coad took Walsh alone to his command jeep to address the hapless lieutenant colonel in private. Coad informed Walsh that he was extremely unhappy with Walsh's performance, his disobedience of the order to deploy a company to secure the bridge and the fact that he withdrew the rifle companies from the ridgeline despite being told that they were to remain in place to protect the brigade's rear. As a result, Walsh was immediately relieved of command and the battalion 2IC, Major Bruce Ferguson, was appointed in his stead.

Walsh was extremely disappointed by Coad's decision. He had only just assumed command of 3 RAR and the decision to strip him of his position now would be clear evidence to all the doubters who believed that he shouldn't have been appointed in the first place, that they were right. Perhaps Walsh also knew, if he was being honest with himself, that it was the right decision. Years later, during an interview, Walsh would say: 'My reaction was, of course, extreme disappointment. He [Coad] told me in fact that he thought, as I did, that Ferguson should have assumed command on the death of Charles Green. I believe he was taking the opportunity to give command to Bruce.'[129]

Upon receiving the news, Walsh briefly returned to the battalion position. He placed his kit and sleeping bag in his jeep and drove off, never to be seen again by the battalion.

It is only here that the 3 RAR War Diary resumes the story. The entry for 6 November 1950 merely states: 'The Battalion Second-in-command Major I B Ferguson MC assumed command of the battalion. Lt-Colonel F S Walsh was re-posted to the Australian Operational Research Team attached to Eighth Army headquarters.' Walsh had been in command of 3 RAR for only five days.

The decision to replace Walsh would in time be seen as a prudent one. Unlike Walsh, Ferguson was a combat leader and well placed through both experience and temperament to lead the battalion. He was a tough and exacting man, particularly to his junior officers, but he was totally devoted to both his battalion and his craft as a soldier. Captain Don Beard, the 3 RAR RMO, recalled that Ferguson 'was respected, but not, shall we say, loved by some members of the Battalion with whom he was very hard. He didn't really have the personality that could get very close to people ... [but it was] clear where his heart was, and that was in the Battalion.'[130] But while Ferguson could be gruff with his officers, he was acknowledged as being tactically very sound, worked hard, got on well with the headquarters at 27 Bde and with the Americans, and 'his work was absolutely tireless'.[131]

The Chinese First Offensive concludes

In one way, the sacking of Walsh and the inevitable disruption that this caused to 3 RAR came at a fortuitous time, as this also marked the end of the Chinese First Offensive. After the heavy attack on 3 RAR's A Company during the night of 5 November, enemy activity suddenly dropped away to almost nothing. This gave the Australian battalion, and indeed the entire brigade, much-needed time to reconstitute and reorganize.

On the Chinese side, the sudden whirlwind of fire and action along the entire front which commenced a mere two weeks previously was now at an end. While the Chinese had been able to infiltrate large numbers of soldiers secretly into North Korea, the lack of a sophisticated logistics train and means of resupplying the front-line troops meant that a sustained offensive could only be conducted for at most two weeks. After about a fortnight of fighting, the Chinese forces were exhausted, being critically low on food, supplies and most importantly ammunition. With nothing left to sustain any further momentum, the Chinese had no choice but to retreat to their hideouts along the mountainous spine of North Korea. This allowed them to evacuate the many thousands of casualties they had sustained during these furious days of combat, as well as bring forward supplies of food and ammunition to the front-line troops.

***

Pakchon was the first major engagement that 27 British Commonwealth Brigade had with the Chinese. It allowed the brigade to learn a few things about their new enemy, who were clearly different to the North Koreans that they had fought to date.

Major Wilson of the Argylls reflected on the Chinese tactics and equipment:

> '[O]ur opponents, though brave, were not tactically clever and were in many cases needlessly killed. They were however, better armed and equipped than anything we had seen before. We captured, amongst other things Bren LMGs, in excellent order, 1943 pattern with 1942 small arms ammunition in the magazine. What strange twist of fate had caused our own guns and ammunition to be used against our men. Two of these guns are now in use in my company.'[132]

To find British Bren guns in the hands of the Chinese was not unusual at this stage of the war. Whereas the North Koreans had been liberally supplied with Soviet sub-machine guns and heavy weaponry, the Chinese instead relied on a mish-mash of weapons captured from the Japanese during the Second World War or from their opponents during the Chinese Civil War, the Kuomintang. There was little standardization of weaponry among the Chinese at this stage, which no doubt added further complication to their already-overburdened logistics tail.

The Chinese high command consisted of very experienced officers who were alive to the strengths and weaknesses of their own men. The Chinese commander, General Peng Dehuai, knew that his men could not compete with the UN forces in terms of weapons and equipment. But one advantage he did have was the sheer number of men at his disposal. Mao too firmly believed that sheer weight of numbers would tell in the end and overwhelm the UN troops. While in many cases mass was determinative, particularly when combined with the element of surprise, success was usually accompanied by an inordinately high cost of dead and wounded soldiers. This was, however, something that Chinese commanders were willing to bare in order to succeed.

In terms of tactics, the combination of speed and night attacks were to be the hallmark of the Chinese way of war during the initial few months of fighting in Korea. General Ma Chang, commander of the Chinese Fourth Army, is reported to have said that 'daylight warfare has become disastrous for the CCF [Chinese Communist Forces] because of lack of airpower, consequently night envelopment must be deployed'.[133] The Chinese became masters of moving silently at night and moving large numbers of men over seemingly impossible distances to attack unsuspecting UN forces.

Nonetheless, mounting an attack at night presented the Chinese command with difficulties in co-ordinating and commanding their men. This was exacerbated by the lack of radios or other means to keep their troops in order. As a result, Chinese tactics settled down to a simple and standard template, easily followed by all levels of soldier. A particularly common feature of Chinese attacks was the heavy use of sound – predominantly bugles, whistles and even gongs – to co-ordinate night attacks. With radio communications almost non-existent at lower levels, commanders relied upon bugles and whistles to co-ordinate troops and signal the start of an attack. Many members of 27 Bde now knew that the sound of a bugle would herald the start of a serious assault on their positions. While this noisy announcement of an impending attack inevitably robbed the Chinese of the element of surprise, these loud and clashing sounds coming suddenly out of a black and frozen night would often strike terror in the hearts of the defending Commonwealth troops – as it was intended to do.

Consequently, careful infiltration tactics, silent marches and skilful use of the night as cover were arguably wasted by the loud bugle and whistle blasts that heralded wave after wave of attacking Chinese. The assaults were also rarely supported by anything more serious than some machine-gun and mortar fire.

Captain Zhou Baoshan, an officer in the Chinese 116th Division, described preparations for a typical attack in late October 1950:

'Ten minutes! Get ready! …The night was on our side, and the enemy dominated the daytime. If we could not … destroy the garrison troops tonight, the enemy would reinforce their troops … with their superior air power ... I asked my soldiers to get rid of all their blankets, food, and water bottles in order to run faster. Our only chance was that some of us might be able to run fast enough and reach the top of the hill before the enemy fire got all of my company. I tried to talk to as many soldiers as I could. This could be the last time I would see them…

'Running, I led my company up to the hill. This was a race between our soldiers and enemy bullets. I saw some of them get shot and fall. But I kept yelling loudly and pressing them hard. "Charge!" "Faster!" "To the top!" The faster they could run, the better chance they had of surviving. I kicked several men who had slowed down. I pushed those who were looking for cover from the enemy machine guns. The hill was pretty flat and totally stripped by the constant firing and shelling from both sides. There was no tree or rock left to hide behind.'[134]

***

The night attacks, human wave tactics and the sounding of bugles and gongs are well reported by many UN and ROK participants in the war. A less-often reported feature of the Chinese way of war was their treatment of POWs and enemy wounded. According to many members of the brigade, the Chinese appeared to treat captive UN soldiers differently to the usual harsh manner adopted by the North Koreans.

When 3 RAR commenced its assault on the ridgeline during the afternoon of 5 November, Wilson decided to leave the US gun position and accompany the Australians:

'I went along with them to see how the wounded had fared. I found to my surprise that the Chinese had done what they could for them: they had put on what dressings they had and moved them into shelter. It was very different conduct from what I remembered of the way the Japanese army had behaved some five years earlier.'[135]

The good treatment of UN soldiers wounded by the Chinese was remarked upon by many commentators, and appeared to be markedly different to the cruelty usually displayed by the North Koreans towards men they had captured – in particular ROK troops.

General Matthew Ridgeway also noted this practice, which he said was 'in happy contrast to the treatment – often a bullet in the back of the head – prisoners had received from the North Koreans'.[136] Ridgeway thought that besides basic humanity, there could be an alternative motive to this good treatment in that the wounded soldier would 'tell his comrades' of the compassion at the hands of the Chinese, which may in time convince them to surrender. But whatever the reason, the generally good and humane conduct displayed by the Chinese towards captured and wounded UN troops was a credit to them.

***

Following the unexpected but welcome withdrawal of Chinese troops after the 3 RAR battle, 27 Bde now entered a short period of relative quiet. Aggressive fighting patrols were sent out daily from the brigade's infantry battalions, which often resulted in a series of sporadic firefights with small elements of North Koreans or Chinese. A number of prisoners were also captured during this time; North Koreans for the most part, who told their captors that their units were in a poor state, with few of their original tanks, guns or heavy equipment still serviceable. This was all very small-scale stuff – especially when compared to the hard fighting of early November. The brigade's actions also seemed to confirm the general intelligence picture that the enemy had withdrawn from fighting.

The sudden disappearance of the Chinese allowed both the brigade and the US 24th Division as a whole to make some tentative advances northwards. By late November, the brigade was once again positioned in the familiar surrounds of Pakchon. However, 27 Bde had changed from being the forward brigade of the division to a reserve position. While the brigade took up duties as I Corps reserve, the 21st Regimental Combat Team (RCT), together with the 11th and 12th ROK Regiments, moved ahead of the brigade position to become the forward edge of the 24th Division.

Chapter 10

The Third Enemy – General Winter

A predictable consequence of China's entry into the war was the decision to delay plans to return the British battalions to Hong Kong. Originally scheduled to leave in early November, they were now to remain in Korea 'indefinitely'. For his part, Willoughby knew that it would be hard to deliver this news to his men, but he decided that there was nothing for it but to do it at once and get the unpleasant task over with. He thus scrambled up through the scrub and went from position to position to tell the men. Surprisingly, most took it well, stoically, although there were 'a few wry smiles' from the soldiers – what did one expect from the Army? Willoughby wrote: 'Only ten days ago we thought that this war had been won; and now no light at the end of the tunnel and the cold is getting hard to bear.'[137]

The thought of remaining in Korea for a further indefinite period was tough on the men. Tougher still was the prospect of enduring the rapidly freezing weather that for many would be the defining feature of their tour to Korea.

***

By mid-November, the icy cold descended on North Korea with a vengeance. Whereas 27 Bde had been merely 'cold' all through October and early November, now the real freeze began, brought southwards by a constant front of icy winds blowing directly from Manchuria. Willoughby noted precisely the day and time when the temperature suddenly plummeted towards freezing:

> 'Monday 13 November 1950: While sitting on the ground alongside my jeep at about 8 o'clock and eating a miserable breakfast of cold beef stew out of a tin, I gradually became aware of a distant drawn out moan. Then almost at once the most ghastly wind ever experienced descended on us from the north. It rushed on us from Manchuria and Siberia. The morning temperature had risen to a few degrees above freezing but within two hours it had dipped 22 degrees. I thought I would lose my ears and to look into it for a few moments brought tears. There was no escape, every shelter discovered and all our winters of yesterday were gentle.'[138]

Willoughby was not alone in commenting about the sudden drop in temperature, with many written records surviving to note this significant change in the weather. Major Wilson described it as follows:

> 'Winter usually comes quickly in North Korea, and November 1950 was no exception. By the first week the padi fields were frozen and there was a white rime on the roads and foliage. For those of us in 27 Brigade without proper winter clothing it was getting bloody cold. In those days the British Army's idea of a sleeping bag was two ordinary blankets fastened together with a bit of tape to tie yourself (and your shivering) in!'[139]

An Australian soldier described the freezing winds in typically laconic Digger style as 'a bit of a mother-in-law's breath'.[140]

***

'General Winter' would soon prove to be as a big an enemy and threat to the UN forces as the combined weight of the Chinese and North Korean armies. Similar to the effect that the Russian winter had on the eventual defeat of Napolean and more recently the German Wehrmacht before Moscow, the intense cold now coming from Siberia had the potential to play an outsized role in the fighting taking place in Korea. Without sufficient supplies of Arctic equipment, weapons and vehicles specially prepared to withstand the freezing temperatures, even the best armies could soon find themselves struggling just to survive – let alone be victorious. Many elements of the UN Command would find that they were insufficiently prepared for the onset of the Korean winter, and such ill-preparedness would have significant consequences for their ability to continue to prosecute the war. General Winter had not only arrived, he could not be ignored.

***

Members of the Commonwealth Brigade clearly lacked the clothing and equipment that they needed if they were to be an effective fighting force over the winter months. Due to the hurried nature of their deployment, all of the British troops had little in the way of effective winter clothing. The jungle greens worn during the summer months had by now mainly given way to a hodge-podge collection of British battledress uniforms (a woollen serge uniform consisting of khaki pants and a short-cropped khaki jacket), layered with woollen jumpers and string vests below. Headdress often consisted of a folded cap comforter (the ubiquitous folded scarf loved by commandos and resembling a beanie) or, if they could get it, the US Army fur-lined pile cap.

Many of the Australians, however, still insisted on wearing their slouch hat, despite it offering at best marginal resistance to the cold. Rugged individuality might explain the practice, but perhaps the reason was partially attributable to the exhortations contained in the 23 November edition of the 3 RAR internal *3 Roger Able Roger* newsletter which called on all of the battalion to 'Look Like An Australian And Wear Your Slouch Hat'.[141] Despite the bitter cold, the Australians were still determined to keep their distinctive identity and proudly display it to all the world.

Slouch hat aside, by mid-November some American field jackets were making their way to the men, and these were often worn directly on top of the battledress and anything else the men could find. The US field jackets were a prized item as they gave superior protection from the elements. The jacket comprised a thick cotton outer shell, which had generous-sized pockets on the breast and front waist. It also had a removable insulated liner which increased the effectiveness of the jacket considerably. Initially only a few men were able to scrounge these jackets, but by late November, when further quantities were found, almost every man in the brigade was seen wearing a US field jacket. Some also acquired insulated American trousers or the lined pile caps. The caps, when worn with their long, fur-lined ear flaps folded and tied on top, would become a signature look of the Korean War.

***

Clothing was not the only cold-weather issue facing the Commonwealth men in mid to late November. Operating in the intense cold of North Korea made even the simplest of tasks challenging. Commanders also had to allocate significantly more time to otherwise routine jobs such as cooking, cleaning and guard duty.

Shelter from the elements was a critical aspect of survival during the winter months. Where they could, men would commandeer what few village huts were available. They would rotate those on guard out in the cold every hour or two so that they could at least get some warmth into their bodies and dry out their boots and clothing before the next stint of guard duty. Even the humblest of rural Korean homes had a simple but ingenious underfloor heating system whereby heat from the cooking fire was channelled under the hard-packed dirt floor to keep the whole place warm. Such houses were prized by all during the winter months.

But village homes were rarely available, and certainly not in the numbers required. By this stage of the war, many villages had already been destroyed, either during fighting, bombing or just from the petty destruction and vandalism visited on them every time an army passed through on its way to the north or back down to the south.

With few buildings left standing, or when they were deployed up on the lonely hilltops in the countryside, the troops had little protection from the wind except for shell scrapes and fighting holes that they had hacked out of the frozen earth. These pits were sometimes lined with bits of foliage or clumps of rice husks to provide a scrap of insulation, and covered with a type of sheeting that could act as a small makeshift individual tent. Despite the usual strictures against lighting fires in the field, the troops often scooped out a small hole in the wall of their trench and built a small fire inside. While fires were generally forbidden at night and at guard positions, some commanders turned a blind eye to this practice, knowing that without the small warmth provided by these fires, they would likely find frozen corpses manning the guard posts in the morning rather than alert soldiers.

The brigade vehicles were likewise succumbing to the cold. Already in relatively poor condition, the intense cold from mid-November was the final nail for many of them. 'A considerable number of 1st line vehicles have been disabled by cracked blocks and cylinder heads. This is due to captured Russian anti-freeze being used in lieu of insufficient supplies of British and American Anti-Freeze, whose one to one solution in 20 degrees of frost is quite ineffective,' lamented the Brigade War Diary of 14 November.[142] Even tanks regularly failed to start in the freezing temperatures, with tank crews forced to turn over the engines every few hours during the night in order to stop them completely freezing up.

***

Overall, November was a cold and miserable time for every man in 27 Bde. As the men on guard duty looked out over a frozen moonscape, all they could think about was the next warm meal. At night, when the winds died away, a ghostly silence fell over the battlefield, amplifying whatever fears the men ordinarily had in the dark. The frozen temperatures would have taken a toll on the men, both physically and mentally, yet there were very few cases of actual frostbite recorded in the brigade, and even fewer of any mental or psychological problems. While many men suffered from the cold, the officers and NCOs were very vigilant in watching for signs of exposure among their men; when found, the afflicted men would often be immediately sent to the rear to warm up in whatever shelter was available at the time.

The arrival of General Winter at the end of November heralded a new UN offensive plan. 'New operational orders were received which puts 27 Brigade in Corp reserve today.' announced the Brigade War Diary of 22 November. 'The new plan outlines an offensive to be launched, comprising of 24 Div and 1 ROK Div, with US I Corp to swing West and North West to the Yalu river.'[143] With UN forces now recovered from the initial shock of the Chinese entry into the war, and with intelligence indicating a general withdrawal of enemy troops, MacArthur judged it was time to resume the offensive and push once again towards the Manchurian border.

The sudden and unexpected disappearance of Chinese forces provided the UN with a window to resupply and replenish forward troops ahead of the planned offensive.

The supremely efficient US logistical machine swung immediately into action, working hard to push forward much-needed supplies. Nevertheless, the combination of weather, terrain and general confusion at the front still made supply an ongoing concern for commanders. By mid-November, fuel in particular was in very short supply, with several tank units told that there simply wasn't enough fuel for them to move. As a result, there was nothing for it but for them to remain stationary. Clearly, this was not ideal; a tank shorn of its mobility is simply a sitting duck to the enemy.

Alive to these dangers, commanders realized that desperate times called for vital fuel supplies to be airlifted north. While the airlift demonstrated the ability of the US to use its considerable air assets to overcome any setback, it was clearly not a sustainable solution. It was estimated that it often used as much aviation fuel to airlift in fuel supplies as was eventually delivered to the forward troops. In any event, airlifting fuel could not supply the vast quantities required to keep an entire army in the field, much less provide it with extra supplies needed for a major offensive – particularly during a freezing North Korean winter.

As usual, MacArthur was determined to resume the offensive. A full Thanksgiving dinner was arranged to be sent to every man in the field (in itself a marvellous demonstration of the US logistics system), after which, on 25 November, UN forces were to commence their new general offensive. It was hoped that this offensive would see ROK and UN forces on the Manchurian border in a mere matter of days.

The pre-offensive Thanksgiving meal was commented on by almost everyone in the Korean theatre at the time. The men, used to primitive living and eating food from a can, were suddenly overwhelmed by US largess – turkey, pumpkin pie and prawn cocktail, in enormous quantities. Some private soldiers, with eyes evidently bigger than their shrunken bellies, attempted manfully to eat half a turkey alone. However, several of those who struggled to spoon yet more of the delicious fare into their mouths were soon to regret their gluttony. Quite a number of men reported being sick after eating so much, so quickly, having previously existed on so little.

The Thanksgiving dinner did have the effect of raising the soldiers' morale. So confident were UN troops at this time that many men believed the advance to the Yalu would proceed smoothly and the war would end shortly thereafter. Lieutenant Barry Reed, serving with the Middlesex Battalion, recalled:

> '[I]t really appeared that the war was coming to a conclusion and the Adjutant gave a lecture, and it was how we would undertake guard duties on the Yalu river, and we would have to think about getting drill right, and everyone would have to bull up and look as smart as possible.'[144]

Dreams of smart uniforms and garrison duties were killed off a mere day into the advance, as the Chinese commanders once again unleashed their troops from their mountain hideouts. The Second Chinese Offensive had begun.

North Korean T-34 Enters Seoul, 1950

General Paik, Commander 1 ROK Division

ROK soldier with American M1 rifle, July 1950

27 British Commonwealth Brigade patch. The '999' led to the Brigade being known as the 'Fire Brigade' (Australian War Memorial)

Chinese border from Hong Kong side 1950 – through 2LT Harrop's Binoculars (Harrop)

2LT David Harrop – Jan 1950 (Harrop)

Argyll & Sutherland Highlanders embarking in Hong Kong for Korea (Australian War Memorial)

Naktong River Valley (Australian War Memorial)

1 MX Officers - Allen (L), Quartermaster (C) and Willoughby (L) wearing cap comforter in distinctive stylish manner (National Army Museum)

LTCOL Andrew Man on Naktong (National Army Museum)

Hill 282 "Argyll Hill" (National Army Museum)

Major Kenny Muir. Muir would be awarded the first Victoria Cross of the war

Lieutenant Colonel Green and Brigadier Coad (Australian War Memorial)

Evacuating casualties at the Broken Bridge (Australian War Memorial)

Chinese soldiers planning an attack

Chinese Attack – note the ubiquitous bugler (Australian War Memorial)

1MX MMG Platoon in Carriers near Chipyong-Ni (National Army Museum)

Hill 112, Padre (L) and Adjutant (R) looking north (National Army Museum)

New Zealand 25 Pounder in action (Australian War Memorial)

New Zealand Gunner reloads 25 pounder field gun (Australian War Memorial)

LTCOL Rangaraj, 60 (Para) Field Ambulance

Indian Medical Officer at Chipyong-ni Aid station, March 1951

Australian Vickers Machine Gun in action (Australian War Memorial)

Typical defensive position in the hills (Australian War Memorial)

3RAR Stretcher Bearers 1951

Robinson (L), Ferguson (C) and Coad (R)– after Ferguson assumed command of 3RAR, Nov 1950 (Australian War Memorial)

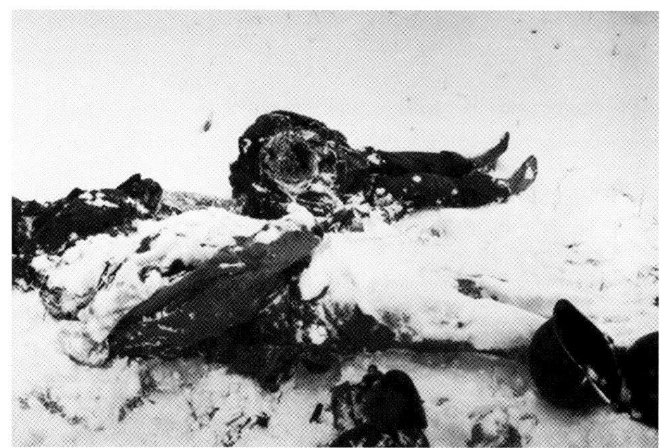

Ambush – Dead American Soldiers following an ambush Feb 1951 – notice all boots taken by Chinese soldiers (Australian War Memorial)

Canadian patrol through Korean village (Australian War Memorial)

Kapyong Valley viewed from A Coy 3RAR position. B Coy 3RAR was located on the lower slopes of the hill in middle ground immediately beyond the road (Australian War Memorial)

View of Hill 677 – just to left of central black line

3RAR 1951 – Note the shallow fighting trenches due to digging in frozen ground (Australian War Memorial)

hermans at Kapyong 23 .pr 1951. On the high round near B Company – hoto by Ray Parry during ıe battle (Australian War Iemorial)

Chinese POW at Kapyong photo taken by Ray Parry a dawn 24 Apr 1951(Australia War Memorial)

Sioux Helicopter landing near 2PPCLI position at Kapyong (Australian War Memorial)

Korean Refugees – the wa displaced millions of civilian who were forced to endur the harsh winters withou shelter and minimal food

Chapter 11

Home by Christmas and the Great Bug Out

For MacArthur, defeat and retreat was something like a trip to the dentist – painful at the time but quickly forgotten. And so it was with the UN forces by late November 1950. Despite the sudden shock of finding several hundred thousand highly motivated Chinese in their midst in early November, less than a month later this seemed to have been all but forgotten. The glaring fact that the nature of the war had been irrevocably changed appeared to have been forgotten by everybody, but most of all by that most supreme and exalted optimist – General Douglas MacArthur.

MacArthur was of course not oblivious to the Chinese threat, but he believed that the UN situation could be rescued and that the offensive to the Yalu must be resumed. Believing that the Chinese had already shot their bolt, he was insistent that the UN forces must resume the advance and liberate all of North Korea. He also grossly underestimated the numbers of troops that the Chinese could place in the front line. When he briefed President Truman at Wake Island in October 1950, MacArthur had estimated that the Chinese could muster no more than 50,000–60,000 troops to fight in Korea. In fact, by November the Chinese had committed over 300,000 men, the great bulk of whom were combat troops.[145] According to General Ridgeway, this failure to properly estimate the number of Chinese amassed against the UN forces was one of the reasons that the 'Home by Christmas' offensive ultimate failed.

In late 1950, and indeed ever since, MacArthur has been widely reported as making a statement that his troops would 'be home by Christmas'. These words were attributed to a discussion he had with some of his field commanders, where it was reported that he said: 'You tell the boys that when they get to the Yalu [river] they are going home. I want to make good on my statement that they are going to eat Christmas dinner at home.'[146]

Of course, MacArthur even at his most confident was not so blind to the situation on the ground that he was totally unaware of the dangers. In an explanation of the remark on 29 November 1950, he said that he 'merely expressed the "universal hope" for a quick and successful end to the fighting in Korea'. He went on to say that 'the evident physical impossibility of fulfilment of the statement attributed to me should be its own best refutation'.[147]

Despite MacArthur's protestations, the advance would come to be known as the 'Home for Christmas' offensive. It was to be an ill-fated moniker, not a description of what happened but a watchword for overconfidence and hubris. In the end, the

UN advance barely resembled an offensive at all. Ridgeway later wrote that although described as 'an "attack" it was really no more than an advance to contact. It is not possible to attack an enemy whose positions are not known, and whose very existence has not been confirmed.'[148]

The Chinese Second Offensive

MacArthur's renewed offensive was doomed almost before it started. His forward units had just commenced their movement north, when a day later the Chinese launched their Second Offensive. Unlike the First Offensive, which began before China was fully ready to strike, the Second Offensive was a well-planned, massive, co-ordinated strike worthy of the name 'offensive'. Taken completely by surprise and shocked by the sheer weight of numbers, UN troops and ROK units in particular crumbled before the onslaught. The flanks of the UN forward lines were torn wide open and great streams of Communist forces pushed relentlessly southwards. With flanks exposed and the threat of encirclement and destruction now very real, UN forces were soon being pushed back all along the front. The withdrawals quickly gathered pace; what started as a few isolated tactical withdrawals soon grew to an army-wide precipitous headlong rush to the south, with troops fleeing as fast as their transport could take them. So fast was the collapse that by 5 December, Pyongyang had been abandoned to the advancing Chinese and North Korean forces. By 15 December, Eighth Army was once again south of the 38th parallel. In the end, it took little more than two weeks before the UN troops were thrown out of North Korea. The scale and speed of the withdrawal would soon earn it the name of 'The Great Bug Out', as bug out fever had infected almost all UN units.

***

The order to withdraw south past Pyongyang was initially met with general disbelief by all members of 27 Bde:

> 'This news was received with amazement by officers and men in the Brigade that so much ground was to be given up without a fight and, at a time when there was no contact with the enemy. However, it was generally felt, although not generally expressed by higher formation, that there were political motives behind this decision and that it was not purely a military decision.'[149]

Time would prove this suspicion correct.

The Great Bug Out was not caused merely by the unexpected presence of so many Chinese troops, but rather was the product of a combination of factors, some found within the UN forces themselves. MacArthur's hubris, the overextension of ROK and US lines, overconfidence and lack of training of some of the replacement troops currently manning the line were all factors that contributed to the collapse. While these might be ignored or papered over during the good times of the general advance, they became stingingly obvious in the face of an enemy as determined and motivated as the Chinese.

There were also larger, geo-political forces at work – or at least considerations that Washington had to take into account and that were not apparent to the men manning the trenches in the frozen hills of Korea. At the start of the Cold War, it was Europe and not Korea that was the primary concern of the Americans (and indeed the British too). Western powers were predominantly concerned about a possible Soviet surprise attack into Western Europe, and their defences were postured mainly to meet that threat. Such concerns were not the wild imaginings of fantasists but were very real risks, clearly demonstrated by Soviet actions such as the Berlin blockade (between June 1948 and May 1949), which saw West Berlin cut off by the Soviets from the rest of West Germany, and which was only relieved by a massive and sustained airlift of supplies into the beleaguered city by the Western Allies.

Such geopolitical considerations had a direct effect on the battlefield in Korea. For example, when MacArthur had asked for an additional 70,000 troops to help hold the line and drive the Chinese out of Korea, his request was denied by Washington. Those numbers simply were not available, as such troops as could be found were held in reserve for possible contingencies in Europe.

Thus faced with both local deficiencies and a tense international situation, MacArthur could not hope for a speedy deployment of sufficient additional forces to help him hold the line. Accordingly, he had little choice but to order a general withdrawal from North Korea.

27 Bde – November–December 1950

27 British Commonwealth Brigade was just one of many units which were buffeted along by the sudden Chinese offensive. Life for the brigade in December consisted of a confusing slew of order and counter-orders as divisional commanders desperately sought to throw 27 Bde at whatever crisis presented itself and as events (read the Chinese Army) overtook the previous day's plans. '[N]othing is really known of the enemy, declared the Brigade War Diary on 1 December 1950, 'and to use an American expression, the situation might be termed as generally fluid.'[150]

But the situation across the front was more serious than just 'generally fluid'. The Operations Log of the brigade noted: 'It is the opinion that certain units are giving false information in order to extract from commands and staff permission or even orders for premature and quite unjustifiable withdrawals. It was just this type of excitable dishonesty which caused some unnecessary and expensive withdrawals in France in 1940.'[151] While the Chinese Second Offensive was certainly an impressive and frightening challenge for the UN forces, the reality was that it was morale and fighting spirit that broke in many UN units well before the Chinese had a chance to test their fighting strength.

For 27 Bde, December was a brutal month. Conditions were made worse by the harshest of winters, which was now being reported as one of the worst in living memory. However, in some respects the brigade was probably luckier than many of its sister units, since it was rarely the focus of a major Chinese encirclement and annihilation campaign. Nevertheless, being regarded as a solid and dependable unit which had resisted the urge to simply flee south, the brigade was inevitably used and misused by divisional and corps commanders desperate to use the Commonwealth troops to try to stem the tide and act as a dependable blocking force.

Dependability and a strong will to try their best was one thing. However, an absence of resources was another thing entirely. For example, lack of sufficient integral transport often resulted in several long and freezing route marches to move the men to blocking positions which they would hold merely to allow other forces to withdraw. As 3 RAR's Ben O'Dowd would sarcastically remark, 'it was our experience that there was never any difficulty in providing transport to insert the Brigade into some nasty situations, but when it came to extracting us for movement south, none was available'.[152]

***

In even the most dangerous of times, there were still moments of relative quiet and the odd surreal experience. For example, at the beginning of December, Major Willoughby's D Company was spending an unexpectedly peaceful moment in the rear. Seizing the rare opportunity, a water truck was found and was brought up to provide some rudimentary washing facilities for the men. Willoughby himself was having a long-overdue wash when he was called to the field telephone to comment on whether his company had seen 'a party of 4 enemy soldiers mounted on white horses' reconnoitring his positions. He had not, came the curt reply from the half-washed major. But as he returned to his position, towelling himself down, Willoughby couldn't help thinking that the four white horses could have been the mythical Four Horsemen of the Apocalypse – war, pestilence, famine and death. His literary turn of mind would once again prove disturbingly prescient, with UN forces just then at the start of a full retreat southwards.

***

The headlong rush south did little to lift the morale of 27 Bde. Despite the brigade's reputation for steadfastness and dedication to duty, it was demoralizing to march back over the same ground that had so recently been taken through the expenditure of much effort and at the expense of many lives. As they trudged through the snow, with the biting Siberian winds pushing at their backs, few of the brigade's men could see any silver linings to this withdrawal.

In one area, however, the move proved useful to the men of the brigade, as they were able to 'liberate' large quantities of sorely needed kit, left behind in great quantities by the retreating US forces. In particular, a large quantity of winter clothing and highly coveted Arctic sleeping bags was found and quickly distributed to the shivering Commonwealth soldiers.

Vehicles had also been abandoned in great numbers, much to the surprise of the Commonwealth soldiers, who had never had enough of them. In the surrounds of Pyongyang, the ever-resourceful 3 RAR, determined to reduce the deficit, was able to secure ten trucks, ten jeeps and three water carts, all in good working order and simply abandoned by the side of the road. This allowed the battalion to finally get rid of its hated Bren gun carriers, which were destroyed by the assault pioneer platoon. According to Ben O'Dowd, 3 RAR's 'path in and out of North Korea was marked by the tin hats discarded by the Diggers on the way north, and by the Bren gun carriers destroyed … on the return journey'.[153] But the acquisition of an adequate number of vehicles was only of limited comfort and did little to assuage the men's nagging questions as to why the UN forces had given up so much ground, apparently without a fight.

By mid-December, the brigade was once more south of the 38th parallel, deployed on the outskirts of Uijongbu and back in IX Corps reserve. The UN lines were now stabilizing south of the 38th parallel as the Chinese Second Offensive started to slow. While the US and UN forces were being reorganized, 27 Bde embarked on an extensive patrolling programme in a radius of up to 20 miles from Uijongbu. 'These patrols are most unpleasant, due to the freezing winds,' recorded the 3 RAR War Diary.[154] The roads were icy or packed with snow and were hazardous to all the brigade's vehicle-mounted patrols. Foot patrols had to contend with freezing winds, snow drifts and the ever-present cold. It was a miserable time to be an infantryman, with all members of the brigade suffering from the elements.

The combination of the weather and constant combat was also taking its toll on the brigade's commanders. By this time, Coad was clearly struggling, exhausted from his constant exertions, lack of sleep and the weight of command. The brigade medical staff finally ordered him to leave his command and take a complete rest with B Echelon for a few days. In the end, Coad would be out of action for about two weeks, with Colonel Man assuming temporary command of the brigade in his absence.

The constant physical and mental pressure on commanders was not limited to Coad, with the effects seen on several other senior officers over the next few months. By January, Man would likewise face serious health problems – chronic exhaustion and stomach ulcers, which would necessitate a spell of recovery in Pusan before eventually being forced to leave Korea and return early to Hong Kong.[155] The pressures of command

and fighting in the freezing countryside of Korea quickly wore down the older men, irrespective of their drive and commitment.

***

By the end of December, the opposing armies had once again settled down to a tense standoff. Both sides now busied themselves in consolidating their positions and reorganizing their lines. Neither had the strength to commence another offensive, so an uneasy stalemate ensued, punctuated by frequent patrolling.

At Uijongbu, much-needed reinforcements started to flow into the brigade, with 3 RAR alone receiving an additional fifty-eight new men who had just arrived from Japan. The end of December also saw the first groups of men sent to Japan for R&R (rest and relaxation). Dubbed 'Operation Relax', the five-day spell often left the soldiers somewhat bewildered when they first touched down in Japan. Having come directly from a war zone, where they had worn the same filthy clothes for months on end and mainly slept in holes in the ground, it was completely disorientating to suddenly find themselves in a peaceful, clean and bustling city. Most dealt with the confusion in the time-honoured way of front-line soldiers – by chasing girls and drinking far too much alcohol.

***

As the year wound down, 27 Bde prepared for the usual celebrations – Christmas and New Year's Eve. Word was also received that the brigade was to be presented with the South Korean Presidential Citation for its actions on the Naktong River. Unfortunately, on the very day on which the citation was to be presented (23 December), Lieutenant General Walton Walker, the commander of Eighth Army, was killed in a jeep accident while en route to the brigade position to present the award. This was yet another example of a senior officer being killed in Korea not by enemy action, but by the deadly road conditions.

Two days later it was Christmas Day, bringing good cheer to all in the brigade. A veritable feast was prepared for the troops, consisting of turkey, plum pudding and – importantly – two bottles of beer per man. As was traditional in Commonwealth units, Christmas Day saw the brigade officers serving the men their Christmas dinner before sitting down themselves to eat. It was a memorable occasion, welcomed by all after the tough conditions of the past few months.

Despite the good cheer and relatively modest enemy activity, there were still serious dangers that threatened the health of the Commonwealth men. Chief among them was the threat posed by the 'consumption of local alcoholic liquors'. This was of such concern that Major Ferguson issued an order to 3 RAR strictly forbidding its consumption: '[O]ne case of moderately severe visual disturbance has occurred as a result of drinking a local spiritous liquor … All personnel are warned that blindness, insanity, muscular paralysis and other disorders may result from this practice.'[156] Given the reputation of the Australian soldiers and their relationship with alcohol, however, one wonders whether it was the contents of this 'spiritous liquor' or rather the quantity of its consumption which had such a deleterious effect on the soldiers.

Nonetheless, celebrations continued and the year ended in the traditional way. At midnight on New Year's Eve, the men of the Argylls were heard to loudly sing 'Auld Lang Syne' and wish each other a more fortuitous 1951.

Chapter 12

A Frozen January

While the Argylls were bidding farewell to the old year in their time-honoured fashion, the Chinese decided to welcome the New Year with fireworks of their own, launching what would in time become known as their Third Offensive.

With 1951 only several hours old, ominous reports started to come into Brigade HQ about heavy fighting breaking out all along the front line. 'At 0615hrs, a message from HQ IX Corp made it clear that the situation was not well,'[157] was the very first entry of 1951 recorded in the 27 British Commonwealth Brigade War Diary. It went on to describe how elements of the 6th ROK Division had already been forced back, with many South Korean troops fleeing south past the brigade defensive areas towards Seoul. This was not an auspicious start to the new year, and as the day dawned the news would only get worse.

While no enemy forces were immediately seen in the 27 Bde area, it was clear that large numbers of Chinese troops were rapidly moving south and would inevitably soon bump up against the brigade. Lines of retreating ROK troops, often in small, scraggly groups rather than formed bodies of men, streamed past the British and Australians manning their defensive positions. As the day progressed, orders were given to the Commonwealth troops to likewise abandon their positions and move south. The Brigade War Diary stated: 'New Years day this year was one which will be long remembered! … the suddenness of the UN retreat and the spectacle of troops in retreat and of refugees in flight the following day were both disheartening and pitiful.'[158]

Massive attacks on the front line by several hundred thousand Chinese troops saw many ROK units simply disintegrate. General Mathew Ridgeway, having now assumed command of Eighth Army after the death of Walker, was concerned about the potential envelopment of his army, so reluctantly ordered a general withdrawal. Events continued to develop so quickly and the fighting escalated so rapidly that by 3 January it was clear that Seoul could not be held. Two days later it was all over, and once again the South Korean capital was in the hands of the Communists.

South Korean units were the main target of this offensive, and some sympathy should be extended to the poor ROK troops who were directly in the firing line. They had been fighting almost continuously since the start of the war – there was little prospect of R&R in Japan for the South Koreans. Furthermore, the Communist forces often targeted the ROK troops, considering them – correctly, as was often the case – to be a softer target than the US or UN soldiers. Almost every ROK unit had suffered significant casualties since the start of the war and by early 1951 was often filled with raw or at best semi-trained troops. In addition, these units frequently had weak commanders. Like their men, the newly commissioned officers only had minimal training, and this lack of skills and experience told against them when tested by the Chinese. They also lacked many of the assets that US troops took for granted – especially vehicles and communications equipment. It was thus no wonder that many of these units simply collapsed when faced with large numbers of highly motivated Chinese troops aggressively moving towards them.

As a consequence, bug out fever once again took hold amongst the ROK and US troops south of the 38th parallel. This was not a replay of the Great Bug Out and the withdrawal was on the whole much more measured and organised, but there was no disguising that this was another victory for the Communists, with UN forces once again on the back foot. Much to the chagrin of the officers and men of 27 Bde, early January 1951 saw further movement south in the face of continued Chinese pressure.

The reason for further withdrawals was almost incomprehensible to many in the brigade. While the brigade proved remarkably resilient and continued to be a dependable fighting force, the soldiers couldn't help but wonder what was going on with an army that had only a month before been on the Chinese border. An entry in the Brigade War Diary accurately captured the mood:

> 'The succession of recent retreats, together with the difficult winter conditions had demoralised the United Nation forces and a general disinterestedness in the war was beginning to creep in. It was unfortunate but true that officers were talking seriously and openly about the superiority of the Chinese troops over those of the Allies and of the possibility of a general evacuation of South Korea. It should be recorded in all fairness, that members of the Brigade were not guilty of this defeatist attitude although the average soldier was puzzled by the poor military situation and had lost confidence in the steadiness of and discipline of some United Nations units … Morale in the Brigade was high and if efficiency was impaired, it was due to the hard winter conditions rather than a drop in morale.'[159]

The winter conditions were indeed hard. By mid-January, average daily temperatures were between minus 20 and minus 25 degrees Centigrade (minus 4 to minus 13 degrees Fahrenheit). Most ground was covered in a thick blanket of snow, and where it was not it was rock hard, making digging in almost impossible without explosives or heavy equipment. There was no let-up from the cold and the biting wind, which only served to further dampen the spirits of already disheartened troops.

General Ridgeway noted: 'Every command post I visited gave me the same sense of lost confidence and lack of spirit.'[160] It was this lack of fighting spirit which concerned

Ridgeway the most; he knew that without restoring pride and confidence in his men, it would be impossible to mount any form of serious counter-attack or general offensive. As a result, restoring morale and martial spirit was his primary focus during his first month in command of Eighth Army.

Fortunately, Ridgeway did not have the same concerns for the Commonwealth troops under his command, whom he found to be full of quiet confidence and not a little wry humour. When visiting 27 Bde in early January while it was holding a relatively isolated position with little cover of its flanks, Ridgeway was met by a young subaltern. Spotting Ridgeway, the lieutenant trotted off a small knoll towards the general and saluted smartly. Ridgeway later recorded:

> '[K]nowing that the British Brigade had hardly more than a handful of men to cover a wide sector of the front line, with a new Chinese offensive expected almost hourly, I asked him how he found the situation. "Quite all right Sir", he replied quickly. But then he added with a pleasant smile: "It is a bit drafty up here". Drafty was the word for it, with gaps in the line wide enough to march an Army through.'[161]

By late January, the front was starting to stabilize south of Seoul. Like the first two offensives, the Chinese Third Offensive soon blew itself out, overreaching its supply lines and casualties continuing to grow. Meanwhile, Ridgeway's efforts in bucking up his command were bearing fruit, and a confidence started to return to Allied ranks. So much so that by February, Ridgeway was starting to turn his mind to the possibility of a measured counter-offensive to push the Communists back northwards.

Before the end of January, Coad would once again need to leave 27 Bde, this time for extended leave in Hong Kong. Despite the rest he took in December, the pressures were again mounting on Coad; being completely exhausted, he required a proper rest. Colonel Man once more assumed command of the brigade. Just before Coad left the brigade, he was given an extremely welcome bit of news. A full regiment of New Zealand artillery would finally join 27 Bde, significantly bolstering its firepower and turning it into a true Commonwealth Brigade.

The New Zealanders

16th New Zealand Field Regiment

Chapter 13

Kayforce

The addition of the Kiwis was welcomed by all in 27 Bde, but none more so than Coad, who had always hated having to beg for artillery resources from his US superiors. With the arrival of the New Zealand gunners, the brigade would now have its own dedicated fire support, available at all times.

It had not always been certain that New Zealand would supply ground forces. While New Zealand agreed to support the UN effort almost as soon as the war was declared, its initial commitment was limited to two of its warships to join UN forces off the coast of Korea. As a very small country with modest military resources, it was felt by many in the New Zealand government that the provision of naval assets was more than sufficient to demonstrate support for the United Nations cause.

Over time, however, requests for ground forces soon became impossible to ignore. Notwithstanding the initial hesitation, both the public and the press in New Zealand expressed their enthusiasm for a ground role. It was Britain's decision to deploy its infantry battalions from Hong Kong that finally convinced the New Zealand government that a Kiwi ground commitment was appropriate.

***

Immediately following the end of the Second World War, New Zealand's defence planning and strategy were still closely entwined with that of the British. This was expressed in many ways, including the continuation of joint patrols and co-operation involving New Zealand's naval and land forces, which were based very closely on the British model in terms of equipment, doctrine and training.

Nevertheless, New Zealand was growing increasingly aware of matters in its own neighbourhood. While Korea may have seemed 'a distant obligation' to Britain,[162] peace and security in Asia was a much more immediate and closer concern for New Zealand, and one which it could not ignore.

In addition, the recent war in the Pacific had made it clear that it was primarily the actions of the United States that would prevent any future invasion of New Zealand. Thus, despite the close and longstanding ties with Great Britain, the post-war reality saw New Zealanders starting to realize that they must now consider the wishes of two great powers when considering matters of national defence and the new world order. As Ian

McGibbon notes in the *Official History of New Zealand in the Korean War*: 'The reasons for New Zealand's commitment, and its easy public acceptance, thus lie largely in its relationship with great powers.' McGibbon continues that while '[t]radition, economic and strategic self-interest, habit – all had their bearing' on the decision to commit forces, so too did the newly emerging strategic reality.[163]

The rapidly deteriorating – or more accurately disintegrating – situation on the ground in Korea during July 1950 prompted the Secretary General of the United Nations to formally ask for ground-force contributions. New Zealand now stepped up and formally committed to send ground troops. Once the decision was made, the commitment was broadly supported by ordinary New Zealanders. The Second World War was a very recent memory, and many had served. To many New Zealanders, the attack on South Korea appeared to be an act of naked aggression by the Communist North. As both the US and Britain were already in support of taking action, it was inconceivable at this time that New Zealand would refuse to do so.

Kayforce

Although the people of New Zealand were in favour of the idea of sending ground troops to Korea as soon as possible, the reality of raising, equipping and sending them would be an entirely different matter. In 1950, New Zealand possessed only a very small regular army, which was patently insufficient or indeed capable of generating any meaningful contribution to the fighting. The New Zealand Army had a total strength of only about 3,000 regular troops, who were all committed to administer the Compulsory Service Scheme (i.e. conscription) or earmarked for a potential role in the Middle East in support of British troops. Thus, an early decision was made that regular troops would not be sent to Korea. This was a very painful decision for many of the regular soldiers and was deeply unpopular. Nevertheless, in the end a small number of regular troops, nineteen in total, would find ways to wheedle their way onto the posted strength of the deployed force.

The decision to exclude regular troops was a curious one, and one wonders at the wisdom of ignoring the most currently trained and experienced troops from the force that was soon to deploy to a very intense war. Instead, it was decided that a specially raised force of volunteers would be established, known as Kayforce, now more frequently written as 'K-Force'. It was recognized, however, that such a force would not be immediately available for service, and would need at least four months to raise, train and prepare for war.

The New Zealand commitment would be a specialist combat arm, an artillery regiment of approximately 1,000 men, rather than another infantry battalion. McGibbon writes:

> '[T]he idea of sending an infantry unit was resisted. This was partly because of an unwillingness, arising from unfortunate experiences during the Second

World War, to have New Zealand soldiers reliant upon other national forces, even British, for artillery or armoured support. It was also recognised that casualties tended to be heavier in an infantry force.'[164]

The commitment of artillery may have appeared a modest contribution in terms of total numbers, but it was very significant in relation to both the total population of New Zealand and in terms of augmenting the combat power of the Commonwealth Brigade.

With K-Force excluding the regulars, volunteers were called for and the response was overwhelming. In less than two weeks, recruiting had to be closed with nearly 6,000 men having already applied for the roughly 1,000 positions. Some of the hopefuls were weeded out pretty quickly – either too young, married or in an important profession that meant they could not be spared.

Reasons for applying were varied, although, like the Australians, a common theme appeared to be a thirst for adventure and comradeship. Also, a sizeable number felt that they had 'missed out' on the Second World War, and now was their chance. Of those finally accepted for training, about 60 per cent had some previous military experience, the remainder being new recruits. The recruits came from all walks of life – some were labourers, farmers or office workers, but there were also a fair number of men with some technical or mechanical training. The latter would prove to be particularly useful for the vital transport and signals sections, without which an artillery unit cannot function.

While previous military experience was certainly an asset, even those who had previously served were a motley lot, with a fair number of former sailors, pilots and infantry joining the ranks. Despite the number of applicants, what was in particularly short supply was anyone who had previous experience serving in an artillery regiment. As a consequence, New Zealand found itself creating a new artillery regiment almost from scratch, one which would soon deploy to an active combat zone.

This insistence on volunteers for K-Force also extended to the officer ranks. Even the man selected to command the force, Lieutenant Colonel John Moodie, was not a regular officer. Moodie was 43 years old and had seen extensive action in the Second World War in an anti-tank battery and later as commander of a battery of guns in a field regiment. However, when the call came to establish K-Force, Moodie had already transitioned back to his civilian career as a clothing manufacturer. However, he still held a commission in the Territorial Force. He was a very well respected and experienced officer, but it is nevertheless still curious that he was selected over currently serving regular soldiers.

Moodie was fortunate in being allocated the services of a core of very experienced battery commanders (an artillery regiment was made up of three batteries of eight guns each, plus a headquarters battery) and senior NCOs, who would prove crucial in forming the nucleus of the new unit.

Outside this small kernel, however, the rest of the men had little or no experience of how to operate in an artillery regiment. The government insisted that this new unit would require a period of intensive training before it could be committed to combat, given the newly raised regiment was clearly in no fit state to fight at this early stage. Even a few months of basic military training, followed by specialized artillery training, produced a unit that was barely able to conduct sophisticated fire missions. It was reported that in the last exercise prior to embarkation in early December 1950, it took the guns approximately thirty minutes to locate targets, calculate firing data and fire rounds down range. This was clearly well below what would be expected of a well-oiled and experienced unit.

That said, the officers accepted that they had been granted very limited time to bring raw recruits up to the level of experienced gunners. Indeed, many of the lessons and training that would ordinarily be included in basic gunnery training had to wait until the men were aboard the transport ships bound for Korea. Even most of the officers were quite new – several were put through a crash course in officer training and only obtained their commissions as a second lieutenant upon reaching Korea. Nevertheless, by December 1950, the 16th NZ Field Regiment was on its way to Korea and to join 27 Bde.

16th NZ Field Regiment

The 16th NZ Field Regiment had three batteries of eight 25-pdr guns, making a total of 24 guns. This was a formidable addition to the Commonwealth Brigade's firepower. Following British doctrine, the artillery commander was usually located in Brigade HQ beside the brigade commander, on hand to provide advice regarding fire support as needed. This arrangement was quite different to the American approach, whereby the artillery commander usually stayed with his troops and only dispatched a liaison officer to the supported unit. The British approach meant that there was usually a very strong and close relationship between the brigade CO and his artillery commander.

Each battery comprised three main components – the guns themselves, the Command Post (CP) and the Forward Observers (FOs) – all working together as a team to deliver rounds, accurately and at the right time, onto the desired target.

The guns used by the Kiwis were the venerable, much-loved 25-pdr. This gun was the mainstay light field gun of British and Commonwealth forces during the Second World War. The name of the gun referred to the weight of the projectile – 25lb (11.3kg) of high explosive and steel. It had a maximum range of about 12km and could fire on a very high trajectory, which was vital in being able to bring rounds down on and over the hills and mountains that were such a part of the landscape in Korea.

Each gun crew was composed of six men, who were expected to be available around the clock to serve the guns and provide fire support at a moment's notice. While six men were more than sufficient to prepare the ammunition, sight the gun and fire it, prolonged twenty-four-hour operations often meant that at any one time no more than three or four men would be on duty. Imagine the physical effort required to move and load the gun during even a rather modest twenty-round fire mission. This would involve shifting 500lb (about 230kg) of ammunition as well as the propellant, and moving the gun itself, by hand, if it was not in quite the right position. It made for hard and heavy work, and gun crews would often lose several pounds of sweat during an extended fire mission, leaving them exhausted and looking for somewhere to sleep at its conclusion.

As important as the guns were the Forward Observer teams. The FOs comprised small teams of two or three men, often just consisting of a junior officer and his radio operator. The FOs would usually accompany the infantry as they advanced or would be located in hides on key features several kilometres in front of the battery. From these positions, the FO would direct artillery fire onto enemy positions. This was very hard and dangerous work, often located very close to the foe. The FO party would be expected to march with the infantry, carrying all their own personal equipment as well as additional radio equipment, and then, in the middle of any battle, coolly radio in targets to the battery so that fire could be brought to bear. As well as courage, it required coolness and the ability to conduct calm analysis in even the most chaotic of situations. Due to their location on the forward edge of the battlefield, it was often the case that the majority of casualties in an artillery unit came from the FO parties.

It may be a statement of the exceedingly obvious, but the guns were also extremely loud. Unlike today, no hearing protection of any sort was available. Men with nothing in their hands would clasp both hands to their ears, while the unfortunate ones carrying things or preparing ammunition for the next mission could do little more than shrug up one shoulder in a vain attempt to at least shelter one of their ears. The well-worn caricature of artillerymen with poor hearing is, unfortunately, rooted in reality.

The gunners, perhaps even more than their infantry brethren, were a particularly small and tight-knit team who spent practically their entire time either firing, serving or caring for their guns. For many of the men of K-Force, their gun crew was their entire world. Almost the entirety of a gunner's tour in Korea revolved around preparing, firing and maintaining their guns.

***

With the 16th NZ Field Regiment now ready, it embarked on its cruise towards Korea, passing through the ports of Brisbane and Manila before arriving in Pusan on New Year's Eve 1950. Shivering as they came down the gangplank, the gunners were welcomed to the strains of the same band that had played for the other Commonwealth contingents over the past few months. However, unlike the British infantry, who were immediately sent to the front, the Kiwis had the relative good fortune to remain in Pusan for three weeks, acclimatizing to the freezing weather and getting their guns and equipment in order before making the journey north to join 27 Bde. In Pusan, the regiment was quartered in a series of long, low and particularly draughty barracks, which had previously served the Imperial Japanese Army during their occupation of Korea. It wasn't particularly luxurious, but at least the men were out of the cold and wind. They were also given plentiful supplies of good American rations to help keep out the chill, which was just as well as their clothing, like most of 27 Bde's, was not of Arctic quality, barely sufficient to deal with the freezing temperatures.

The gunners' initial impressions of Korea were not particularly flattering. Almost all of the men commented on the ramshackle and broken-down state of the city and the ever-present 'stench'. The Kiwis were also struck by the obvious poverty of the Koreans whom they saw all around them. This was something of a shock to the clean, well-fed and newly arrived New Zealanders, and it took some time to realize that most of the townspeople were in fact refugees who had fled the successive waves of fighting over the past few months, arriving in Pusan with little more than whatever they could carry. Even though Pusan was the biggest city in this part of South Korea, shelter for most refugees was crude and ramshackle, often just a makeshift hut made from whatever scrap timber or bits of canvas that could be scrounged. Orphans were everywhere in the city, the children begging for food from the soldiers. It was a particularly hard winter for the Korean civilians in Pusan, and many went hungry. One sight that stayed with some of the new arrivals was the image of women diving into the icy waters of the harbour, desperate to get hold of whatever shellfish or seaweed they could find to supplement their meagre diets, irrespective of the potentially deadly cold of the harbour waters.

***

By mid-January, the regiment's time in Pusan had come to an end and they started to move northwards to join the brigade. Almost immediately, the unit was reminded in the harshest possible manner about the deadly seriousness of what they were about to take on. On their first night out from Pusan, two members of the regiment became separated from their comrades. Alone and in the dark, they were dragged from their vehicles by Communist guerrillas and then stripped, beaten and shot. Looking for the lost men the next day, members of the regiment discovered their naked bodies lying in the snow.

The heady days of enlistment in New Zealand and the expectations of fun and adventure had come face-to-face with the harsh realities of life in a combat zone. McGibbon notes that 'from then on no one had any doubts that we were playing for keeps'.[165]

Chapter 14

The Battle at Hill 112

There was no let-up in the atrocious weather. During the first days of February, the Commonwealth Brigade would be continually subjected to biting winds, cold and then – the infantryman's special enemy – rain. 'Rain, unbelievably cold and miserable. I don't understand the climate or anything else about this benighted country'[166] – that was how Willoughby described his feelings as the brigade faced the new month, one that would see attempts at offensives mounted by both sides.

In early February, some inconclusive northward thrusts were made by both ROK and US forces, but these achieved little and quickly petered out. Of more importance to 27 Bde was the opening of the Chinese Fourth Offensive around 11 February. Fortunately for the brigade, when the offensive began it was once again in reserve and did not feel the full force of the renewed Chinese attack. But while not in immediate danger, the offensive inevitably affected the brigade, being moved hither and thither to shore up a flank, plug a gap or be wherever higher command thought they could be best employed.

By mid-February, a positive change was starting to be observed across the UN forces. While the weight of this latest Chinese offensive had inevitably pushed back US and ROK units in some locations, there was no repeat of the earlier bug outs. Ridgeway's efforts in putting some steel into his subordinates was starting to have an effect, and all along the front there seemed to be a more determined and steadfast approach to dealing with the Chinese threat.

A prime example of this new-found steadfastness was the dogged defence of Chipyong-ni between 13 and 15 February by the US 23rd Infantry Regiment, supported by a French battalion. The US and French forces were attacked by several Chinese divisions. While the overwhelming enemy numbers would have suggested that a retreat was the most sensible option, Ridgeway decided that there would be no withdrawal. Rather, the US forces would make a heroic stand at Chipyong-ni, blunt the Chinese offensive and thus allow the UN to counter-attack. The result of several days of hard fighting was a clear Allied victory and an important morale-booster for the UN cause.

But this was in the future. In the days prior to the battle, 27 Bde found itself located in the surrounds of Tanguri, approximately 20 miles south of Chipyong-ni. Chipyong-ni itself was held by the 23rd Infantry and was facing stiff pressure from the Chinese. Willoughby reported in his diary on 12 February:

'The Chinese are now reported to be making headway in their drive down central Korea ... and we are now getting frantic reports of units being cut off and guns abandoned. It now seems that the 23rd Regiment, which includes the French Battalion, is cut off at Chipyong-ni, 25 miles to the north of us. They are reported to be holding their ground and inflicting heavy losses on the Chinese. This is wonderful news, for this must surely be the first time during this terrible debacle that this has been done.'[167]

On the morning of 14 February, Colonel Man received warning that the brigade would need to move north to Chuam-ni, about halfway between their present position and Chipyong-ni, in order to facilitate the withdrawal of the 23rd RCT from Chipyong-ni if their position became untenable.

At about noon, 1 MX were first to move out. As Man was now leading the brigade, 1 MX was under temporary command of the battalion 2IC, Major Roly Gwyn, bundled in his thick winter clothing complete with trademark cravat. Gwyn was somewhat comforted in having a US tank company in support of the battalion, but nevertheless the advance was very slow. The slowness, often no more than a mile an hour, was partially a product of the need for careful clearance of high ground to the flanks of Route 24 that the battalion was moving along. Like all 27 Bde officers, Gwyn was convinced of the necessity to ensure his flanks were safe, and as such he would not be rushed until they were cleared and his line of advance secured.

After an hour or so, the forward companies spotted some figures, who were obviously Chinese, atop a feature named Point 112 on the righthand side of the road. Point 112 was a long, low feature mainly running on a north–south axis and about 1,000 yards long. Its far end – the northern end – broadened east and west into a T-shape, while a small hamlet lay in the shelter of the southern end – the side closest to the advancing Middlesex men. Contemporary photographs show that snow was still lying on the ground everywhere except for the southern sides of the distant hills, that side having received some sun through the day, causing the snow to melt. Point 112 was also covered with a small number of short, scraggly pines trees as well as the dried husks of last summer's low scrub poking here and there through the snow. Surrounding the feature, the land fell away and opened up to frozen paddy before once again rising to a range of tall, snow-covered ridges to the north.

Inexplicitly, the Chinese atop 112 did not display the excellent daytime camouflage and fieldcraft that was usually second nature to most of their comrades. Rather, these men were wandering around in plain sight, apparently unaware of the Diehards making their way towards them.

Wishing to take advantage of their good fortune, the Middlesex men were ordered to immediately assault the position. They were well spread out and advanced with purpose through the frozen paddy towards the slopes. A Company was in the lead, with 1 Platoon,

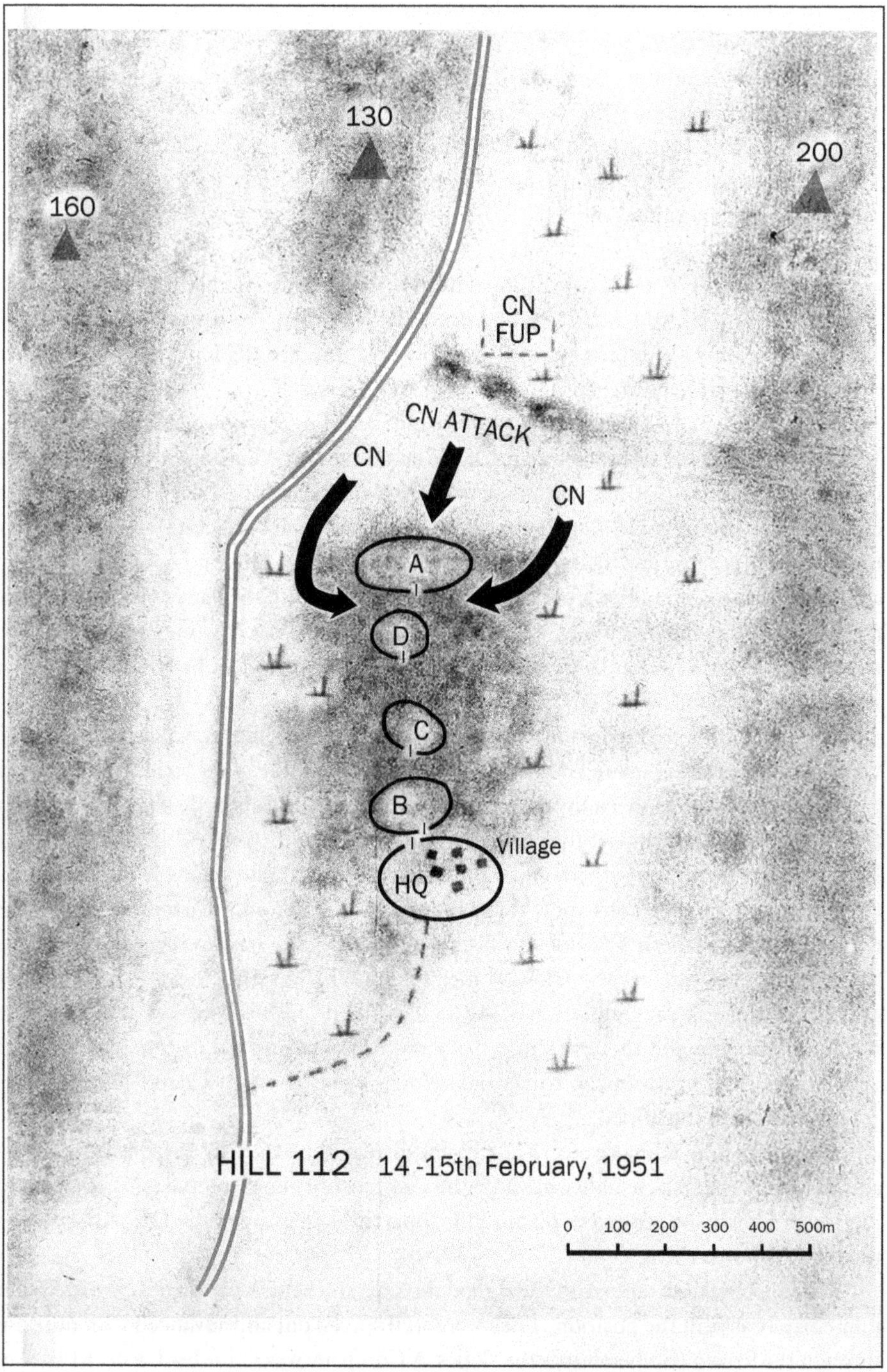

130
200
160
CN
FUP
CN ATTACK
CN
CN
A
D
C
B
Village
HQ
HILL 112 14 -15th February, 1951
0 100 200 300 400 500m

the most forward platoon, being led by the recently arrived Second Lieutenant David Harrop, who had not deployed with the battalion in August due to a question as to whether the time remaining in his National Service commitment would allow it. With a recent change in the rules, Harrop joined the battalion in late December as a replacement officer. Now, just over a month later, he found himself advancing silently at a half-crouch towards the unsuspecting Chinese.

The Middlesex advance was going well and they were undetected by the Chinese. However, the cat was out of the bag as soon as covering fire from the New Zealander gunners started up on the forward (northern) slopes of the ridge. The elongated whistle overhead followed by the crashing explosion of the 25-pdr rounds shook the forward slopes of the hill. This was soon joined by the crumping sound and explosions of the battalion's own 3in mortars, providing even more cover for the advancing infantry. With surprise gone, stealth was abandoned and Harrop's men moved up the hill at a rapid pace. Then one of Harrop's men yelled 'Look out!' and pointed up the slope to where he had spotted an enemy machine gun, seemingly pointing straight at them. Harrop's men immediately went to ground and his Bren gunners let off a burst of rounds to keep the enemy's heads down. The rest of the platoon then smoothly worked its way to a flank to try to get around the side of the machine gun. The manoeuvre worked well and 1 Platoon was soon charging through the machine-gun position, only to find that it was already out of action, its three crewmen lying dead around it – all victims of the wickedly accurate and deadly artillery fire of the New Zealand guns.

The concentration of suppressing artillery fire kept the remaining Chinese heads down long enough for the advancing infantry to gain the foothills. Then, over the next hour or so, the rifle platoons fought their way up the southern slope and onto the crest. The hill narrowed considerably at the top and the men were forced to fight along the ridges and gullies on both sides. About an hour later, after employing excellent infantry tactics, characterized by small outflanking manoeuvres and then an assault on isolated groups of Chinese, the Middlesex men had complete control of the position. The remaining Chinese acknowledged the inevitable and grudgingly gave up their positions. By about 1830hrs, the hill was in British hands.

Man was delighted with the attack and the capture of Point 112. It was a very good tactical position, dominating the road to the west. Accordingly, Man decided to locate the whole battalion in defence around the hill. While concentration in this manner could potentially expose the men to encirclement, the excellent fields of fire in almost all directions for the battalion machine guns provided reassurance to Man that this would be a good and easily defensible position.

Having led the initial assault, A Company remained forward, occupying the forward right edge of the slope (the north-east). D Company was allocated the forward left edge (north-west – closest to the road) and the other companies were placed to the rear (south), with Battalion HQ located at the extreme south end of the feature among the remnants of the small hamlet. Meanwhile, 3 RAR was also moved forward and secured another hill to the left (west) of Route 24.

***

With daylight fading, it was a race against time to get the position properly prepared and defences tied in. Ammunition was brought up the hill to resupply the men who had been engaged in the fighting. The artillery guns were also busy registering defensive fire on likely enemy forming-up points and avenues of attack. This work was essential so that if an attack came, the guns could quickly be aligned with preregistered positions and bring in fire much more rapidly than if calculations had not been worked out in advance. This prior preparation would prove to be a godsend in the hours ahead, compensating to some extent for the lack of white phosphorous shells which would ordinarily be used to illuminate targets at night.

The men started digging in, but as usual the frozen ground was solid and the crust 'was like concrete. But it was surprising what can be managed with enough incentive.'[168] Knowing full well that enemy were still in the vicinity motivated the men to wield their shovels and picks with vigour to dig full trenches and defensive positions. The only concern noted was that Harrop had to have his trench dug considerably wider and deeper in order to accommodate the newly arrived New Zealand artillery Forward Observer team. Captain Arthur Roxburgh, the FO, and his signaller, Lance Bombardier Hec McCubbin, were both quite tall men, which necessitated some extra digging to make room for these vital attachments to the platoon and battalion. The extra effort would prove worthwhile during the upcoming battle for the additional protection it provided to Harrop, Roxburgh and McCubbin.

With the Chinese now chased off the hill and trenches dug, attention could be given to laying phone lines between the companies and Battalion HQ. Hot drinks were also distributed to the men in the forward trenches to supplement their otherwise cold and dreary American C rations. As darkness fell, the men on guard duty were met by a cold but relatively clear night, lit by a bright moon. Those in the slit trenches tried to snatch sleep between turns on piquet, looking out into the cold black distance where they knew the Chinese were located.

By about 0400hrs, the moon had well and truly set and the entire countryside was in darkness. Just then, the men were ordered to 'stand to' – to get up and man their trenches. The sentries had heard noises in the distance, and as a precaution the whole battalion was put on alert, peering out into the gloom. The men stood shivering in their trenches, without breakfast, straining to see what could have alerted the sentries and half-imagining sounds down below on the slopes or in the village.

The quiet was shattered about an hour later by the familiar sound of Chinese bugles, signalling that a major attack would soon be beginning. 'Unnerving' was how Harrop described the sounds,[169] and indeed it would have been since every man in the battalion now knew that a bugle blast meant that hundreds of screaming Chinese infantrymen would soon be amongst them.

The bugles were soon joined by machine-gun rounds ripping through the air above their trenches from a series of Chinese positions on the hills some 400–500 yards to the north. Crumping mortar rounds soon joined in, falling around the battalion defences. It was dark and Harrop could not see too clearly when the first waves of Chinese troops started to charge toward his forward sections. Bright green tracer rounds from the advancing Chinese zipped just to the left and right over the heads of the men in the trenches with alarming frequency, to be met by outbound red tracers from the British Bren guns. The bugles continued to sound, urging the Chinese on. When they got closer, some of them bizarrely called out: 'Are you English?' It is not known what, if anything, the Commonwealth men replied, but it didn't matter as the Chinese were soon among them.

Bren guns opened up with short, sharp bursts, accompanied by the single shots of the .303 rifles, firing rapidly and picking out targets among the darting Chinese assaulting up the hill in the pre-morning gloom. As the Chinese rushed forward, Harrop found it increasingly difficult to contact and keep control of his platoon:

> 'It is quite impossible to describe accurately or in detail what happened in that time. The main attacks, which came in waves, fell on "A" and "D" companies who were at the northern end. The right flank platoon (my platoon) was overrun after they had run out of ammunition, one section was temporarily taken prisoner while the other two sections managed to pull back to higher ground. Everyone stood their ground and there were many cases of hand-to-hand fighting.'[170]

As the Chinese got among the forward trenches, small groups of Chinese and British were locked together in painfully close hand-to-hand combat. Bursts of fire from the Chinese burp guns would briefly illuminate an attacker, bringing answering fire from a British Bren. Both sides flung grenades, a preferred and viciously effective weapon at close quarters. Curiously, neither side employed their bayonets.

The speed, aggression and weight of numbers of the advancing Chinese soon began to tell. With Harrop's men almost out of ammunition, a group of Chinese had manoeuvred around the flank of his platoon and was soon attacking it from the rear. They had used the darker southerly slopes to their full advantage, silently creeping up on 1 Platoon before bursting into their positions. Another group of Chinese had brought up a machine gun and placed it in a recently abandoned British slit trench. With the Chinese relentless in their forward movement, they had overrun Harrop's forward trenches. A number of Harrop's men were surprised and captured by the advancing enemy, with the rest of them stumbling back towards his platoon HQ trench or the trenches behind.

Over to the left in D Company, rounds were being traded with the Chinese as they tried to provide fire support with their weapons across A Company's front. D Company tried to light up the ground with illumination rounds fired from their 2in mortars, but the batch appeared to be duds and none of them worked. Forced to find alternatives, D Company sent out a stream of flares from their Very lights over the battlefield. Further back along the hill, the men of B Company were not directly in the fight, just trying to keep their heads down as stray rounds whipped past their positions. Don Barrett, a B Company sergeant, was forced to move from his trench into a low scrape, with his back against some kind of stone monument. It wouldn't give him much protection from the bullets coming from the front, but the solidity of the stone pillar gave him some small sense of security.

Back at A Company's positions, the battle was becoming critical. Harrop was trying to command his remaining troops while trading the odd shot at darting Chinese soldiers with his .38 revolver. As he freely admitted, his pistol likely did nothing to stop the advancing enemy. And with his telephone and radios destroyed, he had no effective way to communicate with his higher command. He was in a desperate position.

Fortunately, the New Zealand FOs, Roxburgh and McCubbin, now came into their own. Having their own radios connecting them directly to the guns, the two Kiwis were able to call in extremely close and effective fire support from the New Zealand 25-pdrs. They were also now the only radio link between A Company and Battalion Headquarters. The FOs coolly and calmly kept communications flowing between A Company, Battalion HQ and the New Zealand gunners, despite several enemy soldiers being just yards in front of them, occupying what had until recently been the forward positions of the platoon. As the battle raged all around them, Roxburgh sent a steady stream of orders to the guns, all the while firing his own weapon in order to keep the Chinese from making a final dash to the platoon headquarters.

Soon, the HE rounds of the 25pdrs started to fall among the now stationary Chinese. Roxburgh continued to relay coordinates to the guns, carefully adjusting the fire, bringing the rounds closer and closer until they were almost on top of the forward Middlesex trenches. It was a masterful piece of gunnery and caused heavy casualties amongst the Chinese, convincing them that despite their early gains, they would be unable to take – much less hold – the hill. Roxburgh would later be awarded the Military Cross for his part in the action, while McCubbin received the Military Medal. The citations spoke not only of the casualties caused by the Kiwis' shooting skills, but paid tribute to the vital action in keeping communications open between A Company and its Battalion HQ. Both of them had displayed impressive coolness and professionalism under fire.

As dawn broke at around 0645am, the Chinese realized they wouldn't be able to dislodge the British from their positions. A trumpet sounded and the Chinese started to withdraw northwards. This was a dangerous manoeuvre in itself, since the retreating Chinese would now be exposed to fire from the remaining British troops. But as the

Chinese had done many times before, in short order they seemed to simply vanish into the distance.

When the fighting finally died away, Harrop could look around and evaluate the carnage wrought by the scant two hours of fighting. Nearly fifty Chinese soldiers lay dead around the forward slopes and the trenches of A Company. It was unknown how many more had been carried off by the retreating Chinese, or indeed how many wounded they had. The Middlesex men had lost seven killed and some twenty wounded, all from A Company. Seven men killed may appear to be a light butcher's bill in the circumstances, but Willoughby sombrely noted that it was still '6 or 7 too many'.[171]

Furthermore, a number of men in the forward trenches had been spirited away in the night, captured by the Chinese as they made their initial advance and overran 1 Platoon's position. As the Chinese withdrew, most of these men managed to escape, but two remained in enemy hands. However, luck then played a hand, as Harrop recalled in a letter to his family a few days later:

> 'At about 7.15am … we spotted three distant figures moving away across the snowy paddy down below, so I said to my Bren gunner, "right, get those". He shoots and one falls dead, the other two run to a ditch, and after a while we hear them shouting, "don't shoot, we're Butcher and Cotterell" and sure enough they were. My mortar man and my batman had been taken prisoner and we shot their escort so they got away to us. Some escape!'

Butcher and Cotterell were lucky indeed, but the same could not be said for the twelve Chinese soldiers, most of whom were wounded, who found themselves prisoners of the British troops. Some were waving 'safe conduct passes', which had been dropped all over North Korea by UN forces. These passes were part of the psychological war being waged by both sides in an attempt to convince their adversaries to lay down their arms and surrender. Such passes would almost certainly have awarded the holder severe punishment if they had been discovered by their senior officers (to say nothing of the ever-present political officers), but the holders of these passes obviously felt the risk was worth it as they held them over their heads and limped into captivity.

Respite from the cruel winter, continual toil and meagre rations may have encouraged some of the Chinese troops to surrender. As Harrop looked around at the corpses of the Chinese splayed out in the snow, he saw that they were relatively poorly armed, with only a few rifles between them (their arms may have been retrieved by the retreating Chinese troops). Their uniforms, while padded, appeared thin and barely sufficient for the freezing conditions. Paired with the flimsy 'gym shoe' boots they wore and supplied with only the bare minimum of rice and vegetables, it was a wonder how the Chinese had managed to not only survive, but mount such a deadly effective attack on UN forces. But as Harrop noted, 'What the Chinese did have was great quantities of men who seemed to fight with reckless regard for their own lives.'[172]

Willoughby also commented that the Chinese were likely on the last of their supplies and were obviously hungry; during the battle for Hill 112, some Chinese soldiers were seen trying to find tins of British rations to eat, even as the battle raged around them. That said, he also noted the Chinese troops' skills in using the terrain, including capitalizing on the different colour of the ground where there was or wasn't snow, which allowed them to disguise their approach towards the British lines almost unseen.[173] It was fortunate for the Middlesex troops that the Chinese only gave themselves a scant hour or two between the moon setting and the sun rising to conduct their attack. In hindsight, it was clearly insufficient, and with the coming of daylight the Chinese knew that they would be unable to hold on or withstand any counter-attack.

***

The battle at Point 112 can be regarded as a successful but relatively unremarkable action, typical of the type of combat occurring at dozens of locations at that time. It was later assessed that the Chinese had probably attacked in battalion strength. But what this action did demonstrate was the close and intimate co-operation of the various elements of the Commonwealth Brigade, each of the parts helping to bring eventual success. While the steadfastness of the Middlesex men, despite nearly being overrun, was a key factor in their eventual success, it is doubtful if they would have survived but for the actions of the New Zealand gunners – both the FOs in the front line and the crews slaving over their guns several miles to the rear. It was this combined action that saved the day, demonstrating very sharply just how much more effective and deadly the brigade now was with the addition of the New Zealanders. The brigade commander was under no illusions as to the importance of his newly acquired artillery regiment and used it almost continuously to support his operations. In February alone, the New Zealanders fired 11,739 HE 25-pdr shells, compared to only 890 rounds from the brigade's mortars, illustrating clearly the significant increase in fire that 27 Bde could now bring to bear.[174]

'Chinese Disappearing Trick'

The fight at Point 112 also coincided with the end of the Chinese Fourth Offensive. As groups of refugees moved past the brigade over the next twenty-four hours, they reported for the first time that the Chinese seemed to be withdrawing. Patrols were sent out to investigate, but no trace could be found of the large number of enemy troops who had attacked the UN forces so relentlessly for the past two weeks. Even aerial -reconnaissance could not spot the retreating Chinese. The road to Chipyong-ni was now wide open. Willoughby called it the 'Chinese Disappearing Trick',[175] and this proved an apt description.

During the night of 14/15 February, to the west, 3 RAR had also come under attack from the Chinese. However, this attack was of significantly lower intensity than that endured by the British, consisting mainly of trading long-range machine-gun and artillery fire. Nevertheless, 3 RAR still took casualties, with three men killed and a small number wounded, mainly from mortar fire.

Following the disappearance of the enemy, the whole Commonwealth force started to move forward again. As the brigade occupied positions recently abandoned by the Chinese, the Australians noted with concern the large number of significant defensive positions that had been dug, including some tunnels bored into the hillside. Weapons and equipment had also been abandoned, indicating that the Chinese must have withdrawn in great haste. Then, quite unexpectedly, they came upon a group of what they termed 'releasees' – a group of thirty US soldiers who had been captured during the fighting on 13 February but had been let loose during the Chinese retreat. Once again, and to their credit, the Chinese seemed to prefer releasing captured soldiers rather than executing them. Less lucky, however, were the bodies of sixty of their companions, found along the roadside as the Australians advanced, next to the burnt-out wrecks of three light tanks and up to a dozen abandoned jeeps, all that was left of the 2nd Reconnaissance Company of the US 9th Infantry Regiment.

***

Following the end of the Chinese offensive, morale on the UN side improved markedly, with everyone from MacArthur down to the lowliest private heartened that they had stood firm and survived the onslaught.

MacArthur issued a statement on 20 February 1951, stating in his characteristically confident manner: 'I note that Marshal Stalin has just predicted the annihilation of our forces in Korea, but his comrades will have to do lots better than they have yet done to prove him a prophet.'[176] This was followed the next day by General Ridgeway's first major offensive since assuming command, codenamed Operation Killer. It was said that certain politicians in America did not like the term, but Ridgeway was adamant that his name for the operation would stay: 'I did not understand why it was objectionable to acknowledge the fact that war was concerned with killing the enemy.'[177] Despite MacArthur trying to take credit for the UN offensive, this was Ridgeway's show. Operation Killer, with its clear but modest objectives, was designed to drive the Chinese northwards. More importantly, success in this operation was designed to put an end to Eighth Army's bug out mindset of the past several months and instil a determination in the troops to seize the initiative and embrace an offensive mindset. In respect of both of these measures,

Ridgeway would prove to be extremely successful, Killer setting the stage for further victories in the months to come.

The Commonwealth Brigade received further good news with the arrival of yet more forces to bolster its ranks – a battalion of Canadian infantry and a full Field Ambulance contributed by India. With the addition of these two units, 27 Bde was now considerably above full strength. It was no longer a weak scratch force hastily thrown together, but an extremely potent, capable and deadly formation of which the Commonwealth troops could be justifiably proud.

The Canadians

2nd Battalion, Princess Patricia's Canadian Light Infantry

Chapter 15

2 PPCLI – 'Soldier of Fortune Types'

Like many Allied nations, the Canadians had taken full advantage of the post-Second World War peace dividend and had largely dismantled the powerful war machine that it had built during the conflict. From a total Canadian Active Service Force strength of just under half a million men in 1945, Canada's regular ground forces numbered just over 20,000 by early 1950. It had a considerable reserve of ex-servicemen, but only some 43,000 continued to serve on a part-time basis.[178] These already relatively modest figures only tell half the story, as of those officially still serving, only some 7,000 were fighting soldiers, the rest employed mainly in specialist or administrative roles.

Despite the waning of troop numbers, the bonds between British and Canadian troops and their respective militaries were still extremely strong. In 1950, only a few years after the end of the global conflict, the Canadian Army was still highly compatible and almost interchangeable with British units. The Canadians were armed with British weapons, trained along British lines and staffed by officers and men who had gained painful experience in combat alongside their British counterparts. This familiarity did not breed contempt, but rather mutual understanding and respect, which would prove crucial in Korea in early 1951.

Yet despite the previous familiar (and familial) bonds, the strategic international centre of gravity was moving swiftly away from Britain. Canada no longer regarded the United Kingdom as its lodestone; instead, it was irresistible magnetic pull from the great country to its south that was growing ever stronger. 'The country whose policies would now concern us most would not be Great Britain but the United States … Washington, not London, would determine, with Moscow, whether peace, progress and even survival were possible,' declared the Canadian Under-secretary for State, Lester Pearson.[179]

***

Compared to that of the Australians and New Zealanders, the Canadian response to the North Korean invasion of South Korea was slow. In late June and early July 1950, Canada had decided that it would contribute three warships and some transport planes to assist the UN forces. Discussion about a possible ground contribution was not even seriously entertained at this stage. It didn't help that the Canadian government was enjoying its summer recess; a Communist invasion in a far-removed Asian country was not good enough reason to recall politicians to debate the matter.

By mid-July, with the UN position around the Pusan pocket becoming increasingly desperate, the UN Secretary General formally asked Canada to consider contributing ground forces. This coincided with increased calls by the Canadian public to actively contribute to the UN cause and back up its rhetoric of support with actual soldiers. With the US government also making a formal call for support in late July, it was becoming difficult for Canada's leaders to ignore this matter any longer.

As deployment of ground forces became increasingly likely, various options were debated. The initial proposal, most favoured by the government, was the raising of a separate Canadian Brigade, which would fight as part of a Commonwealth Division. It was thought that this option would satisfy the requests for ground troops, but also that 'under this system, the Canadian forces were more likely to retain their identity'.[180]

With numbers in the regular force anaemic and already committed for other tasks, it was finally decided on 8 August that a special force would be specifically raised to deploy to Korea. There was some consternation among the government as to whether sufficient men (estimated at around 10,000 in total, including support and reinforcement troops) could be found, given the high employment rates in post-war Canada and the fact that after just serving in a world war, there may be few men willing to once again put their lives on the line. These fears proved wholly unfounded. Within days of putting out the call for former soldiers to sign up, recruitment centres were swamped with willing volunteers.

As hopefuls flooded into recruitment offices, the terms of service were just being finalized. Men would be recruited for the new Canadian Army Special Force for an initial eighteen-month period, specifically for service in Korea. Approximately 50 per cent of the recruits were ex-servicemen, many having extensive experience in the Second World War. Mirroring the New Zealand experience, even the officers were predominantly volunteers or men currently serving in the reserve.

For example, the commander of the newly raised 2nd Battalion, Princess Patricia's Canadian Light Infantry (2 PPCLI) was an ex-serviceman who had returned to civilian life after the war. Lieutenant Colonel James Stone had an exemplary career during the war, starting as a private in 1939 and ending up as the commanding officer of the Loyal Edmonton Regiment by 1945. His service saw him fight in Italy and Holland, being awarded a Military Cross and DSO with bar. He displayed great personal leadership, initiative and courage, factors that would be vital during the testing times he faced in Korea.

Lieutenant Hub Gray, 2IC of the 2 PPCLI mortar platoon, described Stone as 'a complex individual, self-contained, aloof, intelligent, decidedly imperious, intrepid in battle, and on occasion, unforgiving'.[181] Nevertheless, Stone would prove to be a very able commander who was responsible for shaping the newly raised battalion and quickly forming it into a serious fighting force.

Despite the apparent prohibition on recruiting Active Force officers for the Special Force, a number inevitably found their way into the newly raised units. Some were required in order to fill a particular technical gap, although it is likely that others used their connections or lobbied hard in the background in order to secure a position. It is believed that approximately eighteen officer billets were filled by Active Force officers. The proportion of Active Force officers in the PPCLI was also higher than in other battalions of the Special Force. Besides the CO, Stone and his 2IC, six out of seven of the battalion majors were Active Force officers.[182] While the proportion of Active Force men to volunteers declined as one went down the rank scale, there were nevertheless a large proportion of Active Force members amongst the officers and senior NCOs. Most of these had also seen service during the Second World War, and this combination of experience as well as recent skills and knowledge would pay dividends in the battles to come.

In relation to weapons and equipment, it was decided the Special Force would have predominately British kit to ensure uniformity with other units in the Commonwealth Brigade. While Canada was slowly starting to adopt more US equipment into its Active Force, almost all of the veterans who joined Special Force were intimately familiar with British weapons, so the choice was a prudent one.

With new recruits quickly flowing into depots, training quickly got underway. Much to everyone's surprise, training progressed faster than expected, which was almost certainly due to the high number of veterans filling the ranks. Yet despite the presence of so many experienced men, the training was (and needed to be) very tough and realistic, exposing the men to training on hills, under simulated fire and in relation to all major aspects of the war – attack, defence, patrolling, etc.

***

While the Canadian Brigade was conducting its training in Canada, the situation on the ground in Korea had changed several times. The pendulum had swung from demoralization and almost certain defeat to overconfidence and expected victory. It had then swung back as the Great Bug Out took place in December 1950. These dizzyingly fast changes on the battlefield inevitably had a considerable effect on Canada's plans to deploy its troops. A consequence of Canada's tardiness in contributing soldiers meant that by the time the Canadian Brigade structure was in place, it appeared to many that that their efforts were to be wasted and that the war would soon be over. As a result, there was some preliminary discussion as to whether it would be sufficient to merely send a small token force immediately in order to 'fly the flag'. Then, as the Canadian government was contemplating this option, the tide of battle swung the other way, resulting suddenly in a desperate need for more troops, right now, in order to hold the line.

Such rapid and continual changes did little to ensure smooth planning at the top, resulting in predictable confusion and complaining at the bottom.

***

With battlefield conditions in Korea now desperate, Canada finally decided to despatch a single infantry battalion immediately rather than wait for the entire brigade to be ready. Consequently, on 25 November 1950, 2 PPCLI boarded US troopship *Private Joe P. Martinez* and departed for Korea. Their selection was more due to luck and logistics than anything else. A rail strike had meant that they were the closest to available shipping, and on that basis alone was 2 PPCLI selected to leave for Korea ahead of the rest of the brigade.

Their hasty departure meant that much of the Canadians' initial training had yet to be completed; certainly nothing beyond individual training and small unit tactics. Furthermore, because of the extant policy of training the new officers separately from the other ranks, many of the officers were only able to join the battalion just prior to departure. Not having the chance to meet, let alone train with their men, many of the junior officers only had the time on board the troopship to get familiar with their men.

***

The Canadians did not arrive in Korea at an auspicious time. On 18 December, as they made their way down the gangplank at No 2 wharf in Pusan harbour, UN forces were in retreat and being pushed back south of Seoul. Unbeknownst to the newly arrived Canadians, there was at this time serious talk at the highest levels of a possible full-scale withdrawal from Korea, should the war continued to deteriorate.

Understandably, there were calls from senior UN commanders to commit 2 PPCLI to battle as soon as they arrived – much in the same way as the British forces had been committed four months earlier. But the Canadian government would not hear of it. Still scarred from their last Asian adventure – when they rushed two half-trained battalions to Hong Kong in late 1941, just in time to see them thrown into two weeks of bitter fighting against the Japanese followed by several years of captivity – the Canadians would not be bullied into committing their men before they were ready. Stone had also been provided with strict instructions – orally and in writing – that his men would complete a further ten weeks of intensive lead-up training before they could be put into the line.

When the US Army still tried to commit Stone's men upon arrival, Stone somehow acquired the use of a small aeroplane and made his way to Seoul to see General Walker, the commander of the US Eighth Army. Walker noted, quite fairly, that the Canadians already had more training than many of the US troops under his command and that the situation on the ground was desperate. But Stone stood firm and relied on his instructions. As Stone noted, 'General Walker wanted no political repercussions and agreed with my demand for eight weeks' training time.'[183]

While such prudence is understandable, it did not go down well with the Americans, who 'pointed to the fact that they were throwing in battalions with as much, or even less training time as the Canadians but Stone, under strict instructions from his government, refused to budge and continued to train'.[184]

***

Besides the specifics of Stone's command instruction, this episode is illustrative of the complexities in coalition warfighting. While an overall commander is usually happy to have troops from many nations in order to demonstrate to the world a united front, on a practical level, having troops from many different countries – all of whom are answerable to different masters and who likely have considerably different domestic interests and concerns – can be problematic. Navigating national sensibilities whilst also keeping focus on the overall military objective can try the patience of even the most understanding and even-handed of commanders.

The issue of national differences and the challenges of coalition fighting were likely high among the reasons why the Commonwealth Brigade, made up of units from countries with at least a similar heritage and background, was preferable to the units themselves and their home governments than merely subordinating the national contingents to US leadership.

Training in Miryang

Returning from his successful lobbying efforts, Stone was under no illusions that the time he had managed to secure for his men was precious but could evaporate at a moment's notice. The result was a packed and hard training programme designed to get his men combat-ready as quickly as possible. Stone was initially concerned at the standard of his men's weapon handling, but further drills, range shoots and lessons on newly acquired weapons (including the new US 81mm mortar) quickly addressed the training shortfall. Physical fitness was also emphasized. Stone was aware that most of the action his men would undertake would likely be conducted in rugged hilly or even mountainous terrain, so he wasted no time in insisting on tough training in the hills to build up his men's strength and endurance.

The combination of tough, realistic terrain and the necessity of speed and aggression when assaulting enemy positions on elevated features convinced Stone of the necessity for his men to travel lightly. Accordingly, he ordered that during an attack, heavy packs and all of the men's bulky clothing and equipment should follow them in motor transport, while each soldier's individual load should only consist of ammunition and an extra blanket and poncho as protection against inclement weather. Following on this theme, the 2 PPCLI War Diary noted: 'Rapid execution and exploitation of an attack is essential if the short length of the Korean winter day is to be used to the best advantage.'[185]

Some much-needed realism was also injected into training in mid-January, when B Company was directed to conduct a three-day fighting patrol to root out suspected North Korean guerrillas who were in the area making trouble. It was believed that these bands were the ones who had carried out ambushes on the 16th New Zealand Field Regiment on 14 January, which had resulted in the death of two Kiwi gunners. Despite the dangers, morale rose perceptibly with this new challenge. The attention of all troops was focussed and keen as B Company conducted its sweeps of nearby hills, exchanging fire with small bands of guerrillas. One of the new junior officers, Lieutenant Loss, was slightly wounded by a suspected guerrilla sniper.

The guerrillas were not the only danger facing the Canadians. On 18 January, Regimental Sergeant Major J.D. Wood, DCM, was killed in a training accident involving the demonstration of an anti-personnel mine. The loss of a universally admired and veteran soldier was keenly felt by all members of the battalion.[186] It also reinforced the utter seriousness of their work in Korea, and how death and injury could come at any time, even without the presence of the enemy.

The tough training also had the effect of weeding out quite a number of soldiers who were simply unfit or unready for the trials ahead. In total, more than sixty men would leave the battalion during their time at Miryang, due to illness, injury or inability to keep up with the exacting training regime that Stone had laid down.

While the training was hard, it did have its upsides. Stone described his battalion as 'a singing battalion', as it appears that the men enjoyed making up self-depreciating marching songs to help keep up their spirits during their long and exhausting route marches. One such song included the lines 'we're untrained bums, we're from the slums'.[187] Whether the words were true or not upon arrival in Pusan, after further training in Miryang, the Canadians became a well-oiled fighting machine, keen to join the action.

Operational

Finally, 2 PPCLI was moved up to the front line in mid-February, joining the brigade just after it had conducted its successful actions south of Chipyong-ni and Hill 112.

Still in command of the brigade, Colonel Man wasted no time in sending his newly arrived battalion into action. He gave orders that the Canadians were to assault Hill 404 at 1100hrs the next day, 19 February. Fortunately, the Chinese had departed just before the arrival of the Canadians, so no enemy was discovered on Hill 404 or any of the other battalion objectives that day.

As the battalion shook out over the next few days, it was fortunate to have only fleeting contact with the enemy. The few times the Canadians came under fire from a sniper or distant enemy helped to keep the men on their toes and focussed as they continued patrolling. These sharp little experiences also gave the battalion time to work out any final kinks and become a fully experienced and effective front-line infantry unit.

Unfortunately, despite not being subject to a full enemy attack, 2 PPCLI still suffered a series of injuries caused by the terrain and conditions. In these early days, no fewer than three lieutenants were evacuated with fall and concussions injuries, mainly caused by falling down dangerous slopes after slipping on the snow and ice.[188] It is not known whether the frequency of injuries was exacerbated by an overeager 'lead from the front' style of soldiering exhibited by these junior officers or simply the result of hard and unforgiving terrain. Whatever the case, these injuries were another reminder – if one was needed – of the tough and dangerous conditions faced by all when operating in Korea during winter, even before the enemy was factored in.

John Kolanchey, who was serving as a private with 2 PPCLI, summarised the difficulties of soldiering in Korea:

> '[T]he physical strength we had to have to carry on, it's very hard to realise because of the hills and the mountains, we kept clearing hill after hill … and the packs we carried and the ammunition we carried … and every night we need to dig in … and we had to stay up all night, an hour on and an hour off … lack of sleep and everything else … and when you feel as though you had everything sorted out someone would come up and say "here carry two mortar bombs".'[189]

But the battalion was coming on well. The training at Miryang and the days of patrolling in February were now producing results. Unfortunately, just as his battalion was feeling its legs, Stone fell ill with suspected hepatitis and was evacuated to hospital in Japan. Upon examination, his condition was more serious than initially thought; he would soon be diagnosed with a case of smallpox. Thankfully, it was a relatively mild case, requiring him to spend the next several weeks convalescing and in isolation, only returning to the battalion on 22 April.

The Indians

60 (PARA) FIELD AMBULANCE

Chapter 16

60 (Para) Field Ambulance

The final, and arguably most unique, unit to join 27 British Commonwealth Brigade was 60 (Para) Field Ambulance from India.

What set India's role in the Korean War apart from the other Commonwealth countries was that it had achieved independence from Britain a mere three years earlier. India was rapidly developing an independent foreign policy, which on many issues was veering away from that of Britain and the other 'traditional' Commonwealth countries. While India had decided to remain a member of the Commonwealth, it was at the same time actively advancing a non-aligned policy. It was a staunch supporter of the newly formed United Nations, but would no longer simply follow Britan's lead in international affairs.

India had also established diplomatic relations with Communist China on 1 April 1950, one of the very first non-Communist countries to do so. This would have significance during the Korean War, as the offices of the Indian Ambassador to China were a frequent conduit by which all parties could 'unofficially' communicate. For example, the Chinese Communists would often use this means to signal their displeasure at the movement of UN forces closer to their border and send warnings that any further northward advance could trigger China's entry into the war. While the messages were indeed relayed by the Indians, they were unfortunately largely ignored.

India was both an original member and enthusiastic supporter of the newly formed UN. India believed that the UN could be an important counterweight to the great powers, helping to preserve international peace and security. When North Korea invaded the South in June 1950, India immediately supported the first UN resolution condemning the attack, which demanded that the North withdraw. India abstained, however, from further resolutions in relation to making forces available for a unified, US-led UN Command.

India found itself in a difficult diplomatic position. While it strongly objected to the North Korean invasion, it nevertheless still wished to be seen as non-aligned and neutral. This initial discomfort at having a foot in each camp was a prime reason why India would eventually have an important role to play in final negotiations for an armistice. That, however, is outside the scope of this story.

Nevertheless, in 1950, India's delicate political position meant that it was unable to contribute traditional combat forces to the UN cause. Instead, and in line with several other neutral or non-aligned countries (including Sweden, Norway, Denmark and Germany), India decided to contribute a medical unit – 60 (Parachute) Field Ambulance.

This contribution would prove to be an excellent choice, both bolstering India's humanitarian credentials and adding a significant capability to the UN – in particular the Commonwealth forces.

60 (Parachute) Field Ambulance

60 Field Ambulance was Regular Army unit of the Indian Army Medical Service, comprising approximately 340 men. It was also a parachute-trained unit, which would prove invaluable over the following months when members often accompanied US forces during parachute operations in early 1951.

In command was Lieutenant Colonel A.G. Rangaraj, a veteran officer who had served with distinction during the Second World War. In 1942, he was one of the first Indian officers to be trained in the then relatively new art of parachuting. He saw action as the medical officer for the 152nd Indian Parachute Battalion during the siege of Sangshak in 1944. This action involved intense, bloody and viciously close-quarter combat as the Japanese Army tried to destroy 50 Parachute Brigade at an isolated village in Manipur during the opening salvos of Japan's audacious bid to invade India in 1944. It was the first in a series of battles in which Rangaraj would fight during the war. After independence, Rangaraj remained in the Indian Army and was deployed as the commanding officer of 60 Field Ambulance in operations in Jammu and Kashmir in 1947.

In 1950, the Indian Army still largely looked, operated and acted as it had during the Second World War. Its organization, procedures and equipment were largely British in nature, which allowed the newly arrived 60 Field Ambulance to slot seamlessly into 27 British Commonwealth Brigade. In addition, several of the brigade's senior officers had fought in Burma with the Indian Army, so were used to operating with Indian troops. Overall, it was an excellent match, one that was very much welcomed by the other Commonwealth troops and the Indians themselves. Furthermore, as the Indian unit was a Regular Army formation with recent combat experience, it did not require quite the same pre-deployment training that some of the specially created forces (such as the New Zealanders or Canadians) needed. It could therefore be despatched relatively quickly.

***

The Indian medical personnel arrived at the port of Pusan in November 1950. They spent some time preparing their equipment and acclimatizing to the increasingly cold weather before part of the unit was sent north towards the front lines. At this time, the Field Ambulance comprised seventeen officers, ten Junior Commissioned Officers[190] and 304 other ranks.

The arrival of the Indians and their attachment to 27 Bde was warmly welcomed by all. At last, the brigade would have the services of a combat-ready dedicated medical unit. Coad for one was unstinting in his praise for the work of 60 Field Ambulance: 'The work and general bearing of 60th Indian Field Ambulance was worthy of the highest praise. They were absolutely first class and all members of the Brigade were confident that if they were wounded they would get the very best medical treatment.'[191]

However, the work of Rangaraj and his men got off to a rocky start, as they arrived in Pyongyang on 29 November, only days before the order was given to evacuate the city. Having just arrived, the surprised Indians were now told that they needed to bug out and move south as fast as they could. This was easier said than done. In a refrain that was all too familiar to the rest of the brigade, the Indians arrived in Pyongyang full of enthusiasm, equipped to do a job but sadly lacking any transport, which was critical to move them as required. When the hurried orders to evacuate Pyongyang came through, the Field Ambulance found itself in a difficult situation as it had no way of moving the tons of equipment and medical supplies that it had brought north. Keenly aware that a medical unit is next to useless without its supplies, and unwilling to merely abandon or destroy perfectly good equipment, Rangaraj came up with the idea of 'liberating' one of the small, abandoned trains then lying in the yards at Pyongyang station.

He discovered that two of his medics had some previous experience in driving trains and these men were quickly pressed into service as engineers, while the rest of the unit collected whatever firewood or coal they could scrounge to fuel the machine. The men proceeded to form a human chain, later referred to as 'The Bucket Brigade', to move water, pail by pail, from the river to the station and their newly acquired locomotive in order to fill the train's boilers.

There are stories of US officers trying to dissuade the Indians (there is even mention of threats of court-martial, but this cannot be substantiated), but somehow the medics managed to get their rickety little train operational and were thus able to move the vital medical supplies and the rest of the unit south before the railway lines and bridges were demolished behind them. This amazing story of ingenuity and courage would help to solidify the reputation of the Indian medical personnel and their intrepid commander as brave, creative and utterly dependable members of the brigade.

The 27 Bde War Diary marked the event as follows:

> '60 Indian Field Ambulance, Commanded by Lieutenant Colonel A.G. Rangaraj, joined the Brigade today. This unit is airborne trained and had arrived in Korea from India about a month ago. They had moved up with their equipment by train to Pyongyang early this month and, in the confusion of the retreat at the time, had rounded up some railway men and organised a train, which was one of the last to leave Pyongyang. They have set up their Field Ambulance just south of Uijongbu.'[192]

***

Arriving back in Seoul two days later on 6 December, Rangaraj reorganized his unit into two distinct sections. The mobile section, known to the Indians as the 'Forward Element', was commanded by Rangaraj and comprised one surgical team, two sections and a light medical dressing station, all of which was to be mobile under its own transport. The other section, given the highly misleading title of 'Admin Element', was a much larger unit with the remaining personnel, heavy equipment and stores, and would be based semi-permanently at Taegu under the command of Major Bannerjee. The Admin Element was attached to a Korean hospital and primarily dedicated to treating Commonwealth troops.

The medics in the Forward Element were given little time to restructure themselves after the withdrawal from Pyongyang. Less than a month later, with the Chinese threatening to capture Seoul, Rangaraj and his medics once again found themselves almost in the front lines. Between 1 and 3 January 1950, Rangaraj had to close and reopen his advanced dressing station in three separate locations in order to continue treating the wounded men in his care while staying just ahead of the advancing Communists. For this action (and his subsequent efforts in Operation Tomahawk), his dedication to the care of his patients and his coolness and efficiency under fire, Rangaraj was awarded the Indian Maha Vir Chakra (MVC) Medal, the second-highest Indian military decoration, roughly corresponding to the DSO awarded in other Commonwealth countries.

Operation Tomahawk

One of the most dramatic actions ever undertaken by a Commonwealth medical unit must be the parachute drop of elements of 60 Field Ambulance in support of Operation Tomahawk.

This operation, set to take place on 23 March 1951, was designed to trap the Communist forces retreating northwards. Tomahawk called for the parachute insertion of the US 187th Regimental Combat Team (equivalent to a British brigade formation), together with heavy equipment and artillery. After establishing a bridgehead, the 187th was to block the Chinese from retreating and hold them for between forty-eight and seventy-two hours. During this time, other US forces moving north would attack the trapped Chinese and link up with the paratroopers.

Being the only fully parachute-trained medical team currently in Korea, Rangaraj was asked to supply a parachute Field Ambulance team consisting of himself and twelve officers and men. While all of the Indians were parachute-qualified, when the unit was warned out for deployment to Korea it was only kitted out and prepared for a ground role. The unit thus had none of its specialized airborne equipment in theatre. Accordingly, and with a mere three days before the operation was set to begin, Rangaraj and his small team raced to collect supplies and ready themselves for what would become the biggest, and last, parachute drop of the Korean War.

Operation Tomahawk commenced in the early hours of 23 March and involved an enormous lift of 120 aircraft flying in more than 3,500 troops. Preparing to exit their planes at a relatively low 800ft (in order to minimize the time the parachutists would be in the air and be vulnerable to ground-based fire), the Indians could clearly see machine-gun fire and the explosion of mortars across the DZ (drop zone). This was clearly not going to be an entirely unopposed landing.

Nonetheless, all of the Indian medics landed safely. Throwing off their parachutes and collecting their equipment, they were almost immediately tasked to provide aid to a number of soldiers who had been hurt during the drop or had already been wounded by enemy fire. Rangaraj and his men did what they could with the minimal medical supplies they had to hand. The heavier medical equipment would only arrive with the second wave, some four hours later. When those supplies did arrive, an operating theatre was established and running within thirty minutes of the drop. In the first day alone, the Indian medics performed three major and half-a-dozen minor operations.

As the surgeons worked on the seriously wounded, the rest of the Indian team were busy constructing a more substantial field hospital consisting of multiple trenches to house the various stretcher cases that were being brought in.

Fortunately for the UN forces who were air-dropped, enemy resistance, whilst constant, was relatively light. It appeared that the bulk of the Communist forces had left the area shortly before the Americans arrived. This allowed the deployment of helicopters to evacuate some of the most seriously wounded and transport them south to a field hospital out of immediate harm's way. The helicopters were also instrumental in bringing forward fresh supplies of blood, plasma and other medical necessities.

Over the course of the next few days, the Indian troops continued to perform multiple surgeries, treat the less seriously wounded and then arrange helicopter transfer as and when they became available. This was restricted to daylight hours only, the helicopters being unable to fly at night. Helicopter support ceased altogether on days when heavy mist and rain made flying impossible.

On the night of 24 March, enemy resistance stiffened considerably and the promised link-up with friendly troops from the south did not occur. The optimistic forty-eight-hour timeframe for the relieving troops to arrive had been exceeded, and casualty numbers continued to grow. The Indians continued to work on newly wounded soldiers while also having to care for a growing ward of patients who had been brought in over the past few days but could not yet be evacuated. Most of these men were housed in the trenches constructed by the medics, which were covered by a makeshift canopy of parachute silk to keep out the rain.

The Indians of 60 Field Ambulance were deployed on Operation Tomahawk for six days before they were relieved and rejoined their unit in Seoul. Their efforts were roundly applauded by all the American soldiers and officers with whom they worked. In addition, a number of officers and men were awarded decorations for their part in the operation, both Indian and US awards. Alongside Rangaraj, his deputy, Major Banerjee, was also recognized for his efforts in carrying on operations on badly wounded soldiers in the middle of a particularly nasty mortar barrage. Banerjee's citation reads that showing 'utter disregard for his personal safety, and with amazing power of endurance, he carried on rendering medical aid to casualties and saved many lives'.[193] His citation likely applied equally to all of the men of 60 Field Ambulance who deployed on Operation Tomahawk. They were a dedicated and professional group of doctors and soldiers who were universally respected and applauded by all who had the good fortune of working with them.

The Commonwealth Brigade – March 1951

While not comparable to the excitement of a combat parachute descent, the rest of 27 Bde maintained a steady programme of minor operations during March, steadily moving northwards. For the most part, the weather in March was bad, with the thaw bringing heavy rains. Rain meant mud, and it was this combination of mud and rain that tested even the most resolute of infantrymen. On the plus side, these minor operations and the constant patrolling was exactly what the Canadians needed to put the final touches to the training that Stone had insisted on over the previous months. By the end of March, the Canadians were every bit as experienced as their British and Australian counterparts and were now very much veterans themselves.

While the constant work during March brought challenges and a variety of small actions, each of which was literally a matter of life and death, none of them particularly stood out. Overall, March was thus a period of consolidation for the brigade.

It was also a time to consider the future for 27 British Commonwealth Brigade. Despite having been thrown into battle as a hastily assembled fire brigade, during more than eight months of near-constant combat it had established itself as an excellent and reliable fighting force. Whenever required, irrespective of the terrain, weather or enemy, 27 Bde could always be counted on by its US commanders to deliver. On the other hand, despite the welcome addition of various units between October and February, the months of campaigning and fighting were starting to take their toll on the brigade.

At a strategic level, Britain needed its battalions to return to Hong Kong as soon as possible. China's entry into the war heightened fears of a Chinese threat to the Crown Colony, leading to calls to withdraw the Middlesex and Argylls forthwith.

On a unit and individual level, the eight months in Korea had affected the efficiency and strength of the British battalions. Casualties had continued to afflict both of these battalions, which were understrength to begin with and could not easily absorb large-scale losses. While replacements did enter the field intermittently, the time needed to replace wounded or dead men was overly long. One reason was purely bureaucratic, as policy mandated that a wounded soldier was to stay on the battalion books for twenty-one days after they were injured, with replacements only to be called for if he remained out of action for twenty-two days. So at best, the system only started the process to send a replacement after twenty-two days, and the process itself usually took several weeks more before a man was actually found, transported and present at his new platoon in the field.

Besides casualty replacement, March also saw many members of 27 Bde go on leave. Men would be pulled out of the line, seemingly at random, and told that they had a week's leave in Japan. This respite from the constant demands of the campaign was wholly necessary, but it placed additional demands on the already small pool of men who were serving at the front. A decision was also made that no one would remain in Korea longer than one year – 'one winter was quite enough' was how Field Marshal Sir William Slim, the Chief of the Imperial General Staff, termed it.[194]

One man who had certainly served his winter was Brigadier Coad. Looking much older than his 45 years would suggest, Basil Coad was by now thoroughly worn out by the demands of the campaign and had to be sent back to Hong Kong on compassionate grounds. All who had served under him agreed that he was an excellent soldier who had served 27 Bde faithfully throughout his time in command. Nevertheless, Korea was an unforgiving country, and as such it was time for Coad to leave.

Replacing Coad was Brigadier Brian Burke, DSO, the then second-in-command of 29 Brigade. Interestingly, Burke was also 45 years old when he took over command of the Commonwealth Brigade, and like Coad already had a long and distinguished career in the British Army. He had served in the Second World War, commanded 10 Indian Brigade from 1945–46 and been awarded a DSO in 1944.

Burke was a good choice to take command of the brigade, even though he would lead it for only a little more than a month. But that month was April 1951, which would see 27 Bde face its greatest test yet at the Battle of Kapyong.

Chapter 17

The Chinese Spring offensive

It has become a cliché that 'the enemy has a vote', but that does not make the statement any less true. It was certainly true in respect of the Chinese during March and April 1951. Despite Eighth Army commander Matthew Ridgeway's desire to stabilize the line and minimize casualties, the Chinese leadership had radically different plans. Rather than merely 'holding the line', they intended to conduct another great offensive, a final attack of such size, scale and ferocity that it would crush the UN forces and drive the Americans out of Korea.

During March, China had been rapidly reinforcing its troops, bringing in massive numbers of additional combat soldiers ready for the upcoming offensive. By mid-April, China had close to a million men in the field, a large proportion of whom were fighting troops. Mao believed that with such overwhelming numbers, he would be able to launch a massive attack that would prove decisive, or at the very least would force the Americans to consider withdrawing from Korea. Plans were thus laid for the Chinese Fifth Offensive, often termed the 'Spring Offensive', which was to commence on 22 April and continue until June.

As well as the additional manpower, the Chinese had also taken delivery of more Soviet arms – sub-machine guns, assault rifles, anti-tank weapons, etc – with which they were able to equip their divisions. This rearming was critical, allowing the replacement of most of their old captured Japanese equipment with more modern Russian equivalents. What they continued to lack, however, was communications equipment and motorized transport. Even following the influx of Soviet equipment, there were still few radios available below battalion level. This meant that most attacks would have to be set-piece, tightly scripted affairs, allowing little scope for commanders to exercise initiative or adapt to events as they unfolded. With almost no radio communications available at the very lowest levels, Chinese company commanders would need to continue relying on the basic yet effective expedients of whistle and bugle calls to signal to their men.

Motorized transport was also in very short supply. Movement largely on foot during the surprise attacks of the Chinese First Offensive had caught the UN forces completely by surprise. However, it was another thing entirely to mount an aggressive offensive campaign deep into South Korea mounted only on soldiers' backs. By the start of the Spring Offensive, most Chinese battalions had only a handful of vehicles – at best, a single vehicle per company. This was clearly inadequate to transport the necessary quantities of food and ammunition to the large groups of men engaged in significant combat all along the line and to sustain a major operation. So acute was the shortage – and so clear the effect it would have on the transport of ammunition, supplies and casualties – that in General Peng's 6 April 1951 speech to the Fifth Enlarged Session of the Chinese People's Volunteers Party Committee, the commander of Chinese forces in Korea spent considerable time discussing the need to capture and use as many UN vehicles as possible – together with their drivers if necessary![195]

Even more critical than the lack of vehicles was an acute shortage of rations. Peng knew that the closer his troops got to the UN forces, the longer his logistic lines would be stretched and the less local food would be available for his men. His army could arrange about twenty days' worth of supplies, but beyond that the troops in the field would need to find or scavenge whatever they could from the enemy. Peng stated:

> '[W]hen the campaign is launched, every unit will itself carry field rations for 5 days, and the various logistics detachments must also be ready with another 5 days of field rations to advance along with the troops. At the same time, every effort must be made to overcome the difficulty of 300 li [300 Chinese miles] foodless zone when we advance southwards to ensure that the troops are able to get uninterrupted supplies of food and ammunition.'[196]

Thus, the Chinese faced significant logistical obstacles as they made ready for the Spring Offensive. Peng had originally wanted to delay commencement of the attack until these matters were addressed, but Mao was insistent that the offensive must be opened soon in order to capitalize on previous gains and keep UN forces on the back foot. While neither Mao nor any of the other Chinese leaders were ignorant of the material inferiority of the Chinese forces, they had placed greater store and confidence on their manpower, fighting spirit and skill at night fighting. With a numerical advantage of about three to one over the UN forces, the Chinese did indeed have reason to be optimistic.

On 18 April, Peng issued final orders to his men, including for the encirclement and destruction of specific UN units. Outlining his plan in detail, Peng continued: "For our Spring Offensive, we have decided to make our objective the wiping out of three divisions of the American Army … First of all, we will mass our forces to wipe out the 6th Division of the Puppet Army [and] the British 27th Brigade.'[197]

Kapyong

Chapter 18

Opening Rounds (22 April)

In late April 1951, 27 British Commonwealth Brigade was allocated to IX Corps reserve around the Kapyong Valley. The valley is an extremely strategic position, being one of the traditional invasion routes for armies streaming from the north into southern Korea. Both sides recognized the importance of the Kapyong Valley as a natural 'highway' through the mountainous terrain of this part of central Korea, so it was reinforced with a number of major units in order to provide defence and protection.

To the brigade's immediate north was the 6th ROK Division, which had recently arrived and relieved the 2 PPCLI. The Canadians were not impressed with the relieving force, with 2 PPCLI's Intelligence Officer, Captain MacKenzie, scathing of what he saw. MacKenzie described the South Korean soldiers as having 'poor training, low morale and insufficient equipment'. Moreover, MacKenzie claimed that when the ROK's 17th Regiment was due to take over 2 PPCLI positions on 17 April, they declined to go forward to conduct a thorough reconnaissance, and 'for this reason the ROK knowledge of the area forward of 2 PPCLI was negligible'.[198] This lack of enthusiasm did not earn them any friends amongst the Commonwealth troops.

Despite the Canadian concerns as to the quality of their relief force, the allocation to IX Corps reserve was very much welcomed by Burke. The brigade needed a period of time to undergo some much-needed internal reorganization, as the two long-suffering British battalions were soon to be relieved by fresh units, recently arrived in Korea. Furthermore, it was planned that shortly after this change, the whole brigade would come under new command. No longer would it be an independent brigade allocated to American divisions as and when needed, but rather it would be renamed as 28 Commonwealth Brigade and would form part of the newly raised 1st Commonwealth Division.

However, once again planning was interrupted in spectacular fashion by the Chinese, who executed their plans first, this time with their much-heralded Spring Offensive.

***

When the Chinese struck, 27 Bde was deep into its internal reorganization. The Argylls had already been pulled out of the line in preparation for exchange with the 1st Battalion, King's Own Scottish Borderers, who had just arrived in Korea. As a result, the Argylls were placed well south of the main brigade position and had already begun to hand back weapons and stores, reading themselves for the move back to Pusan and eventually Hong Kong.

The Middlesex men were in a slightly higher state of readiness, having not yet been removed from the front lines. They were, however, operating on a very depleted scale, with most of the companies down to just fifty or so men – barely two understrength platoons. The effects of a long campaign and the steady drip of casualties had taken their toll. Furthermore, with the strong expectation that they would leave Korea very soon, replenishing the Middlesex ranks was not a priority. Thus, while the 1 MX were keen and their morale remained high, they were not operating as a full-strength battalion and thus could only be used by Burke in a limited manner.

The result of this was that when the Chinese started to move towards the Kapyong Valley, Burke only had two full-strength infantry battalions at his disposal – 3 RAR and 2 PPCLI. But he still possessed some elements of 1 MX and, crucially, the entire New Zealand artillery regiment. So while 27 Bde was still a potent force, it was certainly not operating at full strength.

On 22 April, despite the relatively warm and sunny day, the men of the brigade were not completely in 'holiday mode'. They were, after all, a mere 15 miles or so from the front lines. Accordingly, while the units could relax to a certain extent, officially the infantry battalions still remained at three hours' notice to move to reinforce one of the three divisions in the line north of them (6th ROK Division to the north, 1st Marine Division to the north-east and US 24th Division to the north-west). Accordingly, while the Argylls made ready to leave the theatre, the remaining units of the brigade were still very much ready to fight.

Nevertheless, the fact that there were several complete US and ROK infantry divisions to their front did give the brigade and its units some measure of comfort. Being in a rear area provided an opportunity for catching up and some socialising between the battalions. The Argylls held a farewell party, well attended by many of the officers of the brigade, and there was also a steady stream of VIP visitors making calls on the brigade to congratulate them on their efforts to date. These visits were accompanied, ironically in light of later events, by 'The 6 ROK Division Band entertaining the [3 RAR] Battalion'.[199] The somewhat relaxed and festive atmosphere was reinforced by the issue of a beer ration to the thirsty troops.

Much-need reinforcements also arrived, 3 RAR taking in a new intake of soldiers and a number of officers. Captain Laughlin returned from leave and resumed command of B Company, while Captain Gerke, who had been looking after B Company in Laughlin's absence, was transferred to command Support Company. These veterans slotted easily back into the battalion and into their familiar roles.

Likely less sure of himself was Lieutenant Brumfield, a graduate of the Royal Military College (Duntroon), recently arrived in Korea and now posted into B Company.

Despite being a new arrival, he would soon prove to be a cool and clear-headed platoon commander during the trials the battalion faced over the coming days.

Like the Australians, the Canadians were quiet on the 22nd, mainly resting and checking their equipment. During the month since they had joined 27 Bde, the Canadians' vehicles had taken a terrible beating on the unforgiving tracks and rough terrain of Korea. A day of maintenance was absolutely necessary if the Canadians had any hope of using their precious motor transport during the months that lay ahead. They were also able to welcome back their commander, Lieutenant Colonel Stone, who had been pronounced 'cured' after his minor attack of smallpox.

***

While the Australians and Canadians were hard at work with maintenance, Lieutenant Colonel Moodie and his fellow New Zealand gunner officers were becoming nervous. Artillery units are well-known for having their own dedicated communications networks, often superior to the infantry formations they support, essential for ensuring that communications and orders for the guns are never interrupted. Besides transmission of fire orders, the artillery 'net' provided an additional, often faster and more accurate medium for intelligence gathering. And so it proved in the early evening of 22 April when reports started to stream into the New Zealand artillery headquarters of a 'collapse' in the 6th ROK Division sector. Moodie listened intently to the 'squawk box' loudly broadcasting radio messages into the regimental command post throughout the evening. What he heard worried him, as regular updates told of a rapidly deteriorating situation. The radio traffic suggested that 6th ROK Division was under significant pressure, which had already resulted in the beginnings of a hasty retreat. Attempts were made to hold an intermediate line, and when that failed they were forced to move southwards yet again as Chinese pressure increased on their sector. Moodie's concern grew, and as a measure of prudence he reduced his men's notice to move first to ninety minutes and subsequently to sixty minutes as more-frantic reports of ROK collapse came in over the net.

'IX Corp ordered 6 ROK to hold the line,' noted the New Zealand War Diary in its usual matter-of-fact manner. 'It however, became more obvious as time went on that the 6 ROK Div was incapable of holding any line. Stragglers were soon swarming past our guns on their way south without any control being exercised.'[200]

The 6th ROK Division was disintegrating, and it was obvious to Moodie that sooner or later, his guns were likely to be called on to provide some sort of support. At around 0300hrs, he reduced his regiment's notice to move yet again – now to 'immediate notice to move'. His gunners knew what that meant as they packed all unnecessary gear into their Quad vehicles, readied the guns and made plans to leave at a moment's notice.

Chapter 19

The Gunners' Battle (23 April, day and early evening)

All through the night, the Chinese continued to press their aggressive attacks on the South Korean and American divisions to the brigade's north. Brigade HQ was now also receiving reports that the South Koreans were in trouble and in serious danger of total collapse. Burke didn't need to be told that if the Chinese were able to break through, then 27 Bde would be next in line for the full attentions of Peng Dehuai's aggressive and determined army.

As a precaution, in the pre-dawn hours, Burke ordered the 16th New Zealand Field Regiment to move south of his position and establish a new gun line. Yet no sooner had the exhausted gunners reached their new gun lines and commenced setting up, than the orders were reversed. The situation north of the brigade required immediate assistance, so at approximately 1000 hrs, two batteries were ordered to pack up again, hitch the guns to their Quad vehicles and move north to support the beleaguered 6th ROK Division. Meanwhile, 162 Battery and HQ Battery were to remain in place to support the brigade. Recognizing the seriousness of the situation and the likelihood that the gunners might themselves be the subject of Chinese attack, Burke also ordered a company from the Middlesex Regiment to accompany the gunners to act as their close infantry support and protection party.

While the gunners were readying themselves, Burke issued warning orders to both 3 RAR and 2 PPCLI to be prepared to occupy defensive positions to the north and east of the current brigade area, covering the main road and valley routes leading south towards the Kapyong–Pukhan river valleys.

The Kapyong Valley was a relatively narrow and flat sliver of land, tracing the flow of the Kapyong River and dividing the endless series of surrounding hills and ridges to its north, east and west. The Kapyong was not a particularly big river, and certainly did not present much of an obstacle. In April, the river was not deep, with contemporary photographs showing water levels at the many fords barely reaching halfway up a truck's tyre. Relatively flat farmland traced the valley floor on both sides of the river for about a kilometre or so east and west, before the terrain rose abruptly into a series of hills and significant features, many of which ascended to a height of several hundred metres. The hills on both sides dominated the valley floor and gave defenders excellent views, and fields of fire, onto anyone proceeding down the valley. Of course, these hills also gave an attacker multiple covered routes to move south and surround any Allied troops waiting in the valley or the flanking hills. A dirt road wound along the valley floor on the left bank of the river, and the valley also contained a small number of farmhouses and tiny hamlets, generally clustered in the lee of the hills.

While the rumble of artillery could clearly be heard to the north and a steady stream of ROK soldiers moving south confirmed that a great battle was taking place just north of their brigade boundary, the day itself was a pleasant one, about 20 degrees Celsius and with no rain. When the IX Corps commander, General Hodges, visited Burke in the early afternoon to confer and give orders, he found the brigadier in relatively good spirits, unexpectedly wearing a rose in his cap – a gift from members of his staff returning from Tokyo as a token of remembrance for St George's Day.[201]

Neither the confident outlook nor the floral adornment, however, could disguise the seriousness of the situation, and Hodges made it clear that 27 Bde needed to be prepared to absorb a major Chinese thrust down the Kapyong Valley. To that end, 27 Bde was ordered to act as a blocking brigade north and east of Kapyong. To provide Burke with some much-needed additional firepower, Hodges arranged for an American tank unit – A Company, 72nd Tank Battalion – to be available, as were two companies of US 4.2in chemical mortars.

Burke's defensive plan called for the creation of a line running between Hill 677 to the west of the valley floor and the slightly lower feature, Hill 504, to the east. These two features easily dominated the ground in the valley between them, thus constituting key terrain that the brigade must occupy and hold. He ordered 2 PPCLI to occupy the western feature and 3 RAR to take up position further to the west. To complete the brigade defences, Burke situated 1 MX (less one company supporting the Kiwi gunners) on a hill approximately 4km to the south, near the village of Tanghan, while Brigade HQ and the remaining guns would occupy a position south of 1 MX. The defensive plan was sound, considering the likely enemy routes of advance as well as taking advantage of the terrain. However, the downside to having the brigade units spread over such a large area was that the battalions could only provide limited support to each other, as they were several kilometres apart and at the very limits of the range of their heavy machine guns and mortars.

At the same time, 3 RAR and 2 PPCLI's A and B echelons were required to move south of the likely front lines, taking whatever excess supplies and vehicles that they could. This still left a great quantity of stores that could not be moved, which would need to be destroyed. These supplies had been brought forward for the expected refitting of the newly arrived battalions, and it was disheartening to the men moving forward to new defensive positions to see so much useful equipment and ammunition going up in flames.

3 RAR – morning

At mid-morning, Lieutenant Colonel Ferguson returned from the brigade O Group to his 3 RAR Battalion HQ, situated at the small village of Chuktun-ni. This was a small hamlet, adjacent to the ford across the river and near where the main road started to bend towards the south-west. Rightly suspecting that something big was brewing, all of the 3 RAR company commanders were already waiting at the hamlet for Ferguson to arrive. Wasting no time, Ferguson told them that they were to act as the eastern side of a blocking line, focusing their defences on Hill 504, which rose out from the edge of the paddy fields to their immediate north-east. A, C and D Companies were allocated sections of the 504 Hill complex to defend, overlooking the valley floor to the west.

Hill 504 is a rugged feature, comprising a series of ridges and valleys, rising from the valley floor up to a number of 300- and 400–metre-high ridges, with its highest point being 500 metres above the valley. Seen from above, it could be likened to the splayed thumb and first two fingers of the right hand which had been bunched into a fist. Taking the analogy further, Ferguson allocated his companies as follows: A Company on the west forward ridge (i.e. the forefinger), D Company on the east forward ridge (the middle finger) and C Company placed some way to the rear and south of A Company (the thumb). The hill complex rose steeply from the valley floor, had deep gulleys between each of the 'fingers' of the hill and was mainly rocky and covered with low scrub, except for the high points, some of which were covered with small copses of trees, particularly near the D Company position. The steep hill certainly tested the infantrymen's endurance as they struggled to haul their gear and ammunition to the heights. Yet Hill 504 would be equally difficult for any attacking Chinese infantrymen, and had the added advantage of excellent fields of view and lines of fire down into the valley below.

B Company did not join the other units on Hill 504, but rather was allocated a long low hill on the valley floor itself. B Company's hill only rose some 40 metres above the valley floor, but it gave excellent fields of fire onto both the main road and the nearby ford. While this hill was about a thousand metres long, B Company was ordered to focus its defence on its southern end, closer to the expected line of march of the enemy. The reasoning given was that at least on the southern end, B Company could benefit from covering fire from the rest of the Battalion on Hill 504, whereas further north would have left them even more isolated. This position also covered the northern end of the village of Chuktun-ni, down on the flat land at the southern end of B Company's hill. This was the location of Battalion HQ and most of its support weapons, except for the Vickers MMGs, which were split into sections of two guns each and allocated to A, B and D Companies.

It could be argued that B Company was more isolated than its sister companies. Whereas the rest of 3 RAR at least had the comfort of having another company in close proximity, ready to provide mutual support, B Company was on its own, in splendid isolation. Some post-war descriptions suggested that 'B Company's position [w]as a small natural fortress',[202] and while it may have appeared so to an outsider, the positioning also attracted some criticism from the men who had to occupy this small – and isolated – 'fortress'. Captain Reg Saunders, commanding C Company in the depth positions on the southern end of Hill 504, thought that Fergusson had committed an error by placing B Company on the isolated pimple: 'It was obvious that when the enemy came they would attack right where B Company was located – B Company were going to cop the lot … I don't think it was a good position at all.'[203]

Nevertheless, B Company's hill dominated approaches to the valley and it was vital that it was held. Captain Laughlin did his best to position his men to take advantage of the terrain and ensure they were locked in, mutually supporting, and also able to be aided by the Vickers from Ben O'Dowd's A Company up on Hill 504. Laughlin placed two of his platoons forward, one on each side of the ridge, with his other platoon a way further back in defence. He also had a section of two Vickers MMGs, which were deployed facing straight down the valley. These two water-cooled machine guns, while old, produced a terrific rate of fire and could pour effective bursts some 2,000 metres to the company's front.

Some further comfort was provided to the B Company men by the presence of the American Sherman tanks from 72nd Tank Battalion. This powerful armoured unit at the foot of their hill would surely make the enemy think twice before taking on B Company.

If the deployment of B Company raised eyebrows, the location of Ferguson's Battalion HQ caused some of the rifle company commanders to shake their heads. Rather than being up near his fighting companies, Ferguson decided to locate his headquarters over a kilometre to the south at the village of Chuktun-ni. After the battle, Ferguson was to receive some criticism for this decision, which seemed uncharacteristic of a battalion commander who was known to have a very good eye for ground and was capable in deploying his units to their best effect. So the question remains, why would he separate himself so far from his fighting units?

Unbeknownst to the company commanders, the reason – at least in part – appears to stem from orders given to Ferguson by Burke that he was to occupy and hold Chuktun-ni. Holding the hamlet would hopefully provide a positive example to retreating ROK troops and persuade them to carry on the fight. Be that as it may, the effect for 3 RAR was that Battalion HQ would end up having to mount its own defence of another isolated area, removed from the protection of its own companies. Crucially, it would also deny Ferguson the ability to closely monitor and influence the battle that he was only too aware would soon occur.

With orders given, 3 RAR started to move forward and occupy its allotted positions. On the main Hill 504 feature, A Company was located to the north of the position on a long slope. Its first platoon was on the western side of the slope, where it could overlook the road between B Company and Hill 504 and could provide supporting fire to B Company. O'Dowd's other platoons were located further up the incline, facing generally north. There was, however, a big gap between his second and third platoons, necessitated by the steeply rising ground at this location and the need for his company to cover a relatively large area. O'Dowd noted: '[F]rom my point of view, it represented a classical case of "occupy the lot and be weak everywhere or concentrate in strength at a vital point".'[204] Conscious that his main task was to provide support to B Company, O'Dowd decided to accept the risk and disperse his company more thinly than he would ordinarily have liked.

With A Company located at the north of the position, D Company took up a place on the eastern edge of the feature on a long, crescent-shaped line, and C Company was placed on the southern side of Hill 504, providing protection from any attempt to push through the back door.

The entire hill was covered by low-lying rough scrub. It was still dry from the winter and had not yet started to turn green with the coming of spring. Otherwise, the hills were sparsely covered, except for a few stands of low pine trees, particularly near the D Company position. As the men started to dig in, they found the going hard, the soil just below the surface still semi-frozen from the long winter. Even when this barrier was breached, the Diggers discovered that for the most part the ground a few feet down was rocky which made it difficult to construct any deep fighting trenches. Consequently, many positions were only half as deep as they should have been. Keen to build as much protection as possible, the trenches were reinforced above ground with low walls constructed from whatever stones and rubble could be found.

As the men continued with their well-rehearsed and by now automatic routine of digging in and preparing their defences, a hot meal was brought up to them from the valley. The food was appreciated by all. There was, however, an unfortunate side effect, as no ration packs had been brought forward. The result of this oversight would be felt over the next few days, with the conduct of the battle meaning that no further rations could be called forward. Unbeknownst to the 3 RAR men at the time, this would be the last meal that they would get for some time.

The Kiwis – morning and afternoon

The mid-morning order to move north to support the 6th ROK Division must have been deeply annoying to the New Zealand gunners, who had already spent a sleepless night on alert followed by a quick movement south in the morning. No soldier likes to retrace his steps and re-establish a position that he has left a few hours previously. But with orders given, there was no choice but for the reconnaissance parties in their jeeps to immediately head back north to identify likely gun positions, while the rest of 161 and 163 Batteries once again packed their gear and readied their guns for another road move.

It was a long and slow journey over rough tracks towards the 6th ROK, by now less than 10 miles to the north. When the recon parties arrived, they found a division that was on the brink of collapse. The commander of the recon team attempted to link up with the South Korean command post, but 'it was futile as they had little idea where their units were'.[205]

Winding their way slowly behind the recon team, the main elements of 161 and 163 Batteries arrived at their designated positions at about 1630hrs. What they saw did not inspire confidence, the battery commanders realizing that there was a risk that their guns would soon be within small-arms range of the advancing Chinese. Prudently, the riflemen of 1 MX who accompanied the gunners quickly moved up into the hills around the guns in order to provide both early warning and a modicum of protection.

As it happened, the Kiwis were not destined to remain in this position for long. Less than two hours later, the ROK defences became first precarious and then hopeless. The South Korean HQ came under attack and the division then started to collapse, presaging the start of a general retreat southwards.

The gunners continued to provide what fire support they could. But as more and more terrified South Koreans moved past their gun lines, it was becoming obvious that they could not remain in position for long. As the sun set, isolated small-arms fire started to fall among the guns. The battery commanders conferred with the Middlesex company commander and it was decided to bring the riflemen back off the hills and take up position alongside the guns. This precaution would provide intimate protection for the gunners, who were still hard at work responding to fire missions, as well as enabling a faster withdrawal when – not if – the order was given.

Transport was once again a key concern, as the Middlesex men did not have sufficient vehicles of their own at this forward location. As it would be clearly impossible for the Middlesex men to march south in good order amongst the increasing numbers of fleeing South Koreans, it was decided to overload the Quads and pack the riflemen onto the gunners' trucks, limbers and even on top of the towed guns themselves in order to get them out. It would be an uncomfortable ride for the precariously perched infantry, but at least it would move them out of harm's way while at the same time providing some measure of local protection to the gunners.

While preparations to withdraw were being made, enemy units were getting closer still. No longer limited to random rifle fire, larger groups of Chinese soldiers were now making their way ever-closer to the gun line. One large enemy formation had somehow outflanked the retreating Koreans and was spotted close to the Kiwis' position, necessitating firing the guns directly over open sights.

It being clear that nothing further of use could be done, the priority now was to get the gunners away and back to the relative safety of the brigade. Sometime between 2000 and 2100hrs, both 161 and 163 Batteries fired their last rounds and then proceeded to move off the position and begin their move south. It would prove to be a difficult and slow journey due to the poor tracks and roads, which were by now clogged with desperate South Korean troops fleeing as fast as they could. Both the gunners and the attached Middlesex riflemen frequently had to kick and push off panicked ROK troops who tried to clamber aboard their trucks or the guns themselves. With the road packed with troops taking flight, the drivers had to continually push forward through the waves of people, since any slowing down or hesitation on their part would result in the trucks being halted and swamped by ROK soldiers.

The ROK retreat

As the evening progressed, the initially small groups of fleeing ROK soldiers grew more numerous. By 2300hrs, increasingly large numbers of retreating South Koreans were seen streaming south in apparent disorder. MacKenzie, the Canadian Intelligence Officer, saw that the retreat was not limited to the rank and file, as even the Battalion HQ staff were pulling out too. MacKenzie saw that 'vehicles were covered with the usual interesting collection of bric-a-brac and furniture which so characterised the move of any ROK Army formation … it was quite apparent that the regimental and battalion headquarters of 6 Division were pulling out and abandoning their sub-units to their own devices.'[206] There was simply no cohesion among the ROK forces, the hapless South Koreans fleeing as fast as they could, either singly or in small groups.

In an attempt to stem the tide, the general commanding the 6th ROK Division established a checkpoint on the road near Ferguson's headquarters at Chuktun-ni. The South Korean general placed six machine guns facing north, directly into the line of his retreating troops. Desperate to establish some control of his broken division, he was forced to resort to extreme measures. While he was able to corral a certain number of men and force them back into makeshift units, the Canadians nearby on Hill 677 also witnessed a number of ROK troops gunned down by their countrymen as they tried to skirt the checkpoint and continue their flight. The retreating ROKs were becoming more panic stricken and their commanders were becoming more desperate – and ruthless – in their attempts to stop them.

The ROK commander's attempts to stop the flow was even remarked upon by members of the New Zealand artillery, who had by now managed to travel past the Australian positions and were safely back near Brigade HQ. Laurie Valentine, manning No 1 gun in Easy Troop of 163 Battery, recalled:

> 'It was one o'clock or so in the morning, we woke up and there was yelling and shouting and banging and carrying on. What the devil's that? We got up and had a look. The road was just packed solid with people. Not just packed solid with people, but there were people shooting those people. It turned out that the people running down the road were the troops that had replaced us in the front line, the

> Capital Division of the ROKs ... and the shooting was the officers trying to stop them. Shooting them point blank.'[207]

But it was already too late; the retreat was now obviously a rout. No matter how many machine guns the ROK general could point at his men, it was not enough to stop the southerly flow of frightened men.

***

Many Commonwealth Brigade accounts of the ROK retreat at this point also expressed a firm conviction that the advancing Chinese were intermingled with the fleeing South Korean troops, using the ROK exodus as cover for deep infiltration past their lines. The 3 RAR War Diary plainly stated as much: 'Intermingled with the fleeing ROK troops were the enemy and confused fighting broke out in the Headquarters.'[208]

But as historian Anthony Farrar-Hockley quite rightly points out, this impression, whilst firmly held, was most likely wrong: 'Even if many of the British Commonwealth complement found it difficult to differentiate between the Koreans and the Chinese, the Koreans had no difficulty in identifying a Chinese presence. Detection among their columns would have prompted them to abandon the tracks, and of this there was no report.'[209] So while it was unlikely that Chinese forces had intermingled with the fleeing Koreans, it was indisputable that they were close on their heels; in many places they had already got ahead of them and were infiltrating into 27 Bde's rear.

The Canadians

While the New Zealand gunners were having their own private battle north of the brigade defensive line, the Canadians spent most of the afternoon and early evening of 22 February getting into position atop their high fortress on Hill 677. Lieutenant Colonel Stone's month-long absence from the 2 PPCLI and convalescence did not appear to have had a negative effect on his enthusiasm or his determination to get his battalion ready for the upcoming fight. Returning from an O Group at Brigade HQ by mid-morning, Stone assembled his officers and detailed his plan for occupying the high ground to the west of the road, concentrating on the dominant feature of Hill 677. With orders given, and while the battalion was busy preparing to move forward, Stone led a reconnaissance party of his key officers to Hill 677 in order to get a closer look at the ground they would soon occupy.

Stone was acutely aware of the criticality of good reconnaissance. He no doubt recalled the oft-told, yet still true, military aphorism that 'time spent in reconnaissance is never wasted'. Approaching the hill feature, Stone looked at his battalion's new defensive position in detail and spent some time to move past the hill complex and assess it from the perspective of an attacking enemy. Where was the vital ground that must be defended, and what were the likely enemy avenues of approach? These were the questions that Stone needed answers to, and the time he spent on this reconnaissance would reap rich rewards during the upcoming battle. Taking the time to recon and walk the ground prior to occupation was simple and yet excellent soldiering. It demonstrated clearly that Stone knew his craft well and was determined to place his troops to best effect.

In his memoirs, Stone described Hill 677 as follows: 'Hill 677 is about a mile and a half across, gullied, wooded and impossible to defend in the classic manner of deploying companies to support each other. Each company had to develop its own individual defended locality, the platoons being mutually supporting.'[210] Stone realized that there were extensive gaps in the proposed defence, but he proposed to deal with these deficiencies through cover provided by the battalion MMGs, mortars and artillery fire from the New Zealand 25-pdrs. He decided to break up his MMG platoon into small packets, with the six Vickers machine guns deployed in sections of two guns each to cover the gaps between the rifle companies and provide much-needed depth to the battalion's defences.

The reconnaissance itself took several hours to complete. This was in part due to a punishing climb to the summit of Hill 677 but also some 'navigational errors' on the return journey which meant that Stone was only able to return to the battalion and provide full orders at 1800hrs. Fortunately, 2 PPCLI was already packed, prepared and ready for the move. Under cover of darkness, the battalion moved forward at about 1900hrs.

Trucks were allotted to take the Canadian riflemen up to the village Tugmudae, after which the men debussed, shouldered their equipment and started their long slog up the slopes of the feature, carrying as much ammunition as they could. As they assembled, the early evening was illuminated by the village of Naechon burning in the distance. It was not known whether the fires were set by the advancing Chinese or the retreating ROK troops, but whatever the case, the fierce blazes helped cast some pale illumination into the night. As the riflemen began their climb, the Canadians' vehicles returned to Brigade HQ before making a further move south, following the withdrawing A and B echelon transportation.

While the Canadians trudged upwards, loud explosions were heard from the south, towards the valley of the Pukhan River, bright glows of fires showing where the Chinese had already got around 27 Bde and were attacking and setting light to petrol dumps previously stored there by the Americans. This dramatic lighting and ominous soundtrack accompanied the wary riflemen as they went.

The effect of this considerable background illumination was that the men were able to move forward relatively well and quickly. It was only in the deepest gullies, where the light could not penetrate, that the battalion had to resort to guides to gingerly lead the men and the few vehicles of the mortar platoon.

Unlike the rifle platoons, the mortar teams found the going quite tough and slow. The mortars were being transported in US-made half-tracks that the Canadians used as mortar carriers. Stone had found a particularly appealing re-entrant on the southern side of Hill 677 to base his mortars, but even the rugged half-tracks were having difficulty on the tough terrain with its narrow edges. Sharp turns were particularly difficult for the half-tracks to negotiate. Nevertheless, some quick thinking and a few pounds of explosives allowed the hardworking pioneer platoon to blast a useable road that permitted the half-tracks to proceed up into the re-entrant and take up their allotted positions.

As can be imagined, the less encumbered riflemen directed much good-natured banter towards the Battalion HQ and mortar teams due to their slow and noisy occupation of the position. However, the efforts of the pioneers and their smart bit of field engineering would prove their worth over the next twenty-four hours, as the both the mortars and the half-tracks came into their own.

Even on foot, Hill 677 proved a tough climb for the riflemen, who faced a tough ascent as well as lugging heavy loads of weapons, ammunition and personal gear. Lieutenant Brian Munro of A Company, who had already ascended the hill earlier in the day with the recon party, was feeling the effects of another hard climb: 'I became so exhausted my knees seemed to buckle, every step is agonising … the last 100 metres is a dreadful struggle for me.'[211]

Finally, at around 2200hrs, the rifle companies were in position and commenced to dig themselves in. It took another two hours before the mortars had their base plates dug-in and ready for action. By then, the Chinese had already struck in the valley below.

Chapter 20

The Hammer Falls (23 April, evening)

A Company, 72nd Tank Battalion

The Sherman tanks allocated to assist 27 British Commonwealth Brigade were deployed down on the valley floor, just forward of 3 RAR's defensive position on the isolated island fortress. The 35-ton Sherman M4A3E8 tank – also known as the 'Easy Eight' – was a formidable weapon of war, sporting a 76mm main armament as well as two bow-mounted .30 calibre machine guns and a turret-mounted .50 calibre machine gun. The Shermans were rightly feared by the lightly armed Communist forces and would certainly prove their worth at Kapyong.

One tank platoon, 4 Platoon, was positioned a little forward of the rest of A Company as a blocking force. As the numbers of fleeing South Koreans started to peter out, almost immediately the tankers started to take fire from advancing Chinese forces. The Chinese seemed initially surprized to meet the solid force of US tanks astride their line of march. The first Chinese attacks were feeble and unco-ordinated, consisting of little more than a platoon or so of regular infantry. Critically for the Americans, this initial attack was not supported by any stand-off anti-tank weapons. The Chinese had no choice but to try to close the gap between themselves and the Americans as quickly as possible, then clamber on top of the tanks and attempt to disable or destroy them with grenades and other personal weapons. It was a dangerous gamble, but one that Chinese commanders appeared willing to take as they threw their men against the US tanks. This hasty attack was quickly beaten back, but the Chinese considered that time and numbers were on their side as more troops continued to pour south into the valley.

For the Americans, the night fighting, with no Allied infantry in close support, provided its own challenges. As the Chinese started firing, the Americans were concerned about opening up with their main armament in case they mistakenly hit retreating ROK troops rather than the enemy. As it became clear that there were no longer any South Koreans in the vicinity, the Americans started to fire with their .50 calibre machine guns, the dark momentarily lit up by the flames of the gun barrels, silhouetting the imposing metal bulk of the three tanks.

In the gloom and 'buttoned up' in the hold of their tank, it was impossible for the tank commanders to direct their impressive main guns and machine guns to their best effect. They had no choice but to sit halfway out of the turret in order to see the enemy and direct their weapons. While directing their main guns, the tank commanders also had to shoot with their .45 pistols at Chinese clambering up onto their tanks. The result was predictable, two US tank commanders being shot through the head in quick succession by the advancing Chinese. As the enemy closed the gap, the tank crews were forced to close their hatches once more and resort to firing their machine guns directly at their opposite numbers in an attempt to 'hose down' the Chinese infantry clambering up and over the sides of their tanks, desperately looking for any chink in the armour in which to lodge a grenade or explosive charge.

The Shermans battled bravely against the Chinese infantry, but there was a very real danger of them being overrun. As the situation deteriorated, the tanks had no choice but to reverse and lumber off to the south, back in the direction of Chuktung-ni and the remainder of their tank company.

***

Post-war reports were uniform in their high praise for the actions and bravery of the US tank company throughout the Battle of Kapyong. Praise was particularly high for the company commander, Lieutenant Kenneth Koch, who led his men superbly and skillfully throughout the battle. The unstinting support provided by the tank crews over the next few days was also recognized as they made repeated trips between Brigade HQ and the forward companies in order to provide fire support, deliver ammunition and transport wounded men out of harm's way.

That said, it remains something of mystery as to why there was not better – or indeed any – effective co-ordination between the tanks and the infantry during the early stages of the battle. It was widely recognized by commanders at all levels that in a close-quarters fight, particularly at night, tanks by themselves are rarely of much use. But when combined with close-support infantry, they can be a battle-winning force multiplier.

One of the problems was that while the tank company was ordered to assist the brigade in a general sense; it was not formally attached to the brigade nor placed under its command. They were simply in the same location, and it was up to the tank commander, at his complete discretion, as to how he would employ his powerful armoured force. The tank commander had placed 4 Platoon forward as a type of 'trip wire', intending that they should move back to the main position after spotting the enemy. While this may have been a sound strategy during daylight hours when the tanks had good fields of view, it was proven to be less effective at night when the tank crews could see little in the gloom, particularly if they were fighting from inside the tank's armour. In addition, the tank commander had not envisaged that the Chinese infantry would advance so quickly so that instead of being a trip wire, the Shermans became more of an isolated and vulnerable outpost.

Furthermore, there was little means of communication between the tanks and the Australian infantry now defending the surrounds of Hill 504. Nor were infantry specifically allocated to protect the tanks from close-in infantry attacks. Major O'Dowd pithily remarked: 'I've not had much experience with infantry tank cooperation but I distinctly recall it being rammed into me that you do not employ armour against ground troops without infantry cover, particularly at night.'[212] The casualties suffered by the exposed crew commanders proved a deadly reminder of the truth of O'Dowd's remark.

In spite of these fundamental deficiencies, the tank crews of 72nd Tank Battalion performed heroically and bravely during the entirety of the battle, winning great praise from all of the grateful Australians whom they supported.

Chemical mortars

Unlike the praise for the US tank troops, almost all 27 Bde accounts of the Battle of Kapyong are scathing of the actions of the American 2nd Chemical Mortar Battalion that was supposed to provide intimate fire support to the Australians and Canadians. Despite its name, this mortar unit did not have anything to do with 'chemical' weapons, but rather was equipped with the very powerful and extremely useful 4.2in mortar. In many ways, the 4.2in mortar was more reminiscent of artillery than the usual smaller infantry mortars. It could send 13kg shells out to a maximum range of 4km from its rifled barrel, making it a potent weapon which could provide intimate and effective fire support. In addition, it had a very high rate of fire, able to deliver high-explosive shells as well as masking troop movements through the application of smoke or white phosphorous. Each mortar company was equipped with twelve mortars, making them a powerful force indeed.

The 2nd Chemical Mortar Battalion had been reactivated from its reserve status at the start of the Korean War, and had seen service throughout the peninsula. It was an experienced unit, led and staffed by veteran troops who had already endured many months of fighting. It is thus largely inexplicable as to why the unit appeared to suddenly leave all of its equipment and depart on foot, carrying only personal weapons, when attacked by Chinese forces on the evening of 23 April. The unsaid inference in all contemporary 27 Bde accounts is that the mortar men acted just the same as many of their US Army comrades, being infected with bug out fever which caused them to simply run away.

The mortar unit's own records, however, detail a slightly more dangerous turn of events. With enemy forces closing in on the position and with fears of being overrun, the company commander ordered his men to move into the hills east of the position, carrying only their personal weapons. The intention was that after the Chinese had moved through, they would be able to go back down to retrieve their mortars, trucks and heavy weapons. However, when it became clear that the Chinese were here to stay

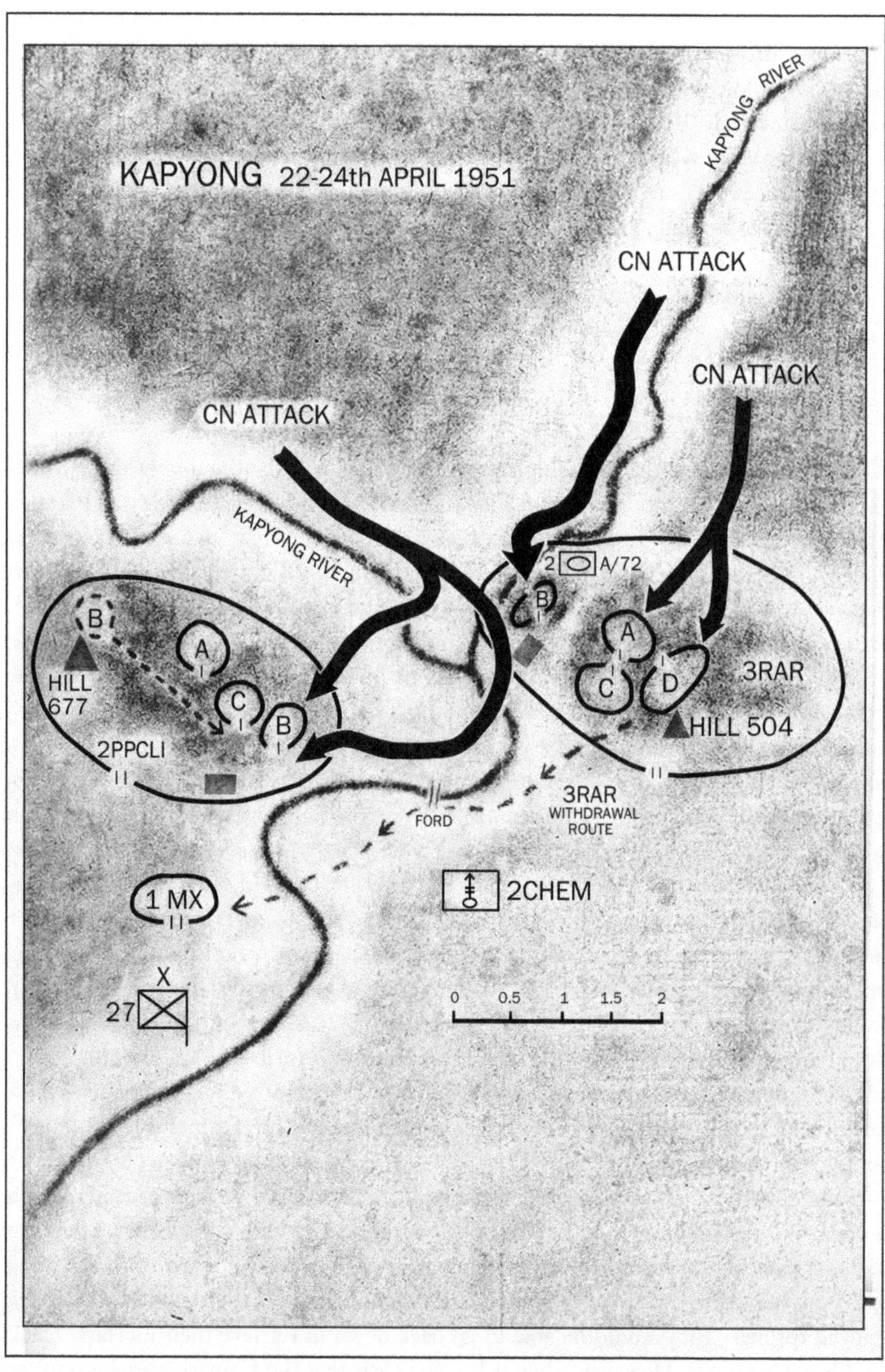
KAPYONG 22-24th APRIL 1951
KAPYONG RIVER
CN ATTACK
CN ATTACK
CN ATTACK
KAPYONG RIVER
2 A/72
B
A
C
D
3RAR
HILL 504
B
A
C
B
HILL
677
2PPCLI
FORD
3RAR
WITHDRAWAL
ROUTE
1 MX
2CHEM
X
27
0 0.5 1 1.5 2

and there was a growing threat to the unprotected mortar men in the hills surrounding their old position, the company commander ordered his men to abandon the position altogether and move east towards Chunchon.

It is not easy, nor fair, to second-guess the decisions of a commander under fire, particularly from a distance of several decades. On the one hand, post-action reports complain that if the mortar company had been equipped with half-tracks and additional .50 calibre machine guns, they may have been able to hold their positions.[213] These comments suggest that the company commander's decision was based on a realization that he could not defend his position from a close-in infantry attack, so he decided that protection of his men took priority over continuing to perform his fire-support mission.

The sterile wording of the 3 RAR War Diary, however, provides a different and altogether more damning interpretation: 'B Company 2nd Chemical Mortar Battalion left all their vehicles packed, but unguarded. The enemy did not reach their position in strength and the vehicles were later driven out by members of the Battalion and an Engineering unit.'[214]

Whatever the cause, by midnight, the mortar men were gone. 'By the time the US 4.2 mortar fire controller joined me [up on Hill 504],' noted 3 RAR's O'Dowd, 'shooting had broken out in the rear and his gun crews had taken to the hills, leaving their vehicles and mortars behind.'[215]

As midnight fell across the 3 RAR position, no further fire support was available from the 4.2in mortars, and none would be forthcoming for the rest of the battle – all of the mortar men were by now making their way eastwards as fast as they could march.

3 RAR – opening moves

The night of 23 April was clear and cool, and despite the time of year there was still some light frost on the ground.

ROK troops continued to pass through and around the 3 RAR Battalion HQ, which was proving a real headache for Ferguson, threatening his control over the area. With heavily laden ROK troops trying to get away, South Korean officers trying to regain control and an inability to determine friend from closely following enemy, the Australian commander was having a difficult time.

As well as threats to his headquarters, Ferguson was able to receive only intermittent signals from his rifle companies defending the slopes of Hill 504. The communications cable which had been so painstakingly laid between the companies and HQ had, like many times before, already been damaged by the increased traffic and troops moving in an unco-ordinated manner through his position. The supporting US tanks also chewed up his telephone cables as they moved back and forth between the forward trip wire position and his HQ. The result was that nearing midnight, Ferguson had abandoned the field telephones and was reduced to relying on the less reliable radio link to communicate with his subordinate units. This was not ideal, especially with it becoming increasingly likely that the main weight of a significant Chinese attack would soon be among them.

The uncertainty of identifying friend and foe was resolved in an abrupt and aggressive manner just before midnight when Chinese forces commenced some confused firing at the 3 RAR Support Company troops which were placed just forward of the main Battalion HQ. The assault pioneer and anti-tank men came under fire, green tracers lazily arching over their heads, clearly signalling that there were unidentified Chinese troops in the area. It was not serious fighting, but it resolved the mystery as to whether the Chinese had penetrated this far south. Their green tracers and flying rounds confirmed they had.

Up on Hill 504, O'Dowd and his men also started to feel the first probes of the advancing Chinese infantry. The flitting shadows and probing shots were relatively small beer, intended to draw the Australians out, return fire and thus give away their positions. But the 3 RAR men were not so easily taken in. They were by now very experienced soldiers who knew full well what their opponents were up to. They held their fire and did not simply waste ammunition by blasting away at shadows.

Nevertheless, the Chinese probes must have been successful, as they were soon forming up to put in a characteristic main attack, this time directed straight up the hill towards A Company.

O'Dowd described the standard form of a Chinese attack, which was to be repeated time and again at Kapyong for the remainder of the night:

> 'From somewhere down in the gully below us a discordant flurry of bugles and whistles would be heard, as the commanders assembled their soldiers and organized them for the attack. Then there was silence, as they crept up the hill towards us.
>
> 'Next came a hail of hand grenades, intended to put the defenders' heads down.
>
> 'Finally, there was the assault, launched with determination and ferocity, wave upon wave.'[216]

Following the familiar pattern, O'Dowd's men knew what to expect as the attacking Chinese came screaming towards them up the hill. The moonlight helped identify the enemy but also aided the Chinese in locating their targets. O'Dowd recalled that this 'was to be a very personal affair, soldier against soldier in the dark'.[217] The Chinese, nearing the top of the slope, rushed forward, urged on by their officers, spraying ahead of them with bursts of bullets from their fast-action burp guns.

The Diggers, half-crouched in their pits and stone sangars, returned fire. Crack, re-cock, crack, re-cock came the rhythmic sounds of the riflemen's .303s, only to be overshadowed by sharp three-round bursts from the section's Bren guns or the quicker spray of bullets from the section commanders' Owen sub-machine guns.

The attack was quickly beaten back, the Chinese withdrawing a short distance down the hill into a protected gulley to collect themselves and get ready for another charge. During the pause, but with the sounds of battle still ringing in their ears, 3 RAR section commanders went from pit to pit to check on their men. A number had been hit during the initial assault, and these were quietly dragged by the company medic, Nobby Clark, and his stretcher bearers back towards Company HQ. The wounded were placed on the reverse slope of the hill in order to provide some protection from the next assault that was almost certain to follow. The medical orderlies swiftly went to work, bandaging wounds and giving what aid they could. But medical supplies were not plentiful, and as the night progressed the orderlies would see their stocks of all medicines dwindling, in particular morphine, meaning that although the wounded were now out of the direct line of fire, they still had to endure the pain from their injuries while lying on the cold ground and without even the minimal comforts of a stretcher or blanket. It would prove to be a long and cold night for many of these men.

Back in the forward pits, platoon commanders rearranged their defences and moved men from the rear sections to fill gaps, readying themselves for the next wave. Ammunition was redistributed, magazines charged and grenades arranged on the forward edge of their pits.

As midnight passed, O'Dowd's 1 Platoon, being closest to the road and a natural reference point for the attacking Chinese, bore the brunt of renewed assaults from the still enthusiastic enemy. Lieutenant Freddie Gardner's men saw off a number of assaults, but these were nevertheless taking a toll as more of his men were being killed or wounded in the close-contact actions. Finally, in the early hours, Gardner told O'Dowd that he simply didn't have enough men left to hold his position. Torn between the desire to continue covering the road and the need to protect his remaining men, O'Dowd reluctantly ordered Gardner to abandon his position and pull further back up the slope to reinforce Company HQ and 3 Platoon.

Chapter 21

Main Assault (24 April, pre-dawn and day)

3 RAR – A Company

Having already endured multiple charges and intense hand-to-hand fighting for several hours, the 3 RAR men were encouraged when the enemy fire and attacks seemed to peter out from around 0200hrs. But hopes that the Chinese attack had run out of steam or been called off were soon dashed when a barrage of HE and incendiary shells started to pepper the Australians' position. Flattening themselves even lower into their pits, the high-explosive shells did little damage to the dug-in riflemen. Of more concern were the incendiary rounds, some of which set the dry heather alight and caused a thick blanket of smoke to descend over the battlefield. The smoke was of particular annoyance to the wounded, stinging their eyes and causing them to cough continuously, threatening to rupture temporarily bandaged wounds and generally adding to their misery.

At least one small band of enterprising Chinese used the cover of the makeshift smokescreen to thread their way back up the slope. Moving silently and masked by the smoke, they found a large gap between 2 and 3 Platoons and were able to set up and dig in. They set up a light machine gun and started to pour fire into the Australian positions, almost from within A Company's position. This sudden and unexpected development was a dangerous threat to the Australians, and O'Dowd knew that he had to deal with it immediately lest it split his company and provide a foothold for successive waves of enemy forces.

An immediate counter-attack was needed to neutralize this threat, and O'Dowd assigned the fiercely anti-Communist and God-fearing Lieutenant Mulry the task. All the while, the commander of the Chinese machine-gun team, perhaps realizing the precariousness of his situation, proceeded to blast on his whistle with increasingly desperate tones, calling for assistance and reinforcements from his compatriots further down the slopes. Despite his whistle blasts and the longer bursts from his team's machine gun, he was soon winkled out of the position and dispatched by a section of determined Diggers. Employing classic fire and movement, Mulry's men leapfrogged in small groups towards the Chinese. As they got closer, grenades were hurled by one team to keep the enemy's heads down, followed in quick succession by an aggressive bayonet charge by another section. The machine gun was silenced, with the few surviving Chinese hotfooting it back down the slope.

The counter-attack revealed another surprise in the form of one of their own wounded who had been briefly captured by the Chinese machine-gun team. The wounded man was from 1 Platoon and had been discovered by the Chinese when they were setting up their machine gun. When they saw that Mulry was preparing his counter-attack, they placed the wounded Digger in a nearby shell scrape to give him some protection from the coming fight. The Australians were uniformly impressed by this small act of kindness from the Chinese. 'Savage as they could be,' remarked O'Dowd, 'they also had compassion.'[218]

3 RAR Headquarters

At the same time as the enemy attacks on O'Dowd's company were tailing off, the Chinese were turning their attention towards Battalion HQ at the southern end of Hill 504. A large group had carefully infiltrated around the lower slopes of the hill and were now threatening the village of Chuktung-ni. What was previously sporadic firing into Battalion HQ suddenly picked up at around 0400hrs, with concerted pressure brought to bear. Using the darkness to their advantage, groups of Chinese got among the small houses of the village and established several machine gun positions. They also brought up a mortar, which they used to good effect on the men of Support Company.

Battalion HQ had managed to retain a number of the retreating South Koreans, who were now pressed into service. It is not known if they were forced to stay, but more likely they felt it safer to stay and fight with a unit that was actively resisting the advancing Communists than merely leaving their fate to chance, alone on the road and in the dark.

The newly recruited ROKs were used to deal with the fleeting shadows to the front of the 3 RAR men, who were busy trying to silence each of the newly positioned enemy machine guns. Infuriatingly for the Aussies, no mortar support from the attached 4.2in chemical mortar company was available. They tried time and again to raise the American mortarmen on the radio, but all they received in return was a crackle of static and silence.

What they would not know until after the battle was that Brigadier Burke had ordered a company of the Middlesex Regiment to go forward to support 3 RAR's HQ Company. 3 RAR records suggest the Middlesex men never arrived at Battalion Headquarters, but rather found their way to the Americans of the 4.2in mortar company and departed with them when they abandoned their position.

However, Middlesex records are very clear that not only did they arrive at Ferguson's headquarters, but they were also engaged in very heavy fighting against the Chinese. At around 0430hrs, Lieutenant Barry Reed was ordered to take his 1 MX platoon to the western side of the HQ position near the road. As he did so, they came under intense machine-gun fire and were targeted by a recoilless rifle, likely a captured US Army 75mm M20. While largely ineffective against heavy armour, the M20 could cause devastating effects on enemy bunkers or unprotected infantry – such as Reed's platoon. In short order, four men in Reed's forward section were hit and wounded. With the section beginning to crumble and the Chinese threatening to envelop it, Reed dashed forward to rally his men. By his example, the platoon was able to hold and stave off the follow-up Chinese assault. With the immediate danger abating, Reed organized the evacuation of his wounded men and then pulled back to the 3 RAR HQ defensive position. For his actions that morning and his inspirational leadership of the platoon over nearly six months, Reed was awarded the Military Cross.[219]

Despite actions such as Reed's, the 3 RAR HQ position was becoming untenable. As more enemy troops moved forward and took up positions in the village, and with daylight soon to break, it was becoming clear that the headquarters was in danger of being overrun. After seeking permission from Burke, Ferguson ordered a withdrawal to the Middlesex defensive position, a relatively safe location several kilometres to the rear of the current Battalion HQ.

As dawn broke, the Support Company men began their withdrawal. But it was touch and go, as daylight made their movement increasingly easy to spot by the growing numbers of advancing Chinese. Many men were understandably reluctant to leave their established and currently safe fighting positions to make the uncertain and dangerous move in the open. Fortunately, the Shermans from 72nd Tank Battalion once again provided sterling service, covering the withdrawal and carrying many of the Aussies out of the immediate danger area to the rear.

Casualties were once more a major concern. Those from Battalion HQ were loaded onto several vehicles, including an ambulance which was marked with its distinctive red cross. Don Beard, the 3 RAR Medical Officer, commented: 'It was notable that we were loading casualties onto the ambulance prominently displaying the red cross; firing on us ceased, only to start again when the ambulance had gone.'[220] This respect for the red cross symbol was another example of the general compassion shown by the Chinese towards wounded Allied soldiers, and it was of great credit to the Chinese that they showed such care, even in the midst of battle.

B Company, 3 RAR

While Battalion HQ had been hit hard during the early morning, B Company on its isolated island hilltop had also been on the receiving end of Chinese attention throughout the night. These night attacks were in the form of infiltration attempts rather than a concerted or deliberate assault, and were easily beaten off.[221] The most dangerous attempt was at approximately 0430hrs, when a group of around fifty Chinese infantry somehow worked their way silently to the rear of the company position. Using great stealth and skill, the Chinese got into position behind B Company, then split into three columns for a multi-pronged assault.

Manning the rearmost south-western corner of the company's position was Lance Corporal Ray Parry and his small team, consisting of a Bren gunner, two riflemen and himself. Parry, a native of Perth, Western Australia, was another very experienced Second World War veteran. He was a former commando who had seen action in the South-West Pacific and had previously been Mentioned in Despatches. His section was defending in what appeared to be the remnants of a former North Korean trench complex, what Parry suspected was likely their old command post. The defences were worked in among some granite outcrops and included winding trenches and fighting positions, as well as an anomalous hole positioned just in front of Parry.

The Chinese attacked Parry's section in waves, streaming up the short hill before hurling stick grenades and then charging behind a stream of automatic fire. As the Chinese gained height up the hill, they would soon be silhouetted enough for Parry and his men to get a clear shot. Some did make it all the way up the hill, when they suddenly spotted the large hole to the front of Parry's section. A moment of disorientation or surprise was all it took for Parry's men to be afforded a split second to shoot at the puzzled attackers. The air quickly filled with the smell of cordite, the darkness frequently broken by a burst of light as a grenade exploded or a machine gun ripped off a burst. The attack continued.

Parry's men were holding on, but ammunition was running low. Parry later recalled that he had the constant headache of trying to get his men to conserve ammunition while at the same time trying to fend off so many targets. The fact that the Chinese were all armed with automatic weapons while his section only had two (the Bren gun and his Owen sub-machine gun) did not help, as his two men armed with bolt action rifles simply could not keep up with the number of enemy coming towards them.

Then calamity struck. The Bren gun barrel began to glow, a sure sign that it was overheating from the number of rounds being fired. Parry was contemplating whether they should urinate on the barrel in a desperate attempt to cool it when the Bren completely broke down, meaning the section's firepower was effectively halved. While Parry was occupied with this problem, he received a smack on the shoulder from one of his privates, making him spin around quickly, just in time to see a large, well-built Chinese soldier wielding an American Browning automatic rifle running straight for him, firing as he came. Parry had been warned just in time. He remembered feeling no fear, reacting instinctively and cutting the Chinese soldier down with a burst from his Owen gun.

Fortunately for B Company, and despite the bravery of the Chinese assault, it did not match the skill of the earlier infiltration. After a fierce fight with the Australian's rearmost platoon, and particularly Parry's section guarding the 'back door', the assault fell apart. The ground was littered with Chinese corpses strewn across the lower approach slopes to the company position. After the battle, twenty-three enemy dead would be found in front of Parry's section, a testament to the ferocity of the fight there. Amazingly, B Company did not suffer a single casualty. Ammunition was, however, perilously low. Parry recalled that his men were down to a handful of rounds between them, and he was getting ready to fight on with only bayonets.[222]

Dawn

Dawn broke just before 0500hrs on 24 April, the start of a fine and cloudless day. The light spreading across the horizon must have helped bolster the spirits of the hungry and tired 3 RAR soldiers. It would be easier to face an attack from identifiable, and targetable, men rather than defend against faceless ghosts that came in the night.

The Chinese were less welcoming of dawn's light, which robbed them of the invaluable cover that they had thus far been able to use to such good effect. As the sun continued to rise, O'Dowd's troops quickly retook the original 1 Platoon position that was abandoned during the night's fighting. Once again able to look down into the valley between Hill 504 and B Company, the A Company soldiers saw a welcome sight. Between the two positions and now clearly visible, large groups of Chinese infantrymen were in the open area between the two Australian companies, some attempting in vain to hide among the heather or in the folds of the ground in the paddy fields.

After enduring a night of fierce Chinese attacks, the Australians needed no encouragement, instantly pouring fire into the hapless Chinese from both flanks. They were joined by machine-gun fire from Lieutenant Koch's tanks, now located just south of the B Company position. Every time a Chinese soldier popped his head up or tried to make a run for better cover, he was tracked by half-a-dozen Australian rifles before being felled by a series of well-aimed shots. Many Chinese were seen to fall, cut down by the unforgiving crossfire. The murderous attentions of the Australians only let up when O'Dowd reluctantly called a halt to the killing. Despite his men enjoying what O'Dowd termed a 'turkey shoot', he was concerned about his dwindling ammunition stocks, which he knew would be vital once the Chinese regained their breath and made another attempt on the Australian defences.

Early morning saw the Australians still in command of their various defensive positions, but under strain. B Company was holding firm on its island fortress, its only concern being ammunition. The companies on the hill, however, were suffering from both a shortage of ammunition and a large number of casualties, which were mostly still held at the aid stations on the position.

The Chinese had also taken considerable casualties, and there were many crumpled bodies littering the slopes in front of the position. As usual, the Chinese had made significant efforts to remove their wounded and dead during the night. Nevertheless, it was clear that they had suffered heavily. In a lull during the fighting, Private Knowles of A Company was ordered forward to check the dead and wounded and collect whatever ammunition he could find. He recalled:

> 'This was one job that I did not relish …as I did the rounds of the hill I was amazed at the drag marks, blood, cotton wool and bandages where the Chinese had dragged their dead and wounded during the night. After collecting the ammo and distributing the same, we ended up with 15 rounds each.'[223]

At about 0800hrs, Ferguson came on the radio net. Without any prior indication of what he was about to do, the major ordered Laughlin's B Company to abandon its hill fortress and join the rest of the battalion on the main Hill 504, taking up a new position near to C Company.

The decision to withdraw B Company has subsequently attracted much criticism. O'Dowd in particular has questioned why B Company needed to be moved when it was still in excellent fighting order, continued to dominate the valley floor and was able to count on support from the companies located on the hill above. It was not, in his view, in any immediate danger of being overrun. After the war, O'Dowd raised pointed questions about Ferguson's decision, given that at the time he was not with his rifle companies but rather was several miles to the south at the Middlesex positions. The implication was that Ferguson wasn't really in a position to know what was going on with B Company at the time, and thus his order was not grounded on the actual situation.

On the other hand, Ferguson had seen his Battalion HQ forced to move during the morning due to strong enemy attacks, and was likely concerned about B Company's isolation, ripe for being cut off and attacked in detail from the west. While concentration of forces is a basic principle of war (and thus a positive reason to consider moving B Company), on balance it made little sense to relocate a unit that was already occupying a good defensive position and for it to commence a move under the eyes of the enemy to another location which had not been so well prepared.

Soon after the order was given, O'Dowd also came on the radio and suggested to Ferguson that B Company *must* remain in place. O'Dowd was likely concerned about his own left flank and was certainly already tired from a night of heavy fighting. Nevertheless, questioning orders in this manner over an open radio link was bordering on insubordination, and was not the sort of behaviour to be tolerated. Ferguson for his part chose not to respond to O'Dowd over the radio or to get into a debate with him. He either just ignored the comments from a clearly agitated company commander who was still in a difficult situation, or else he just reserved his comments until he could see O'Dowd face to face.

Nevertheless, the order was given and Laughlin at B Company set out putting it into action. He quickly briefed his platoon commanders and prepared the company to move across the open ground to their east and then up the hill towards C Company. As he was doing so, his tall, red-headed Company Sergeant Major, Eric Bradley, was attending to unit administration, redistributing ammunition and counting the dead Chinese soldiers lying on the slopes and down in the valley beyond. Bradley counted approximately

173 dead Chinese in the vicinity of the B Company fortress, an appallingly large number, many of whom had fallen to O'Dowd's morning 'snipe shoot'.

As he moved around the perimeter to conduct his checks, Bradley noticed some Chinese soldiers trying, and failing, to remain hidden among the small scraps of cover in the paddy field below. Spotting a poorly hidden Chinese soldier, a Digger quickly fired a short burst of his Owen gun towards him. However, instead of killing the man, and much to everyone's surprise, a large number of shy and nervous Chinese soldiers gingerly stood up – well over thirty in number. In ones and twos, the Chinese emerged from folds in the ground or from behind scant cover with their hands up, obviously intent on surrendering. It is proof of their amazing fieldcraft that the Diggers had not previously noticed such a large concentration of enemy troops until they quite literally walked onto them.

Sadly, one dedicated Communist foolishly flung a grenade at the advancing Australians even as all of the rest of his countrymen were surrendering. While the grenade did little damage, 'the Australians were in no mood for this type of behaviour'[224] and a short, sharp burst of fire from an Owen gun immediately cut him down. Unfortunately, a number of other Chinese, desperately trying to surrender, were also killed before Bradley could regain control of the men and stop the killing. The rest of the prisoners, even more frightened of the Diggers than before, instinctively huddled towards Bradley, with their arms still held straight overhead. These men obviously did not wish to be associated with their recently departed martyr and looked to Bradley to protect them from the enraged and murderous riflemen. In all, more than forty shocked and frightened prisoners were captured by Bradley and his men, and they closely followed the tall CSM as the company made its way across the paddy fields towards their new positions on Hill 504.[225]

As B Company climbed the hill, O'Dowd and A Company looked back across the valley. They saw large numbers of Chinese soldiers, close behind the departing Australians, moving through the scraggly pine trees and now taking over the excellent defensive positions so recently occupied by B Company.

***

With the tempo of fighting now reduced somewhat, attention could be paid to the dire ammunition situation and care for the large number of wounded, many of whom were still lying on the cold ground on Hill 504 and awaiting evacuation.

O'Dowd's men had suffered approximately thirty casualties (both dead and wounded) during the fighting in the night. This represented approximately 22 per cent of his company strength (A Company was listed as having 133 men just prior to Kapyong). While these were significant losses, O'Dowd remained confident that his men could hold. He is also reported as saying that despite the casualties and low ammunition, his men's morale was nevertheless surprisingly good.

Morale would certainly have improved as Shermans from the 72nd Tank Battalion started to return to the southern end of Hill 504. Now refuelled and rearmed, the tanks again moved forward to help evacuate the wounded. They became in effect the armoured transport company of the battalion, ferrying ammunition and medical support (in the form of the RMO, Captain Don Beard) forward to the rifle companies before transporting the wounded back to Brigade HQ. The tanks completed several trips in this manner, but it was not an easy ride for the wounded, either perched precariously across the rear deck of the vehicle or pushed – in spite of their wounds, and often painfully – down into the already cramped interior of the tank itself. Despite the discomfort, the armoured ambulance service was a godsend, another reason for the Australians to be grateful to the Americans.

***

At some stage during the morning after B Company had withdrawn towards Hill 504, Ferguson sent another order that the company should turn around and reoccupy their recently abandoned position on the fortress. Accounts suggest that Ferguson was ordered by Burke to reoccupy the old B Company position, likely because he now understood that there was a possible relief force from the US 5th Cavalry Regiment arriving in the next twenty-four hours.[226]

Between Hill 504 and the old B Company position was a small knoll that was criss-crossed with old trenches and bunkers, previously home to some long-forgotten group of soldiers also trying to defend this vital route towards Seoul. The criss-cross nature of the defences earned the knoll the nickname of the 'Honeycomb'. As B Company moved forward in extended formation, Laughlin could see that a large group of Chinese troops had already taken possession of the Honeycomb and would need to be cleared if they had any hope of reclaiming their old hilltop home.

Nearing the Honeycomb, a trench was spotted manned by an estimated ten Chinese soldiers, who started shooting at the advancing Australians. Deciding that speed and aggression was the only way to silence this trench, Lieutenant Ken MacGregor of 5 Platoon lined up his men and immediately dashed forward. In the lead was 5 Section, with MacGregor and his Platoon Sergeant close behind. As 5 Section leapfrogged their way in fast bounds, they realized to their horror that the trench contained many more than ten men, all of whom were now furiously firing towards the advancing Aussies. But the Australians were committed and could not turn back without risking even more casualties. So they charged on, firing at the trench in the hope of keeping heads down for long enough to allow them to get into the trench and go to work with their long 18in bayonets, grenades and sub-machine guns.

The forward section started to take a furious fusillade of fire. The Bren gunner, Private Stan Connelly, saw men fall to his left and right, shot down by the wall of fire. He sensed that his turn was next, and so it was; he took a .30 calibre round straight through his thigh and out of the back of his leg near his buttock. 'I was knocked completely off my feet,' recalled Connelly, '… it was like being hit by a truck. I was completely stunned.'[227]

Connelly fell forward within feet of the Chinese-held trench. How he was not hit again is a mystery, but perhaps the Chinese were so focussed on those who were still advancing towards them that they didn't think to waste a further few rounds on a man who was obviously down and out of the fight. But Connelly knew he would not be ignored for long. Seeing a piece of cover to the rear, he somehow found the strength to cast off his heavy Bren and ammunition pouches and, in stages, stagger, limp and crawl to the covered position, whereupon he crouched, making himself as small as possible while waiting for assistance and a medic.

Connelly was not the only man hit, and MacGregor's platoon was quickly cut down, its advance stopped dead in its tracks. MacGregor himself was shot through the jaw. He fell, stunned and bleeding profusely from his wound.

With the advance abruptly stopped, attention turned to extracting the wounded and pulling back towards Hill 504. The section of Vickers machine guns accompanying Laughlin's company quickly assembled their weapons and started to pour accurate streams of fire towards the Chinese, trying to keep them occupied long enough for their comrades to dash forward and drag MacGregor's stricken men to the rear.

The attempt to retake the Honeycomb and the fortress with a mere section had proven a costly mistake, it now being realized that it was occupied by at least eighty Chinese soldiers. Amazingly, none of the men who fell around the Honeycomb died, but several were very seriously wounded. MacGregor would have his jaw wired and need to be fed by a straw for fourteen months afterwards. As historian Bob Breen notes in his analysis of the battle, the men of B Company 'were victims of poor tactical decision making [and the] consequences were the misfortunes of war'.[228]

Repulsed but still determined, Loughlin decided to put in another attack, this time using a full platoon, supported by fire from his remaining platoons. The assault was led by Lieutenant Len Montgomerie, a Second World War veteran and former commando. Montgomerie had his men fix their fearsome 18in bayonets to their rifles and then, under covering fire, proceeded to charge at the enemy in 'one of the finest and most aggressive actions'[229] carried out by the Australians during the entire Korean War. The citation for Montgomerie's subsequent Military Cross, awarded for this action, included the following:

> 'Montgomerie leading 4 Platoon advanced over open ground towards the enemy strongpoint. During the advance his Platoon came under fire from the objective and from the right flank. Despite casualties he pressed on the attack. When his platoon was approximately thirty yards from the objective they came under intense fire from LMG, rifle, submachine gun and hand grenades. Showing complete

disregard for his personal safety and although outnumbered by approximately two to one, he led a bayonet charge against the first line of trenches.'[230]

This was not the only bayonet charge, and further assaults were put in on the Chinese defenders, who were eventually overcome by the sheer guts and aggression of the assaulting Australians. As Breen describes it: 'The use of bayonets … had the psychological effect of forcing many Chinese to flee in terror across the valley floor and run the gauntlet of small arms fire from those supporting the attack – the chance of a bullet better than the probability of a bayonet thrust.'[231] Besides Montgomerie's Military Cross, his leading section commander, Corporal Davie, was also awarded the Military Medal for his fearless actions that day.

The Honeycomb was recovered, with more than eighty Chinese bodies counted on or around the position. It was a fearsome death toll, revealing the intensity of the fighting over these few pits, trenches and bunkers. Montgomerie's men also suffered, with three of them killed and a further two wounded. While battles are not won by simply tallying up the dead and wounded on each side, the scale of the Chinese losses were out of all proportion to those suffered by the Diggers.

***

Ferguson arrived back near Hill 504 in one of the tanks, just after Laughlin had captured the Honeycomb. It was now clear to him that further attacks towards the old B Company position would be very costly in terms of casualties, now that the Chinese held the hill in strength. The expected arrival of the 5th Cavalry Regiment was not a sufficient reason to expend the lives of so many more Diggers, particularly when 5th Cavalry had three full-strength battalions under its command. Weighing up the costs and benefits, Ferguson reluctantly decided that B Company should withdraw from the Honeycomb. It is not recorded what the B Company men said or thought in response to this new order, but after a morning of heavy and deadly fighting, one can only imagine.

As ammunition was unloaded from the tanks and humped up the hill by parties of tired and hungry men, Ferguson informed O'Dowd that going forward he would be in overall charge of the defence of Hill 504 and any eventual withdrawal if that was ordered. He also informed O'Dowd that plans were being prepared to move up an entire US regiment (5th Cavalry) to push through the 3 RAR position and force the Chinese back north. O'Dowd was asked whether 3 RAR could hold Hill 504 and stop any further advance by the Chinese. 'Possibly', was O'Dowd's answer. He believed that they might be able to hold on for another night now that ammunition had been brought forward, but the combination of casualties which had weakened the battalion and an enemy now acutely aware of the Australians' position and likely preparing for even larger attacks, meant that it would be a near-run thing.

Morning – the Canadians prepare

Lieutenant Colonel Stone was keenly aware from monitoring the 3 RAR radio traffic that his battalion, the 2 PPCLI, would very likely be next in line to receive the attentions of the rapidly advancing Chinese. At first light, keen to obtain a clearer picture of the enemy situation around him, Stone dispatched a number of small reconnaissance parties to survey the ground and bring back reports of enemy movements. One patrol under his Intelligence Officer, Captain MacKenzie, almost immediately came under fire from Chinese troops as he worked his way south towards the small village of Tugmudae. The Chinese had already occupied the village and looked ready to advance further. Likewise, recon parties to the west of the Canadian battalion's position also reported that small parties of Chinese could be seen moving forward.

While the Canadians had been relatively unmolested during the daytime of 24 April, Stone knew that enemy forces would eventually switch from probing his Australian comrades and focus on his own battalion as they tried to find a weak spot in 27 Bde's defences. Sensing that the weight of attack would likely come from his right flank and right rear, which was along the main line of march of the Chinese, he used the lull to reallocate his Baker Company from its current positions north of Dog Company to reinforce the ridgelines to the east of the battalion, in an effort to further strengthen his right flank. It would prove to be a prescient move, one that would greatly assist the Canadians in fending off attacks from that direction.

With the recon patrols returned, the rest of the morning was spent developing the defences of the position and getting ready for whatever the Chinese would throw at them. At approximately 1100hrs, Brigadier Burke flew over the Patricias' position in a light US Army aircraft and proceeded to address the battalion from the air via a loud hailer. Burke is reported to have said that he knew the Patricias would do their duty and fight hard, being a credit to their regiment. According to Hub Gray of the mortar platoon, the Canadian soldiers were impressed and quite touched by this uniquely delivered address on the eve of battle.[232] While perhaps useful for maintaining morale, one wonders about the wisdom of clearly broadcasting the exact location of a small defensive force to a large Chinese army which was rapidly approaching from the north.

The Chinese who had already been committed the previous day and night were about to be massively reinforced. Many reports noted the scale of the approaching Chinese forces, lined up six abreast like a solid Roman legion, trotting down the valley's roads and tracks as fast as they could. It appeared that speed was paramount to the Chinese, and it was only when enemy aircraft came near that they tried to hide and take cover. Major Mason, the New Zealand FOO, recalled: 'The Chinese camouflaged with pine branches were moving on the road of the valley and every time a plane flew over they would lie still.'[233] But the intermittent overflights did little to discourage the Chinese, who were intent on their march southwards towards the Commonwealth Brigade.

Daytime – Chinese attack D Company, 3 RAR

Having failed to dislodge A Company from its positions on the western slopes of Hill 504, the Chinese now turned their attention to D Company. This was a bold move and not in accordance with their usual practice of only attacking at night. It says much about the pressure on senior commanders to push through the 3 RAR blocking position that they decided to attack in broad daylight, forgoing all of the usual protections of the night.

Captain Norm Gravener, in command of D Company, had spread out his platoons in almost linear fashion, only slightly curving his pits and sangars to follow the natural contours of the eastern slopes of Hill 504. This was not at all a textbook defensive position, but was thought necessary in order to cover all the approaches from the northern and eastern sides of the hill. Depth was provided by Gravener's Company HQ, located on the reverse slope of the high point of the hill. Further support was available from the most easterly positioned platoon of A Company, located just over the ridge.

D Company's most forward unit, 12 Platoon, was located on a small spur which jutted out on the northern side of the hill. The ground on both sides of the spur fell away quite sharply and the summit was covered by trees, all of which gave the men some welcome protection and concealment.

Gravener's company had already received some attention during the night, but it was small-scale and sporadic, and his men were still in good shape. But while D Company had got off lightly during the night and early morning, it was now very much its turn to feel the full weight of a Chinese assault. After a brief exchange of fire from a reconnaissance team at around 0700hrs, the Chinese lined up in strength for what would prove merely the first of many attacks they would put in against D Company that morning.

'12 Platoon was hit hard,' recalled Gravener, describing the first big attack. The platoon was located out on the forward spur and was heavily outnumbered by the charging Chinese. It took all of the platoon's firepower and discipline to see off the initial assault. But numbers alone did not determine the battle: '[T]he Chinese also had a hard time locating [the] position in the trees after they came over the edge of the feature. To get to the … perimeter the Chinese had a long, hard climb followed by a 50 metre dash.'[234] The exposed run and initial confusion of the Chinese, desperately trying to locate the Australians, gave the Diggers in their defensive trenches time to pour out deadly fire, leaving a string of Chinese bodies on the open ground. At the same time, the company commander had been able to call in artillery fire from the Kiwis' 25-pdr guns against the Chinese second wave that was still clambering up the slope.

Caught out in the open, the first Chinese attack stalled and then failed under the fire from 12 Platoon. Chinese officers were unable to press home the attack, and those who were still alive were soon seen backing up and trying to seek cover down the slope. Catching their breath, the repulsed troops were reorganized and pressed back into lines, ready for another effort.

Further probes and brutal human wave assaults continued to be put in on D Company all morning. The whistles and bugles sounded the start of each attack, chilling the waiting Diggers but at the same time alerting them to what was coming. A nervous silence followed as the rubber-shod Chinese ran up the slopes, ducking between cover and trying to remain hidden until the waiting Australians finally heard 'the rattle of metal striking stone as a shower of stick grenades fell about them. When they ducked to avoid the effect of the explosion that would quickly follow, the Chinese attacked.'[235]

D Company was holding on, but the forward platoon in particular was suffering; it had already lost eight men either killed or wounded during the initial actions. Because of the shape of the slope to their front, the platoon was unable to bring much fire to bear onto the attackers until the Chinese were almost on top of the ridge and dashing towards them. On the other hand, the good view down the slopes and into the valley beyond helped Gravener to call in accurate artillery fire. Seeing exactly where the Chinese were assembling, he called for fire to break up large groups of Chinese as they assembled and made ready for another push towards the Australians.

D Company was under heavy pressure. By mid-morning, Lieutenant Johnny Ward, the commander of the forward 12 Platoon, raised Gravener on the telephone link (amazingly, the land line connecting the platoons to Company HQ was still working) and told him in no uncertain terms: 'Boss, the bastards are all over the place. I think perhaps we should be moved.' Nonetheless, Gravener knew it was vital to hold. Any wavering now could be the start of a general panic and give the Chinese a vital foothold on top of the ridge that they would be sure to exploit. He calmly replied to his young platoon commander: 'Johnny, all we need to do is sit tight and it will be alright.'[236]

The regular attacks now included fire from a Chinese mortar team. While the Chinese launched at least six separate assaults throughout the morning, the Australians were fortunate that each followed the same predictable drill. Thus, despite the large numbers of enemy and a huge weight of fire, each attack saw Gravener's men well prepared and ready to repulse it. Bodies were piling up in large numbers in front of D Company's forward pits, yet still the Chinese had the appetite for more.

Inevitably, Gravener's company was also taking casualties. Several seriously wounded men had to be pulled out of the forward pits and taken to the medics in the rear. Gravener plugged the holes as best he could with fresher men brought forward from other sections, but it was still very much touch and go and his perimeter was being sorely tested.

Fortunately for the Australians, just after 1330hrs, the pressure on D Company lessened somewhat, giving Gravener an opportunity to move his forward platoon rearward in anticipation of a general withdrawal which the commander had just been made aware of. There was another dose of luck shortly thereafter, when a number of US Marine Corsair fighter-bombers started an attack run against the position where the D Company men had just been located.

It remains unclear exactly who ordered the airstrike, but it was most likely Ferguson, hoping to relieve pressure on his battalion. Nevertheless, and in what could easily have been a repeat of the deadly 'friendly' attack on the Argylls earlier in the war, the US Marine aircraft missed their intended target and dropped their fiery loads just forward of D Company. D Company's Sergeant Ray McKenzie later exclaimed:

> 'I was angry about this … our marker panels were clearly visible. I saw the big silver bomb [napalm] leave the plane and watched it fall on the D Company area … where I had been two minutes before. The napalm exploded and took all of the oxygen out of the air. I felt like I was just breathing heat.'[237]

Tragically, one of Gravener's men was killed in the strike and several others wounded, suffering severe burns from the fiery liquid. These men only added to the already long list of casualties who would have to be either carried by stretcher or assisted in the long withdrawal that was to come.

Withdrawal of 3 RAR

Besides the current need to evacuate the growing numbers of battalion wounded, Ferguson was also becoming more concerned about 3 RAR's ability to hold out for another night. Many sources note that Ferguson was a thoughtful and considerate commander who was not wont to make rash decisions. On the one hand, he wanted to continue to hold Hill 504, continue with his mission to block the enemy advance down the valley and act as a firm base for the US 5th Cavalry Regiment that he knew was making its way forward to help relieve 27 Bde. Ferguson was not, however, a commander who would uselessly squander his men's lives. Faced with the certainty of an even bigger assault after nightfall and possible catastrophic losses, Ferguson thus had a very tough decision to make.

He appears to have discussed the matter with O'Dowd during one of his forays forward on the US tanks to collect wounded. Ferguson was crouching in a bit of cover and had a radio propped up next to him while he spoke to O'Dowd. The pair spoke at length about the possibility that 5th Cavalry might not be able to relieve them in time, so it was very likely that 3 RAR would be left alone to face the Chinese for another evening. In such circumstances, he felt it might be necessary to withdraw rather than take another night's hammering. Ferguson did not give O'Dowd firm orders to withdraw at this time, but rather O'Dowd was warned that if it came down to it and a withdrawal was necessary, then he, O'Dowd, would need to be ready to assume command of it.

By mid-afternoon, it was clear that the Chinese were located in force near the old B Company position and forward of D Company. It was now a certainty, rather than a possibility, that 5th Cavalry would not be able to break through that day. Consequently, the order was given and 3 RAR was told to prepare to move back to the 1 MX lines.

***

A withdrawal from an active and close fight is an inherently dangerous manoeuvre. As troops leave their prepared defensive positions, they become more exposed to attacking enemy and indirect enemy fire. Confusion can ensue if the withdrawal is not well planned and orchestrated. It is also possible for the enemy to use the withdrawal as an opportunity to rush forward, take advantage of the confusion and viciously maul the retreating troops. O'Dowd remarked with his characteristic frankness: 'Withdrawals are always tough on morale and discipline. The urge to run, to put distance between oneself and danger is instinctive.'[238]

O'Dowd, as an extremely experienced company commander, knew what he must do to ensure the withdrawal went smoothly. He formulated his plan and gave orders to the other company commanders in what would be acknowledged as a textbook example of how to withdraw from a position even though still in contact and under fire from the enemy.

O'Dowd and Ferguson had already decided the route of the withdrawal during their earlier discussion. O'Dowd recognized that it would be impossible to go straight down the western side of the hill to the road leading south, as this route was now completely covered by enemy fire – particularly from the Chinese now sat on the old B Company position. Instead, it was decided that 3 RAR would move south, along and down the ridgeline of Hill 504, before descending to a ford in the river approximately 2km south of the battalion's current location. From here, there would be a further 2km march skirting the foothills south of the river before marrying up with 1 MX.

With orders issued, O'Dowd sent an advance party including one lieutenant down the back of the hill to secure the ford and ensure it was still safe for the rest of the battalion to pass through. At around 1600hrs, with the ford secured, a diversionary artillery strike and heavy smokescreen was fired into the area around the Honeycomb and the old B Company positions. At the same time, with the Chinese diverted, the first company started its withdrawal. Utilizing a series of leapfrog manoeuvres, O'Dowd moved the battalion back in a series of bounds, at all times having one company firm on the ground and covering the others as they moved. Each time a withdrawing company moved to the rear, it too took up a new defensive position, allowing the previously defending company to pick up and move backwards through the newly defending unit.

The withdrawal of 3 RAR along the ridge back to the Middlesex lines went off extremely well and was complete some six hours later, by 2200hrs. The men had withdrawn in an extremely organized and disciplined manner, which allowed the battalion to be extricated as planned despite having large numbers of extremely motivated Chinese hot on their heels. The use of the leapfrogging manoeuvres, as well as calling in heavy artillery fire on former positions, allowed the battalion to make a clean break. This was in spite of having been in almost constant combat for more than twenty-four hours and whilst transporting a large number of wounded men over very rough terrain.

The withdrawal was not completely without incident, however. As O'Dowd moved back and forth along the route to locate positions for each withdrawing company, he suddenly found himself near a large group of Chinese, all carrying arms. O'Dowd recalled that he 'got a hell of a shock' until he realized that these were the Chinese prisoners captured earlier in the day, who were now helpfully assisting to carry the wounded men to safety. Nevertheless, he was not well pleased to see that the prisoners were all carrying weapons. When he sharply questioned the escorts as to what they thought they were doing, one of them sardonically replied: '[W]ell you don't expect the bloody wounded to carry them do you?'[239]

***

The Australian withdrawal from Hill 504 was thus completed in exemplary fashion. This was no 'every man for himself' bug out. Rather, the withdrawal was a well-planned and executed rearwards manoeuvre by disciplined men.

O'Dowd singled out his soldiers for the success of the Kapyong withdrawal. He believed that the makeup of his battalion, predominantly experienced Second World War men, made a significant difference. 'The diggers won the battle of Kapyong, he declared. 'There was nothing the officers could do. It was a matter of whether the diggers had the guts to go on with it or not. And they did.'[240]

While O'Dowd was on the one hand correct, he was altogether too humble. Undoubtedly, the fighting spirit and skill of the 3 RAR men contributed to their eventual success, but so too did the actions, clear-headedness and professionalism of officers such as O'Dowd. It was due to their combined efforts that Kapyong is still remembered today as a great success by Australian forces, often being held up as an exemplar of Australian infantry courage and skill.

Chapter 22

The Fight for Hill 677 (24 April, evening)

For the best part of twenty-four hours, the Canadians had a ringside seat to the vicious fight between the Australians and Chinese on Hill 504. Watching on as the Chinese put in wave after wave of attacks, the men of 2 PPCLI were under no illusions as to what they could expect when the Chinese inevitably turned towards them.

The commander of the Canadians' B Company, Major Vince Lilley, assembled his platoon commanders at approximately 1700hrs for an O Group. Bunched up close together, Lilley quietly told his lieutenants that 3 RAR had been hit hard on multiple occasions throughout the day and taken serious casualties. In preparation for a similar attack, Lilley ordered: 'Extra ammo is to be kept about each soldier's neck (ie in bandoliers), wireless watch is to be maintained at all times, all soldiers are to remain in their slit trenches, shoot anything that moves and "prepare for continuous engagement without relief".'[241] Lilley was very well regarded by his troops, being known as a practical and capable officer. The holder of a Military Cross for his actions in the Second World War, his orders were exactly what his men needed to prepare for the fight ahead – they were simple, practical and honest.

B Company engaged

As the evening wore on, Stone's supposition about Chinese intentions would prove correct. At around 2130hrs, a large enemy group – estimated at approximately 400 troops – was seen forming up on the valley floor opposite the right forward platoon of B Company. In the bright moonlight, the anxious men of the company could see the Chinese organizing and making themselves ready for the assault.

Wasting no time, Lilley radioed for a fire mission to be conducted on the assembling enemy. With a considerable amount of artillery support now available (US 105mm and 155mm guns, in addition to the Kiwi 25-pdrs), rounds were quickly brought down onto the Chinese in the valley, disrupting their neat formations as soldiers scattered in an attempt to find cover from the incoming fire.

Inevitably, however, with the end of the barrage, the assault commenced. Negotiating the steep slopes to the front of B Company, the Chinese had a gruelling climb which sapped some of their strength before they got close to the company lines. Nearing the crest, the Chinese flung multiple grenades towards the Canadians before charging forward, their burp guns shouting their tell-tale noises and spewing a great mass of bullets before them.

Crouched ready in their pits and stone-lined sangars, the Patricias fought back, maintaining a constant rate of fire from their rifles and Brens. Critically, the riflemen were supported by the deadly Vickers medium machine guns located near Company HQ to their rear. The high rate of fire from the Vickers guns did much to break up the attacking Chinese, their constant knocking sound giving much comfort to the Canadians in the forward line of pits.

The Canadians were having a difficult time as the masses of Chinese broke over them. Nearest to the edge of the ridge was 6 Platoon, which suffered greatly. The forward section was soon overrun, leaving behind one dead Canadian with another wounded. Also wounded was the Bren gunner, Private Wayne Mitchell, who sustained a serious injury over an eye, leaving his face covered in blood and making it difficult for him to fire his weapon, let alone see where the enemy was coming from. With no prospect of holding this forward edge, the survivors were forced to pull back and join their comrades further back up the ridge.

For their part, the Chinese showed no sign of flagging, still aggressively pushing forward. Lilley was seen at this time moving about his battered platoons, encouraging, leading and inspiring. 'Lilley's example is an inspiration to every man under his command,' recalled Schuler, one of the medics attached to B Company. 'His calm attitude under fire reinforces the confidence of our harassed troops.'[242]

Reassuring he may have been to his troops, but Lilley was also clear-eyed about the danger and what needed to be done if he was to retain control of his company position. At one point, as he neared the stretcher bearers, Lilley told them in no uncertain terms that with so many enemy troops lining up against them, he needed every man who could hold a rifle in the firing line. Any wounded man who could still hold a rifle or fight in any way was to be patched up and immediately sent back into the fight. It was not the time to evacuate men who could still help with defending the position.

With the Chinese now occupying their previous pit, the situation was getting increasingly tense for 6 Platoon. For a time, the Chinese and Canadians traded rifle fire back and forth, but this was soon shattered when the Chinese brought forward a machine gun to put extra pressure on 6 Platoon. Chinese mortar fire also started to find its range, with the deadly rounds peppering the remaining platoons and sections further back in the defensive position.

The tense stalemate on the edge of the 6 Platoon position lasted about an hour. While each side continued to take pot shots, it was clear that the balance was subtly shifting in the Chinese troops' favour as they brought steadily more men and fire to the fore. If this continued, 6 Platoon was in danger of being completely overrun and destroyed. The commander of 6 Platoon, Lieutenant Ross, knew something drastic needed to be done to save his unit. A counter-attack was rapidly planned. Bayonets were fixed and, with covering fire from the Vickers and Bren guns, the platoon rushed forward in an attempt to retake their previous position.

Lieutenant Hub Gray described the Canadian attack: '[D]uring the charge you try to stay close to your buddy, to kill as many of the bastards as you can. It is a matter of ensuring your own safety and survival.'[243] While this description accurately represented the experience of most of the men during the action, some men demonstrated uncommon courage. Chief among them was Private Wayne Mitchell, a 21-year-old Manitoba native who had already been wounded over the eye during the original Chinese push that forced his section out of their forward defences. As required by Lilley, and despite the blood flowing from his head wound, Mitchell continued to man his Bren gun, causing severe casualties among the Chinese.

During the assault to recapture the lost 6 Platoon positions, Mitchell was hit once more, this time in the chest. It was a serious wound, yet incredibly, he got up and kept on fighting. At some point, he had his wounds roughly bound up, but rather than allowing himself to be evacuated to the rear – which even Lilley would agree was necessary in respect of a chest wound – Mitchell refused to leave his post.

Mitchell was then ordered to move to Company HQ to have his wounds attended to. He reluctantly agreed, but as he made his way back he also managed to carry a wounded comrade with him to the aid post.

Later that evening, just after midnight and seeing that pressure on his comrades was becoming critical with the Chinese advancing on the Platoon HQ, Mitchell 'again skilfully brought his Bren Gun into action … seeing his Platoon Sergeant with six wounded men pinned down by enemy fire, [he] voluntarily, without regard for his safety, rushed towards the enemy firing the Bren Gun from the hip, thus allowing the wounded men to escape.'[244] His gallant attack resulted in yet another wound, this time from fragments of an exploding grenade.

The uncommon grit and determination of men such as Mitchell eventually turned the tide, enabling Lilley's men to beat back the Chinese and retake their forward pits. However, even among the many brave men in Lilley's company, Mitchell's courageous actions stand out. He would eventually be awarded the Distinguished Conduct Medal (DCM) for his actions that night. It was, however, a very hard-fought battle, and even though there now followed a short lull in the fighting, both sides were merely regaining their strength for the next round.

***

While B Company was engaged in its furious counter-attack, another assault was brewing at the southern end of the feature near Battalion HQ. Somehow, a strong body of Chinese had worked their way around the hill complex and were now threatening both the headquarters and the nearby mortar platoon.

Lilley spotted the advancing Chinese and informed Stone that a large enemy group was trying to make for his headquarters. Unfortunately for the Chinese, they either had no idea that the headquarters was defended by the six half-tracks of the mortar platoon or perhaps thought they were normal US Army transport trucks. They would quickly learn to their cost that this was not the case:

> 'Each half-track was equipped with one .50 and one .30 Browning machine gun. These were loaded one tracer to four ball. We held fire until the Chinamen broke through the trees about 200 yards away, and then 12 machine guns cut loose together … the enemy never had a chance.'[245]

Hub Gray also recalled how effective the concentrated fire from the half-tracks was against the Chinese. He noted that when the machine guns opened up, with their long lines of bright red tracers arcing out towards the defenceless Chinese, someone was heard to say: '[M]y god, it looks like someone took the top off an anthill.'[246]

Chapter 23

Final Rounds (25 April)

While the Chinese attacks on B Company and Battalion HQ had been dangerous affairs, they were clearly only the opening shots. Having now gained a complete picture of the Canadian defences, the Chinese were setting up for their main attack against D Company on the far north-western spur of the hill.

It began at around 0130hrs, when members of 10 Platoon, the furthermost platoon, spotted large numbers of enemy concentrating to the west and north of D Company. The men in 10 Platoon strained to see in the gloom, but even at night it was clear that the enemy were gathering – some 200 or more.

Less than an hour later, the hammer fell. With bugles and whistles blowing, accompanied by a preliminary mortar barrage and machine-gun fire, the Chinese went in. They attacked D Company from three sides simultaneously, hoping that sheer weight of numbers and aggression would carry them up the hill and through the Canadian defences.

The Canadians, however, were dug-in and ready. Fatigue disappeared as they fired furious bursts at the attackers. Grenade after grenade, carefully arranged on the front lip of their trenches, were flung at the Chinese, bursting amongst them and stopping many of the attackers before they reached the summit of the steep slope.

But as Stalin is rumoured to have said, 'quantity has a quality of its own', and soon the Chinese were among the forward pits of 10 and 12 Platoon. They overran the critical Vickers machine-gun crew which was located near 12 Platoon, killing both of its members.

Also killed were two Korean ammunition porters, who had been taking cover nearby. Most official accounts completely forget to mention that there were a number of Korean porters on Hill 677, who had been instrumental in transporting the huge amount of ammunition required to service the Vickers machine guns. It is also likely that additional Korean porters remained in the vicinity of Battalion HQ, but again most records ignore both their presence and their contributions to the battalion.[247]

As more Chinese were swarming up the hill, desperate measures were called for. Lieutenant Mike Levy, commanding the exposed 10 Platoon, realized that their weapons were insufficient on their own to win this fight. He needed to bring in the 'big guns', both figuratively and literally. He knew that the only solution was to call in artillery support from the Kiwi gunners dangerously close to his own position in order to break up the Chinese attacks and give his men a fighting chance to hold their hill.

A 'danger close' fire mission is a call for artillery fire to be laid either within the usual safety distance of an artillery strike or, in extreme cases, right on top of your own position. Safety distances vary depending on the type and calibre of the ordinance used, but ordinarily an observer would not call a fire mission closer than 500 metres from his position unless he was either in an extremely well dug-in and fortified position or the danger of being overrun was so acute that it was worth the risk of a 'danger close' mission and the possibility of causing casualties to your own troops.

D Company now found itself in the latter position, a desperate situation that required desperate measures. Levy contacted Captain Mills, his company commander, and asked that artillery be brought down inside the safety distance and along the front of his forward sections. It was a dangerous move – unorthodox but necessary. The somewhat startled New Zealand signaller in the Regiment Command Post instinctively replied, 'but that's your own position', to which the Canadian on Hill 677 replied, 'correct ... and my Sunray [i.e. the commanding officer] wants that fire now'.[248]

Over the next forty minutes or so, the New Zealand batteries launched salvo after salvo of shells just forward of and right on top of D Company's position. Thankfully, the Canadians had dug good, strong trenches and defensive positions, so despite the noise, explosions and thunderous concussion of the shells falling all around them, they remained mightily shaken but largely unharmed.

In addition to the high-explosive 25-pdr shells which were set to detonate at ground level upon impact (also known as PD, or Point Detonation), the Canadians were lucky to have support from nearby American batteries. This was critical, since the Americans, unlike their New Zealand counterparts, also had a quantity of VT, or Variable Time, shells that would wreak untold havoc on the Chinese. A VT shell does not explode upon impact, but rather at a pre-set time above the ground, generally 50 metres, whereupon it explodes and sends a burst of hot metal shards and shrapnel towards the unfortunate enemy below. This is sometimes called an 'airburst', and the effect on unprotected infantry is frightening and deadly.

The combination of PD and VT shells raining down on the unprepared Chinese threw their initial charges into disarray. Unable to advance or even to hold their position under the deadly hail of artillery, the Chinese commander reluctantly withdrew his men back down the slope, leaving a trail of dead and wounded behind. However, as the shelling eventually slackened, the Chinese officer somehow whipped up his men and encouraged them forward for another attack. Bugles signalled the start of another attempt, but this too was stopped dead in its tracks by more dangerously close and deadly effective artillery fire.

Over the next few hours, the Chinese attempted at least six rushes against the hill, and were met on each occasion by both stubborn resistance from the defending Canadians and the deadly rain of artillery that made their efforts fruitless.

Numerous commentators singled out Lieutenant Levy of 10 Platoon for his coolness under fire and courageous decision to recommend that fire be brought down on or near his forward sections. By all accounts, his leadership in the forward lines was instrumental in directing the battle and keeping the morale of his men high, despite the very real danger that they were in. Levy commented after the battle: 'The Chinese are so aggressive they are taking heavy casualties. I am proud of my men, although greatly outnumbered and out gunned, they are holding the enemy. The artillery support is awesome, without it we could not sustain ourselves.'[249]

In addition to inspiring his men, Levy had to expose himself to enemy fire time and again as he tried to relay information to his company commander, Captain Mills. Levy only had a US walkie-talkie for communication with Mills, a simple but relatively weak radio that worked best in a 'line of sight' mode. With the intervening hill line and rocks between Levy and Mills, Levy had to keep bobbing left and right around the position to try to improve the radio signals. Each time he did so, he exposed himself to the advancing Chinese. But the risk paid off, allowing him to radio through clear and accurate descriptions of the battle to Mills, which were then relayed to the artillery units.

Levy was not the only one displaying unusual heroism during the morning's fighting. Private Kenneth Barwise would eventually be awarded the Military Medal for several actions that night and morning, including close-quarter fighting with the Chinese which killed several attackers, leading a platoon of C Company alone to the help reinforce D Company and dashing forward in the face of the enemy to retrieve ammunition for his comrades when they were desperately short of bullets and grenades.

Levy recalled:

> 'Through my field glasses I observed bandoleers of .303 ammo lying on the ground at 12 [Platoon]. Some of the men are out of ammunition. I called for volunteers to run the gauntlet of enemy fire to retrieve them. Private Barwise, who was earlier at that position, dashed though enemy fire to retrieve 10 or so bandoleers. He returned again to retrieve a box of grenades … Barwise dashed through the gully separating the two positions to run a distance of about 50 meters. He was also dodging enemy sniper fire.'[250]

The Canadians' steadfastness, combined with the gutsy move by Levy and Captain Mills to call in the deadly close artillery fire had made the difference and allowed the defenders to retain their position. The New Zealand gunners claimed they fired around 2,300 rounds of HE during the support mission for D Company.[251] It is likely that the Americans also fired a large number of shells, perhaps a similar amount. With such a weight of fire, it is unsurprising that it stymied even the most determined Chinese assaults. It is amazing that the Canadians did not suffer more from these tactics; their 'danger close' gamble – and gamble it surely was – had paid off.

With the coming of daylight, the Chinese attacks petered out and then stopped altogether as they withdrew from the immediate surrounds of Hill 677. As the day wore on, they pulled back further into the hills and protected gullies to the north. Desultory mortar fire and half-hearted sniping continued for a few hours, but when Stone sent a patrol from B Company to survey the base of his hill, they found there were no significant concentrations of enemy in the vicinity. The Chinese appeared to have withdrawn.

***

Despite the reduction in fire, lack of supplies and in particular ammunition weighed heavily on Stone's mind in the early hours of 25 April. The 2 PPCLI had expended a prodigious amount of ammunition of all types over the past twenty-four hours, and without an urgent resupply they would not be able to hold Hill 677 for much longer should the Chinese return. Road transport and resupply from Brigade HQ was not possible, given the continued threat of enemy action around the brigade position and in particular between Stone's location and A echelon (which held additional ammunition supplies) to the rear. Accordingly, Stone requested that an airdrop of ammunition and food be made directly onto his position. He recalled that 'six hours later, four C-119s dropped, by parachute, everything requested, including 81mm mortar ammunition. When it comes to supply, you cannot beat the US forces.'[252] On this point, Stone was wholly correct. The C-119s had flown all the way from Japan; the ability to receive an order, assemble the necessary supplies (including ammunition from two different sources – British and American), fly to Korea and then drop the ammunition and other stores with pinpoint accuracy on Stone's position was a testament to just how slick and sophisticated the US supply system was at this stage of the war.

Stone's other key concern was care for his casualties. After the war, Stone noted the *relatively* low casualties suffered by the Patricias at Kapyong – ten killed in action and twenty-eight wounded. But nearly forty dead and injured cannot in any way be considered a trivial number, and it would tax the surviving members of the battalion to arrange sufficient stretcher parties to care for the wounded, especially as the route back to the Field Ambulance was not immediately open.

As soldiers know all too well, the chances of a wounded man fatally succumbing to his wounds increases exponentially with the length of time he remains untreated. It is therefore critical that severely wounded men are evacuated to a Field Ambulance or hospital for specialist care as soon as possible. Fortunately, a helicopter was available for the Canadians, and in the early morning it was able to land near Stone's headquarters and evacuate some of the most seriously wounded.

***

As the day progressed, the enemy melted back into the hills to the north of Kapyong, the pressure on the Canadians thus being released. By mid-afternoon, the road south to Brigade HQ was once again open, meaning that additional supplies were able to be trucked up to the Canadians on Hill 677 and the wounded evacuated.

Later on the 25th, the long-promised Americans from the 5th Cavalry arrived and were able to retake Hill 504. As darkness fell, the Patricias noticed small groups of Chinese in the hills to the north and readied themselves for another night of combat. But it never came. The Chinese had had enough, using the darkness to withdraw their remaining troops and move their wounded and dead back to the north. The Battle of Kapyong had ended.

Chapter 24

Kapyong – The Assessment

The clashes at Kapyong is rightly regarded as 27 British Commonwealth Brigade's most significant battle. It involved stubborn and tough fighting against a determined enemy, as well as a professionally executed defence by the brigade's commanders and men.

To understand the scale of the battle, it is useful to consider some figures.

In terms of the Chinese troops involved in the attack on the brigade, the true figure will likely never be known. However, accounts suggest that it was the best part of the Chinese 118th Division which broke through the 6th ROK Division lines and attacked the Commonwealth troops, intent on annihilating them. If so, then there may have been up to 20,000 Chinese soldiers in the vicinity of Kapyong during the battle, facing the 3,000-plus men of the Commonwealth Brigade. On the other hand, the official Canadian account suggests that US intelligence sources had estimated Chinese attacking forces at around two regiments, approximately 6,000 or so.[253] Of course, neither side had its entire strength concentrated at any particular point during the battle, so overall numerical comparisons are in some ways unhelpful. A better comparison is between the numbers of troops opposing each other in a particular location. Again, exact numbers are unknown, but it is clear that there was an overall mismatch in troop numbers, with the Chinese able to muster several times the numbers that the Commonwealth and UN forces could bring to bear.

Other ways to understand the intensity of the battle are to look at ammunition expenditure and casualties. In relation to heavy ammunition expended, while it is not known how many rounds the supporting US artillery fired, the New Zealanders alone fired some 14,500 rounds of 25-pdr ammunition between 22 and 25 April, which is a prodigious amount of artillery shells for just four days. Fortunately, the Kiwis were sitting on a reasonable stockpile due to the expected refitting in the Kapyong Valley. But even so, still more ammunition needed to be flown in from Hong Kong and brought forward by the US Air Force in very short order in order to keep feeding the guns.[254]

Likewise, the invaluable Sherman tanks of A Company, 72nd Tank Battalion, expended more than 30,000 .30 calibre machine-gun rounds and 11,830 .50 calibre bullets. This was in addition to 162 rounds of 76mm ammunition from their main guns.[255]

There are better statistics in relation to casualties. The Aussies of 3 RAR in particular had endured a serious pummelling, suffering a high level of casualties. Just over thirty men were either killed outright or died shortly thereafter from wounds, and a further sixty were wounded.[256] Together, these casualties represent nearly a full company of men. The Patricias, meanwhile, lost ten men killed and twenty-three wounded,[257] and a further three men were killed in the attached US tank company, with twelve others wounded.

There is no way of knowing how many Chinese soldiers lost their lives in these actions. However, the number of dead Chinese estimated at different times during the battle suggest that the total must have been extremely high. For example, over 170 dead Chinese were counted after the attack on B Company in the early morning of 24 April. If it is accepted that the B Company attack was not the biggest and most costly assault on the Commonwealth forces at Kapyong, it can easily be assumed that the total number of Chinese killed must have been in the region of several hundred at the very least.

While exact statistics will likely never be available for this battle, all of the indicators (troops numbers, ammunition expended and casualties) clearly demonstrate that this was a very significant and consequential action for both sides. For the Chinese, defeat here marked the limit of exploitation of their Spring Offensive. Never again for the rest of the war would they be able to mount such an ambitious and large-scale offensive.

***

The commanders on the ground had differing views as to the significance of events at Kapyong. Many years later, in 1992, Lieutenant Colonel Stone looked back on the clash in which his 2 PPCLI was involved:

> 'Kapyong was not a great battle, as battles go. It was a good battle, well planned and well fought. Personally, I believe that Kapyong was the limit of the planned offensive of the Chinese at that time. Had that limit been five miles further south we should have been annihilated, as were the Gloucesters. The numbers that the Chinese were prepared to sacrifice against a position meant that eventually any unsupported battalion in defence must be overrun. The Chinese soldier is tough and brave. All that he lacked at the time of Kapyong were communications and supply … therefore, I say we were lucky that he did not persist with his attacks.'[258]

In the author's view, Stone's comments are a little too dismissive of the actions at Kapyong and the consequences of the battle. His words probably did not win him any friends among the men who endured the battle, in particular those who were wounded or the families of those who died. However, the comments reflect Stone's character – he was a brusque and straightforward man. The significance of Kapyong was only really understood sometime later. At the time, while it was regarded as a particularly tough and sticky battle, it was nevertheless felt to be just one of many similar actions that the Commonwealth Brigade had endured in nearly nine months of fighting.

For assessment of the impact of Kapyong, the author prefers the comments of Major Ben O'Dowd of 3 RAR: '[I]f the Kapyong battle was important it was because it was a well fought defensive battle against a numerically superior force ... it was a fighting withdrawal, not a rout.'[259] O'Dowd goes on to consider the strategic implications of the battle: 'The time bought by 3 RAR and later The Princess Patricia's Canadian Light Infantry Battalion allowed the United Nations Command to redeploy a force in the Chinese Army's path, averting the threat to Seoul from that direction.'[260]

What is undeniable is that 27 British Commonwealth Brigade performed magnificently and was instrumental in blunting the Chinese offensive in its sector. It would be dangerous to overemphasize the strategic importance of the battle, or to ascribe to 27 Bde's stand the only reason why the Chinese were stopped. That is not the case; it was the combination of huge losses and overextended supply lines that played the major part in General Peng's ultimate failure. On the other hand, it is undeniable that 27 Bde's stubborn defence was significant, playing its part in halting the previously headlong Chinese advance.

Recognizing the magnificent stand at Kapyong, both the Australian and Canadian battalions were honoured through a US Presidential Citation, which is still worn by members of those battalions to this day.

Controversies

There was never a big battle that did not generate its share controversies. Kapyong was no different, but the number of controversies were relatively limited and mainly revolved around the actions of certain key officers.

On the Australian side, there has been some speculation and minor criticism about Lieutenant Colonel Bruce Ferguson's actions in the first twenty-four hours at Kapyong. Questions mainly relate to his location during the critical opening hours of the battle – why had he failed to place himself in close co-ordination with his rifle companies, and why did he fail to at least establish a Tactical HQ forward?

Legitimate questions as they are, there is no doubt that Ferguson was heavily involved in this battle and showed a serious and sustained concern for his troops. Throughout the engagement, Ferguson brought the supplies they needed and ensured that the casualties were evacuated as soon as possible. Wilfred Millar from the US 72nd Tank Battalion remarked in correspondence after the war:

> 'I observed him personally as we continued our forays into and out of the area ... Colonel Ferguson was calm, acted like he was in total command of the situation and [showed by his demeanour that he believed] that his organisation would triumph. He demonstrated great concern for his wounded and encircled men and had no apparent regard for his personal safety.'[261]

Robert O'Neill, in the official history of Australia's part in the Korean War, also praises Ferguson as 'an outstanding soldier and battalion commander'[262] and appears to fully endorse the award of an immediate DSO for 'outstanding leadership', which was presented to him within a record-setting one week of the battle.[263] Overall, despite some minor criticisms, the record is clear that Ferguson was fully in command of his battalion and performed extremely well and bravely at Kapyong.

On the Canadian side, no criticism of Lieutenant Colonel Stone has been levelled. Whilst regarded as a tough and unforgiving soldier, all accounts of him note that he was a thoroughly professional and effective battlefield commander; it was his professionalism in setting the defence and his steadfastness throughout the ordeal which set the conditions for the Canadians' successful stand at Kapyong.

At the other end of the spectrum, opprobrium was reserved for the Canadian officer commanding D Company, Captain John 'Wally' Mills. Whilst Lieutenant Gray's detailed but slightly erratic account of the battle raises Lieutenant Mike Levy to almost hero status, the reverse is true for Mills. Gray's book is a distinct 'hatchet job' intended to demonstrate that Mills did not have the training or experience to be company commander and performed extremely poorly at Kapyong. The thrust of Gray's argument is that Mills placed his Company HQ rearward of his three rifle platoons, behind a relatively large stone feature. This feature gave his HQ additional protection but also, in Gray's view, cut him off from effectively leading his men. Besides being unable to directly see the battle in his forward platoons, it is said that Mills only placed one platoon on the ground and during the battle rarely went forward to see what was happening or give orders. When Levy asked to call in fire support almost on top of the D Company position, the implication is that Mills called through the request for fire, merely repeating what Levy has asked rather than considering it himself.

But is this criticism of Mills fair? While Gray's complaints appear to have some superficial merit and have been supported by a number of eyewitnesses, it needs to be recognized that different commanders have different approaches to leading their men. Captain Lilley, for example, inspired his B Company by frequently moving around the perimeter and directly encouraging his men. This was brave and admirable, but another school of thought says that it was foolhardy and needlessly exposed him to danger when his chief concern should have been to understand the battle, lead his men and arrange for the additional support that they required. This line of reasoning suggests that a commander needs to be close enough to see, but should not himself be, on the front line.

Furthermore, someone's view of a battle and what they believe is worthwhile – or not – can vary greatly depending on their location during the fighting, their experiences, their background, etc. In relation to the criminal law, it is often said that if you have ten eyewitnesses to any accident, you will get ten different accounts of what they saw. This is similarly true of a significant battle when most people are spending the greater part of their time worried about themselves and trying to stay alive, rather than closely monitoring and recording the actions of their fellows. It should also be noted that Gray himself, located with the battalion mortars, was not in a position to closely observe Mills' actions throughout the battle. Without any records left by Mills, we simply do not have his side of the story. It is thus impossible, after so long and without any better evidence, to have a clear answer to Gray's allegations.

***

All of these controversies only arose after the war, many years later. Of more immediate concern was the reorganization of the brigade which took place immediately following the battle.

At 0001hrs on 26 April 1951, 27 British Commonwealth Brigade ceased to be. The newly arrived Brigadier G. Taylor, DSO, took over command of the brigade, which was now renamed as 28 British Commonwealth Brigade. It too came under a new command, the newly raised 1st Commonwealth Division.

There was little time to commemorate their former brigade or celebrate the creation of the new one, as the whole unit was still in the process of pulling out of Kapyong, refitting and being relieved by the incoming US division. The men were also preparing themselves for an orderly move 8 miles south down the valley of the Pukhan River.

Nevertheless, the change of command was marked in some small ways. Brigadier Burke presented Ferguson with a captured North Korean flag, and also issued a special order of the day to all the men who had served in 27 British Commonwealth Brigade:

> 'Special Order of the Day by Brigadier BA Burke, DSO Commanding Officer 27 Bde
>
> '27 British Commonwealth Brigade ceases as such to exist but this is far from the case in respect of its units and personnel …
>
> 'The bonds and friendship formed in battle between British, Australia, Canadian, New Zealand and Indian soldiers of all ranks in 27 British Commonwealth Brigade during the last months can never be severed, and must be of lasting service to our King and Commonwealth which we serve.
>
> 'It has been my pride and honour to command this Brigade for the past month, spent nearly all in action as usual, and I venture to think that the splendid stand, and wholesome destruction of the enemy during the past action, will rank amongst their achievements and has been an appropriate finale.'[264]

Chapter 25

The Summing Up

The addition of the 28 British Commonwealth Brigade to the newly created 1st Commonwealth Division coincidentally marked the commencement of a wholly new phase in the fighting in South Korea. Never again would Communist forces attempt such enormous and costly offensives. Likewise, all further UN advances would be conservative and have limited objectives. Within a few months of the fighting at Kapyong, the war would solidify into a static, positional battle along the 38th parallel, where both sides would remain until the armistice was declared on 27 July 1953. Following Kapyong, the war would continue for a further two years while the diplomats attempted to hammer out an acceptable agreement. Neither side would again attempt the enormous manoeuvre battles that characterized the first nine months of the conflict. Rather, a nasty struggle of attrition now ensued, characterized by constant patrolling, a dark subterranean existence in deep dugouts and unceasing artillery fire.

When the war ended in 1953, the final ceasefire line was essentially at the same place where it had begun. Hardly any land had been gained by either side during three years of combat. However, the war caused colossal losses and the entire country was in ruins. It is estimated that over half a million South Korean soldiers died, as did a similar number of North Korean troops. More than 100,000 Chinese were killed (and hundreds of thousand wounded), while UN force fatalities amounted to nearly 40,000. Tragically, almost 2 million Korean civilians also lost their lives. In 1953, South Korea was ranked as one of the poorest countries in the world, with its economy shattered and industrial output well below its 1940 level.

Now, more than seventy years later, what is to be made of this enormous slaughter and destruction? What did the men of 27 British Commonwealth Brigade think of their part in this war, and what was achieved?

***

Korea is often referred to as the 'Forgotten War', and indeed it was forgotten by most of the citizens of the Commonwealth countries. Gray recalled: 'When I came home, people were more interested in talking about their tennis game rather than Korea.'[265] While the press was absorbed by stories of Korea in late 1950, by the end of the war in 1953, most of the citizenry around the Commonwealth and in the US had moved on and were more focused on domestic matters rather than a static and grinding conflict in a far-off Asian land. When Gunner John Christophers returned home to New Zealand in 1951, he would run into friends in his hometown who would say: 'Hey, I haven't seen you for a while. Where have you been?'[266]

Few of the returning Commonwealth Brigade troops expressed much in the way of concern, anger or outrage at apparent public apathy towards their efforts in Korea. Unlike the negative and often openly hostile reception that returning servicemen would endure a decade later during the Vietnam War, most Korean War veterans returned to a home that simply ignored them. Yet this was largely accepted by many of the returning Commonwealth veterans. 'I was a child of the Second World War, brought up on King and Country,' recalled Private Robert Searl of the Argylls. 'My generation was brought up as though [it was] almost a normal thing to have a war.'[267]

However, despite the apparent apathy of the general public and the stoic acceptance indicated by Searl's statement, the war had a profound effect on the men, the military and the countries of all who served with 27 British Commonwealth Brigade, and most importantly, on the country of South Korea.

The men

War affects every participant; no man escapes unscathed. The Korean War was no exception, and the experiences of that conflict would live with and affect every man who served with 27 Bde.

Experiences were varied, but Captain Allan Cull, a dental officer attached to the New Zealand contingent, summarised his experiences in Korea as follows:

> 'I think going to Korea had a great impact on my life. I think you grow up very quickly and learn to do things yourself and get on with things ... Under the same circumstances, I would volunteer again. It didn't affect me psychologically at all. I was one of the lucky ones.'[268]

Similar sentiment was reflected in the memoirs of a number of veterans, and most (but certainly not all) recorded that they believed what they did was worthwhile and would likely have still gone, even after everything they had been through.

On the other hand, and taking nothing away from Cull or any of the veterans who came away unscathed, there were a large number of men for whom the Korean War would leave an indelible mark. These included those killed or wounded during 27 Bde's tour in Korea. In his post-war report, Brigadier Coad listed the brigade casualties:[269]

26 Aug 1950 – 26 April 1951

	Officers			Other ranks		
Unit	**Killed**	**Missing**	**Wounded**	**Killed**	**Missing**	**Wounded**
Bde HQ	1	-	-	5	-	10
1 MX	5	-	3	26	2	91
1 ASH	5	-	9	25	3	121
3 RAR	4	-	5	83	2	286
2 PPCLI	1	-	2	31	-	78
16 Fd Regt	1	-	-	2	-	4
Total:	**17**	**-**	**19**	**172**	**7**	**590**

These casualty figures, some 800 men in total, represent an entire battalion's worth of soldiers either killed or wounded. The numbers killed are almost unthinkable by today's standards, but in the aftermath of the Second World War were seen as tragic but largely 'to be expected'. What is often overlooked, however, are the very many wounded, some of them terribly so with injuries from which they would never fully recover. Often when a man was wounded, he would effectively 'disappear from history', and it is rare to find any further mention of him in the histories of the war. It is only occasionally, for example the case of Lieutenant Ken MacGregor and the wounds he suffered when assaulting the Honeycomb at Kapyong, that we learn about the consequences of such injuries; MacGregor had his jaw wired and was fed through a straw for fourteen months. But for the men who endured these wounds, as well as their families, the injuries kept the war alive and 'real' for them for many years – even decades – to come.

Even men who escaped Korea with no visible wounds were also changed. Private Searl said: 'The war in Korea changed me. I never gloated over seeing enemy dead. I always felt it was some poor sods father, brother, son.'[270] Others also became melancholic when remembering the war. James Stone was obviously in a reflective mood when he quoted the Robert Southey poem *The Battle of Blenheim* in his 1992 memoir of the Battle of Kapyong. The poem, which discusses the horrors of the fighting at Blenheim in 1704, ends with the lines:

'What they killed each other for
I cannot well make out.
But men say, quoth he,
It was a famous victory.'

It is a poem imbibed with much pathos, one that is regularly quoted in relation to the ultimate futility of war. I am not sure if a soldier such as Stone would agree that all war was futile or unnecessary in every case, but even he recognized the very great cost that was to be paid when engaging in conflict. I suspect that many of his fellow veterans held similar views.

Commonwealth soldiers

One area of unanimity amongst the 27 Bde veterans was the high regard in which each force held their fellow Commonwealth soldiers. All of the memoirs and histories note the almost universal appreciation for each other, with many commenting that they very much enjoyed working with the other Commonwealth units. On a professional level, the common doctrine, weapons, equipment and general ways of working all likely contributed to an affinity between the contributing countries and troops. Likewise, success in battle and a constant steadfastness in the face of the enemy, which was displayed by all of the contingents, also played a part. Soldiers respect other soldiers who do their bit and fight on in the face of adversity. All the Commonwealth soldiers in 27 Bde showed this grit and determination, and this likely helped in fostering warm ties between the units.

Besides professionalism and success in battle, many 27 Bde veterans also noted the great warmth, friendship, comradeship and respect between the contingents. Such mutual respect and friendship appears to have operated at all levels, from brigade commander all the way down to private. Willoughby commented in his *Diaries* that the troops of the various Commonwealth countries became very tight, and as a result there were rarely any serious jokes or sharp comments at each other's expense.[271] However, he went on to say that all other countries were 'fair game', with the Commonwealth troops delighting in pointing out the supposed failings of their Americans allies. Yet such jokes were generally good-natured, as all of the Commonwealth soldiers realized that the Americans – for all their failings – were shouldering the bulk of the burden of supporting South Korea; without their lifesaving logistical prowess, provision of artillery and air support, all UN operations would have quickly ground to a halt.

With all the above said, there were perhaps more prosaic reasons to prefer soldiering within a Commonwealth unit rather than a US one. Private Kolanchey of 2 PPCLI wryly noted: '[W]e got the rum ration and the odd beer ration [in 27 BCB] … if we were with a US unit we would only have got a Pepsi Cola!'[272]

A Commonwealth force?

In a memo noting the formation of a Commonwealth Division for Korea, an excited under-secretary of the Commonwealth Relations Office wrote: 'An integrated Division comprising Canadian, Australian, New Zealand and possibly Indian units, besides those from the United Kingdom, would most powerfully demonstrate to world opinion the capacity of the Commonwealth to act in concert in times of need.'[273]

While the unnamed official was correct in that the Commonwealth Brigades, and eventually Division, did demonstrate the ability of Commonwealth forces to act together, the effect should not be overstated. Nor was the remarkable co-operation in 1950–51 a harbinger of further and closer military ties. The modern Commonwealth was never intended to be a military alliance, and the experiences in Korea in 1950–51 did not turn it into one. Historian Ian McGibbon noted: '[T]he Commonwealth as a framework for military cooperation was on the wane, even as Commonwealth troops stood shoulder to shoulder in Korea.'[274]

While the troop-contributing countries all appreciated the overarching Commonwealth structure that 27 Bde provided, it was only an expedient and did not lead to the forming of any permanent Commonwealth military alliance. Although familial bonds and common military background between the five Commonwealth armies were strong, the fact was that each country's national interest in relation to defence was becoming more divergent.

India was the clearest example of this growing divergence, indicated clearly by its decision to only send medical rather than fighting troops. India's recent independence from Britain and avowed neutrality suggested that it should no longer be aligned with other Commonwealth forces. However, the close ties between the British and Indian militaries and the need for an overarching administrative and protection structure within which to base the Indian Field Ambulance, made service with the Commonwealth forces a logical and prudent step. This would, however, be the high point of India's post-independence military co-operation with Britain; never again would India serve within a Commonwealth military structure.

Even the 'traditional' dominion countries (Australia, Canada and New Zealand) were in the process of pulling further away from Britain in a military sense. Some of this was due to experiences during the Second World War and a growing desire in each country that their military forces be led by their own nationals rather than British commanders. This sentiment was particularly acute in respect of the Canadians, who felt that their troops had sometimes been badly let down during the global war and thrown into hopeless situations, such as the disastrous last-ditch defence of Hong Kong or the Dieppe raid.

The other, and perhaps more important, factor was that Australia, Canada and New Zealand were becoming more closely aligned to the US in a strategic sense. The Second World War had seen the relative decline of Britain and the ascendency of the United States, so it was logical that there would be realignment towards the US. In addition, geography and recognition of a new world order played a role. In the case of Canada, it was logical to look to the US, its immediate neighbour and a superpower, as the likely lynchpin of its future defence. Likewise, sustained fighting in the Pacific during the Second World War and the threat of invasion rammed home to Australians (and New Zealanders, to a lesser degree) that the US, as a Pacific nation, was of infinitely more strategic relevance to its future security than the old ties to Britain.

That said, in the 1950s, the Commonwealth still held great value to Australians, Canadians and New Zealanders, allowing them to obtain information and participate in international affairs at a higher level than they might have if attempting to go it alone. Australian historian Robert O'Neill noted:

> 'The United States consulted Britain on most sensitive issues but Australia had to follow events at a distance when urgent action was taken. Australia's membership of the Commonwealth enhanced its potential for influence on the United States through both the direct relationship between Australia and Britain and through Australia's capacity to argue the case for allied unity within Commonwealth councils.'[275]

Win, loss, draw?

When the armistice was signed in 1953, there was little in the way of celebration amongst the UN forces. Long gone were the heady days of clear operational victories such as the Inchon landings or even Kapyong. Rather, amongst all of the parties, the armistice merely signified a ceasefire, and not much else. The almost two years of negotiations had worn down all of the participants, to the point that even when signatures were finally put to paper, it was all a bit of an anti-climax. The citizens of most UN countries had already mentally moved on and largely forgotten the war several years ago. The politicians were close behind. Korea was not a victory, but neither was it exactly a loss. It was at the time regarded as at best a draw, one that was soon to be forgotten by almost all of the participants.

There was also very little done to jog the collective memory within UN force-contributing countries. Unlike the clear victories following the Second World War, there were no parades, marches or official recognition of any kind to mark the end of the war. Men who signed up specifically to serve in Korea were quietly demobilized upon completion of their contracts, after which they slipped back into civilian life.

Even the many UN war dead did little to remind anyone outside of their immediate families of the sacrifices and courage displayed by the UN troops during the war. This was particularly marked in relation to Commonwealth dead, who, in accordance with common practice at the time, were not repatriated to their home countries for burial, but rather were interred in Korea at the Busan (Pusan) UN Military Cemetery. Being so far away from their families, particularly at a time when international air travel was not common, they were soon forgotten.

This immediate post-conflict amnesia and collective forgetting would continue for decades. As an example, official memorials to the veterans who fought in Korea would only be erected in national capitals decades later: Washington in 1995, Canberra in 1999 and London in 2014, some sixty years after the conclusion of the war. Considering the scale of the fighting, the enormous contribution of men and materiel and the consequences if the UN had lost, it is difficult to understand why so little attention or official recognition was given to the conflict until many decades after its conclusion.

Did this lead to bitterness and disappointment on the part of the Commonwealth men who served with 27 Bde? It would certainly be understandable if it did so, and perhaps it did, at least initially. Men often rankled at the suggestion that Korea was nothing more than a 'police action' – not a 'real' war like the World Wars. Ray Parry for one bridled at this type of talk, saying: '[It] wasn't a policing action [and it is] ignorance on [the] part of people who say this. The casualties on both sides were appalling.'[276]. But the early 1950s was a time when people tended to just get on with their lives, and return to either their civilian careers or peacetime soldiering following their deployment abroad.

Nevertheless, with the passage of time, it appears now that almost all of the veterans from the Commonwealth Brigade universally say that what they did was worthwhile. One of the key reasons is the clear impact that the defence of South Korea has had on the modern Republic of Korea. Sergeant Alex Sim of 2 PPCLI made the very good point that however much the war was forgotten in Canada (and the UK, Australia, etc), it was certainly not forgotten by the Koreans. To this day, South Koreans actively commemorate the war, contribute to war memorials around the world and regularly invite UN and Commonwealth veterans back to Korea for commemoration services. The South Koreans know that their modern and highly successful nation, while certainly a product of their own hard work and ingenuity, would have nevertheless been still-born if UN forces had not come to the young country's rescue in the dark days of 1950.

With the benefit of some seventy-five years of hindsight, it is plain to see that the Korean War was a stunning strategic victory for the UN forces. Irrespective of the fact that the war ended basically where it had started, South Korea is now one of the most prosperous, advanced and democratic countries in the world. The North failed in its aims to unify the Koreas, and even with the massive assistance of its neighbour to the north, China, was unable to defeat the South.

Far from being a draw, I would characterize the effect of the UN forces fighting in Korea as an overwhelming victory – at least strategically. Of course, there are many factors which have contributed to South Korea's current prosperity, but without the efforts of the UN troops between 1950 and 1953 – including the work of 27 Bde – it could have been very different indeed.

***

The Korean War would be the last time that Britain, Australia, New Zealand, India and Canada fought together as a combined force under a Commonwealth banner. It was a final Commonwealth military hurrah, but it was far from being a token force. Rather, the men of 27 British Commonwealth Brigade made a very real and substantial contribution to the UN effort and the defence of South Korea. Their skill and bravery are still rightly and appropriately remembered by the people of today's South Korea.

In 2005, 3 RAR's Ray Parry summed up his feelings about the war: 'I don't have any regrets. But I thank the Lord I got out of it in once piece … I just want people to remember that their freedom doesn't come free. It is pretty expensive.'[277]

Bibliography

Books

1. Barclay, C.N., *First Commonwealth Division* (Aldershot: Gale & Polden Limited, 1954)
2. Bartlett, Norman, *With the Australians in Korea* (Canberra: Australian War Memorial, 1954)
3. Bowers, William, *Passing the Test* (Lexington: University Press of Kentucky, 2011) (see Chapter 4, 'Tanks Above Kapyong')
4. Breen, Bob, *The Battle of Kapyong* (Australia: Headquarters Training Command, 1992)
5. Collins, Michael, *Having Been a Soldier* (Hamish Hamilton, 1969)
6. Cunningham-Boothe, Ashley & Farrar, Peter, *British Forces in the Korean War* (British Korean Veterans Association, 1988)
7. Desmond, Pip, *The War that Never Ended* (London: Penguin Books, 2013)
8. Gallaway, Jack, *The Last Call of the Bugle – The Long Road to Kapyong* (Brisbane: University of Queensland Press, 1994)
9. Farrar-Hockley, Anthony, *The British Part in the Korean War Vols 1 & 2* (London: HMSO, 1995) London
10. Gray, Hub, *Beyond the Danger Close* (Calgary, Alberta: Bunker to Bunker Publishing, 2003)
11. Grey, Jeffery, *The Australian Army* (Oxford University Press, 2001)
12. Grey, Jeffery, *The Commonwealth Armies and the Korean War* (Manchester: Manchester University Press, 1988)
13. Hastings, Max, *The Korean War* (Simon & Schuster, 1987)
14. Heinl, Robert Debs, *Victory at High Tide* (London: Leo Cooper, 1972)
15. Johnston, William, *A War of Patrols – Canadian Army Operations in Korea* (Vancouver: UBC Press, 2003)
16. Li Xiaobing, *China's Battle for Korea: The 1951 Spring Offensive* (Bloomington: Indiana University Press, 2014)
17. Malcolm, George Ian of Poltalloch, *The Argylls in Korea* (Edinburgh: Thomas Nelson and Sons, 1952)
18. Mattis, Jim & West, Bing, *Call Sign Chaos* (New York: Random House Publishing Group, 2019)
19. MacArthur, Douglas, *A Soldier Speaks* (New York: Fredrick A. Praeger, 1965)

20. McGibbon, Ian, *New Zealand and the Korean War Vols 1 and 2* (Oxford University Press, 1992/1996)
21. O'Dowd, Ben, *In Valiant Company* (Brisbane: University of Queensland Press, 2000)
22. O'Neill, Robert, *Australia in the Korean War Vols I & II* (The Australian War Memorial, 1985)
23. Paik Sun Yup, *From Pusan to Panmunjom* (Brassey's US Inc, 1992)
24. Peters, Richard & Li, Xiaobing, *Voices from the Korean War: Personal Stories of American, Korean, and Chinese Soldiers* (Lexington: The University Press of Kentucky, 2004)
25. Ridgeway, Matthew, *The Korean War* (Doubleday, 1967)
26. Shipster, John, *Mist Over the Rice Fields* (Barnsley: Pen & Sword, 2000)
27. Shipster, John (ed.), *The Diehards in Korea* (1975)
28. Stratemeyer, George, *The Three Wars of LT GEN George E Stratemeyer – His Korean War Diary* (Air Force History and Museums Program, US Govt Printing Office, 1999)
29. Wilson, David, *The Sum of Things* (Kent: Staplehurst, 2001)
30. Wood, Herbert Fairley, *Strange Battleground – The Official History of the Canadian Army in Korea* (Ottawa: Queen's Printer and Controller of Stationary, 1966)

Articles

1. Argent, Alf, '4.2 Inch Mortar in Korea', *The Australian Army Journal* (Nov 1951)
2. Banerjee, N.B., '60 Para Field Ambulance', *Army Medical Corp Reunion Souvenir Brochure* (1959)
3. Coad, B.A., 'The Land Campaign in Korea, *The Journal of the Royal United Services Institute*, Vol. XCVII (Feb 1952)
4. Farrar-Hockley, A., 'Reminiscence of the Chinese People's Volunteers in the Korean War', *The China Quarterly*, No. 98 (June 1984)
5. Goswami, P.K., 'India's Contribution in the UN Peacekeeping Mission in Korea: Role of 60 Parachute (Para) Field Ambulance', *Journal of the United Services Institution of India*, Vol. CLIII, No. 631 (Jan–Mar 2023)
6. Harrison, Mark, 'Casualty Evacuation in Korea, 1950–53: The British Experience', *Korean Journal of Medical History* (Aug 2023)
7. O'Dowd, Ben, 'The Battle of Kapyong: From the Inside', Australian War Memorial 2020.22.250 (1991)
8. Stone, J.R., 'Memoir: Kapyong', *Infantry Journal* (Autumn 1992)
9. Willoughby, J., 'Korea – Point 112', *British Army Journal*, Vol. 7 (1952), p.76

War Diaries

1. HQ 27 British Commonwealth Brigade, Aug 1950 – Apr 1951 (WO 281/1233)
2. 1st Battalion, The Middlesex Regiment, Aug 1950 – Nov 1950 (WO 281/1164)
3. 1st Battalion, Argyll and Sutherland Highlanders, Aug 1950 – Mar 1951 (WO 281/1166)

4. 3rd Battalion, Royal Australian Regiment, Jul 1950 – Apr 1951 (AWM85)
5. 16 Field Regiment, Apr 1951 – Dec 1951 (NZ National Archives R10131808)
6. 2nd Battalion, Princess Patricia's Canadian Light Infantry, Dec 1950 – Apr 1951

Official papers

1. 'ATIS Interrogation Report No. 2092, Hong, Kwan To' (26 Oct 1950)
2. 'CAOD Correspondence with LTCOL Joslen (19 Dec 1956)
3. 'COAD Report on the Operations of the 27th British Infantry Brigade by MAJ-GEN Coad' (IWM 18379)
4. 'Command Reports of the 2nd Chemical Mortar Battalion in Korea', https://www.4point2.org/2cmb.htm
5. 'DEFE 11/201 Bouchier CAB 58 to MOD (Chiefs of Staff)' (25 Sept 1950)
6. 'DEFE 11/201 Bouchier CAB 61 to MOD (Chiefs of Staff)' (27 Sept 1950)
7. 'DEFE 11/201 Bouchier to MOD' (2 Oct 1950)
8. 'MacKenzie Report – 2 PPCLI Action Kapyong Area – 23-26 Apr 1951' (26 Nov 1954), DHH 145. 2P7013(05)
9. 'Enemy Tactics, Techniques and Doctrine' (Sept 1951), Headquarters IX Corp, G-2 Section, US Army, Korea
10. 'UN Security Council Resolution No. 82 (25 July 1950), https://undocs.org/
11. 'UN Security Council Resolution No. 83' (27 July 1950), https://undocs.org/

Recommendations/ Citations for Honours and Awards

1. MAJ Muir, VC, Jan 1951 (WO 32-14012)
2. MAJ Banerjee, MVC, 29 Mar 1951 (https://www.gallantryawards.gov.in/)
3. PTE Barwise, MM (reproduced in Gray, p.233)
4. BRIG Coad, DSO, May 1945 (WO 373-55-2)
5. WO2 Collett, MM, Nov 1950 (WO 373-114-7)
6. PTE Fairhurst – Bronze Star – Nov 1950 (27Bde WD)
7. 2LT Lawrence, MC, Jan 1951 (WO 373-114-6)
8. LTCOL Mann, DSO, Nov 1950 (WO 373-114-3)
9. CAPT Moore (US Army), MC, Nov 1950 (WO 373/142/37)
10. LBDR McCubbin, MM, Apr 1951 (WO 373-114-69)
11. PTE Mitchell, DCM (reproduced in Gray, p.230)
12. LT Montgomerie, MC (WO 373-114-107)
13. CPL Parry, MM, Jan 1952 (WO 373-115/20)
14. LTCOL Rangaraj, MVC, Mar 1951 (https://www.gallantryawards.gov.in/)
15. 2LT Reed, MC, Jun 1951 (WO 373-114-100)
16. CAPT Roxburgh, MC, Apr 1951 (WO 373-114-45)
17. CPL Sweeny, MM, Nov 1950 (WO 373-114-5)
18. PTE Watts, Bronze Star – Nov 1950 (1 ASH WD)

Interviews and Oral Recordings

1. Beard, Don (3 RAR), Oral History (AWM No. 9157730)
2. Fairhurst, Joseph Levi (1 ASH), Oral History (IWM No. 18347)
3. Gray, Hub (2 PPCLI), The Military Museums of Calgary, Alberta (https://youtu.be/yspKwhL_4nE)
4. Kolanchey, John (2 PPCLI), Oral History (IWM No. 19386)
5. Man, Andrew (1 MX), Oral History (IWM No. 9537)
6. Morrison, Alan (3 RAR), Oral History Recording (AWM No. S02655)
7. Parry, Raymond (3 RAR), Oral History (AWM No. 25572)
8. Peet, Richard (1 ASH), Oral History (IWM No. 18344)
9. Reed, Barry, (1 MX), Oral History Transcript, National Army Museum, 2001-02-397
10. Rendell, Dennis Bossey, Oral History (IWM No. 19055)
11. Searl, Robert (1 ASH), Oral History (IWM No. 18470)
12. Sim, Alexander (2 PPCLI), The Military Museums of Calgary, Alberta, (https://youtu.be/8Jc0dChdNe0)

Diaries and Personal Papers

1. Coad to Sexton, Letter (20 Jan 1973)
2. Harrop, David, *Life Story*, Ch. 13 and 14 (Author's collection)
3. Harrop, David, *Korean War Diary December 15 1950 – May 27 1951* (Author's collection)
4. Willoughby Diaries (IWM 12980)
5. Man, Andrew Morrice, *The Life Story of Andrew Morrice Man DSO OBE* (1990) (IWM 4482)
6. Lewtas, Keith, *Bengazi to Sinanjui – A True Account of a Soldier's Experiences* (Lewtas Memoir) (AWM 2019.22.109)
7. Knowles, Pat, *A Rifleman's View of the Battle of Kapyong* (AWM 2020.22.249)

Other

1. *The Die-Hards – The Journal of the Middlesex Regiment* (1950)
2. *New York Times*, 'US Planes Strafe British in Error; 60 Are Casualties' (24 Sept 1950)
3. *The Times*, 'Accidental Attack of British' (25 Sept 1950)
4. Peter C. Le P. Jones, 'The Argylls in Korea, August 1950 – April 1951, https://members.optusnet.com.au/~simjones/pjkorea/index.htm#hill282
5. 'A Hill in Korea', Britain's Small Wars website, www.britains-smallwars.com
6. *Washington Evening Star*, 'Home by Christmas remark just "Hope" MacArthur explains' (29 Nov 1950)

Acknowledgments

Writing a book which hopes to explore in any detail those harrowing first nine months of the war in Korea could not be accomplished by the efforts of one person alone. And so it was with this book, which only came to fruition with the work, generosity and support of a great many people.

My thanks firstly go to David Harrop. David was a young second lieutenant in the Middlesex Regiment in 1950/1951, serving in both Hong Kong and Korea. David has been very generous in sharing his war diaries with me as well as reviewing and commenting on sections of the manuscript relating to actions which he participated in. Thank you, David.

In terms of finding and collating a large portion of primary sources, appreciation goes to my long-suffering UK-based researcher, Dr Kevin Jones. This is our second project together, and this book would have been the poorer without Kevin's dogged persistence in digging up sources. I am also grateful to Richard Palimaka of the Canadian Army Command and Staff College for providing hard-to-find documents relating to the Canadian contribution, and to current and former officers of India's 60 Para Field Hospital for providing information and images relating to India's contribution during the war.

Dr Rob Lyman, MBE, who has also published a highly regarded work on the Korean War, has been a strong supporter of this project and to my development as a historian more generally. I have expressed it before, but once again, thank you.

Finally, while it is customary to thank one's family, saying it here doesn't make it any less heartfelt. This book simply would not have been possible without the support and patience of my family. Thank you, Sasha, Daniel, Catherine and Andrew.

Notes

1. Technically, the term 'British Commonwealth' was abolished in 1949 following the London Declaration, and the simple word 'Commonwealth' was to be used instead. Nevertheless, 'British Commonwealth' was frequently used colloquially in the early 1950s, particularly in relation to 27 Commonwealth Brigade, which was more often referred to as 27 British Commonwealth Brigade.
2. Operation Pokpung, or Pokpung-ho, was the North Korean name for the invasion – literally 'Operation Storm'.
3. Paik, *From Pusan to Panmunjom*, p.7.
4. 1st ROK Artillery Battalion consisted of fifteen old 105mm field guns. While welcome, these were completely inadequate for the task at hand, being seriously outranged by the larger field guns of the NKPA. Just as importantly, ammunition was in very short supply, such that it was totally exhausted by the end of the third day of fighting.
5. Paik, p.14.
6. Paik, p.15.
7. Ridgeway, p.12.
8. UN Security Council Resolution No. 82, 25 July 1950.
9. UN Security Council Resolution No. 83, 27 July 1950.
10. Paik, p.20.
11. The Chinese name for Hong Kong means 'fragrant harbour'. The brigade would soon learn that their destination, Pusan in South Korea, also had a certain 'fragrance' of its own.
12. The 57th refers to one of 1 MX's former regiments, the 57th West Middlesex Regiment of Foot.
13. David Harrop Diary, p.15.
14. Willoughby Diary 3.4, 19 Apr 1950. The Duchess of Richmond's Ball was a famous party hosted for British officers in Brussels on 15 June 1815, the night before the Battle of Quatre Bras.
15. Correspondence Coad to Sexton, 20 Jan 1973.
16. Correspondence Coad to Sexton, 20 Jan 1973.
17. *The Die Hards Journal*, vol. 9-7, Sept 1950, p.216.
18. Willoughby Diary 3.5, 31 Aug 1951.
19. CAOD Correspondence with LTCOL Joslen, 19 Dec 1956.
20. *War of Patrols*, p.79.

21. CAOD Correspondence with LTCOL Joslen, 19 Dec 1956.
22. COAD Report – Schedule – British rations brought by Brigade.
23. Andrew Man, Oral History.
24. Ridgeway, *The Korean War*, p.2.
25. Willoughby Diary 3.5, 5 Sept 1950.
26. *The Argylls in Korea*, p.14.
27. ATIS Interrogation Report No. 2092, Hong, Kwan To.
28. Paik, p.37.
29. Paik, p.41.
30. Ridgeway, p.33.
31. Farrar-Hockley, *The British Part in the Korean War Part 1*, p.146, quoting from Heinl, Robert Debs, *Victory at High Tide*, p.43.
32. Coad's report was originally classified 'TOP SECRET'. Even when reclassified at a later date, it was still marked as 'GUARD', meaning that it was only to be released to British readers and not to Americans. Noting some of the less-than-complimentary comments about his US allies, it is not hard to see why the GUARD classification was thought necessary.
33. 27 Bde War Diary, 21 Sept 1950.
34. 27 Bde War Diary, 20 Sept 1950.
35. Coad Report, Part II.
36. *The Diehards in Korea*, p.11.
37. Willoughby Diary 3.6, 12 Sept 1950.
38. *The Die-Hards in Korea*, p.11.
39. Fairhurst, Oral History.
40. While not a critical discrepancy, the American fire support brought down in aid of Willoughby's assault is a good example of how two 'eyewitness accounts' can differ wildly. While both Willoughby and Man note that the American fire support was called in by an American spotter plane, without a call for fire from the British, Man claims that it was brought too close to Willoughby's men and that it was only Man's actions which resulted in it being called off. Willoughby, on the other hand, credits it for giving him additional suppressing fire to get his men towards the hill. I have preferred Willoughby's account, as it was written in his diary shortly after the attack, whereas Man's account featured in an article he penned many years after the fact.
41. Rendell, Oral History
42. Willoughby Diary 3.7, 25 Sept 1950.
43. Lawrence, MC recommendation.
44. Willoughby Diary 3.7, 25 Sept 1950.
45. Willoughby Diary 3.7, 27 Sept 1950.
46. 1 ASH War Diary, 22 Sept 1950, Appendix E2.
47. As an interesting side note, as the war progressed, tank dozers were frequently used to create a type of dirt ramp upon which tanks could place themselves to allow their main guns to be angled higher than normal. This allowed the tanks

to provide support at higher elevations on the numerous hills and features of the Korean landscape. See for example Gray, p.26.

48. Kolanchey says that the Canadians also quickly disposed of their steel helmets, feeling that they were just too heavy and a useless encumbrance; see Kolanchey, Oral History, Reel 2.
49. Fairhurst, Oral History.
50. CPL Sweeny, Military Medal recommendation.
51. 1 ASH War Diary.
52. *The Argylls in Korea*, p.21.
53. Peet, Oral History.
54. DEFE 11-201 Cable 58 from Bouchier to Chief of Staff, 25 Sept 1950.
55. Willoughby Diary 3.7, 25 Sept 1950.
56· Peter C. Le P. Jones, *Argylls in Korea*, online.
57. 1 ASH War Diary, 23 Sept 1950, Gordon-Ingram Report.
58. Peet, Oral History.
59. Watts, Bronze Star citation.
60. 1 ASH War Diary, 23 Sept 1950, Gordon-Ingram Report.
61. 1 ASH War Diary, Appendix F.
62. 1 ASH War Diary, 23 Sept 1950, Gordon-Ingram Report.
63. WO2 Collett, Military Medal citation.
64. Fairhurst Oral History and 27 Bde War Diary.
65. DEFE 11-201 Cable 63 from Bouchier to Chief of Staff, 28 Sept 1950.
66. Casualties were: 1 ASH: Officers 2 KIA, 4 WIA; OR 12 KIA, 72 WIA and 4 missing. 1 MX: OR 1 KIA, 3 WIA – see Bouchier to MOD, 2 Oct 1950.
67. 1 ASH War Diary, 23 Sept 1950.
68. DEFE 11-201 Cable 61 from Bouchier to Chief of Staff, 27 Sept 1950.
69. Muir, VC citation.
70. 1 ASH War Diary, Appendix F.
71. *New York Times*, 'US Planes Strafe British in Error; 60 Are Casualties', 24 Sept 1950.
72. *The Times*, 'Accidental Attack of British', 25 Sept 1950.
73. *The Times*, 'Accidental Attack of British', 25 Sept 1950.
74. Wilson, Oral History.
75. DEFE 11-201 Cable 59 from Bouchier to Chief of Staff, 26 Sept 1950.
76. Wilson, Oral History.
77. Stratemeyer, p.205.
78. *The Argylls in Korea*, p.25.
79. Wilson, *The Sum of Things*, p.165.
80. Peet, Oral History.
81. *The Australian Army*, p.170.
82. Lewtas Memoir, p.130.
83. 3 RAR War Diary, 21 July 1950.
84. O'Dowd, *In Valiant Company*, p.33.

85. 3 RAR War Diary, 8 Sept 1950.
86. Gallaway, p.95.
87. O'Dowd, *In Valiant Company*, p.7.
88. DEFE 11-201 Cable 58 from Bouchier to Chief of Staff, 25 Sept 1950.
89. DEFE 11-201 Cable 58 from Bouchier to Chief of Staff, 25 Sept 1950.
90. COAD Report, Part II.
91. MacArthur, *A Soldier Speaks*, p.225.
92. 3 RAR War Diary, 13 Oct 1950.
93. 3 RAR War Diary, 6 Oct 1950.
94. COAD Report, Part II.
95. COAD Report, Part III.
96. Morrison, Oral Interview.
97. Morrison, Oral Interview.
98. George Cross Warrants, 24 Sept 1940.
99. Gallaway, p.87.
100. It is a tradition in many Commonwealth armies that the band members become stretcher bearers and first aiders during times of conflict.
101. *With the Australians in Korea*, p.33.
102. 3 RAR War Diary, 26 Oct 1950
103. 3 RAR War Diary, Oct 1950.
104. 3 RAR War Diary, Oct 1950.
105. Several accounts note that Coad was very moved by Green's death and kept a photograph of the two of them on his desk for the rest of his life.
106. Gallaway notes that despite Green being widely regarded as the very best battalion commander in 27 Bde, he received no awards or medals for his service in Korea besides the usual campaign medal awarded to all participants. Due to Ministry of Defence policy at that time, only the Victoria Cross or a Mentioned in Dispatches – the very highest and very lowest rung on the Commonwealth honours list – could be awarded posthumously. As Charlie Green fitted neither category, he got nothing – at least from the British or Australians. He was, however, awarded a posthumous Silver Star from the more generous Americans – some small consolation and recognition of Green's short but outsized contribution to 27 Bde and the UN forces' efforts in Korea.
107. Gallaway, p.98.
108. Li Xiaobing, p.xvi.
109. Paik, p.89.
110. Paik, p.86.
111. Paik, p.95.
112. Paik, p.97, quoting an article written by Chinese Deputy Commander Teng Hua entitled 'Military Lessons Bulletin', dated 20 Nov 1950.
113. This maxim is attributed to the ancient Chinese military scholar Sun Tzu in his book *The Art of War*. The full quote is: 'If you know the enemy and know yourself, you need not fear the result of a hundred battles. If you know yourself but not the

enemy, for every victory gained you will also suffer a defeat. If you know neither the enemy nor yourself, you will succumb in every battle.'

114. Paik, p.89.
115. 27 Bde War Diary, 1 Nov 1950.
116. Grey, *Commonwealth Armies*, p.76.
117. Wilson, p.174.
118. Moore, MC citation.
119. 1 ASH War Diary, Nov 1950, Appendix K, 'A Noisy Guy Fawkes Day'.
120. Coad Report, p.18.
121. Gallaway, p.114.
122. 'A Hill in Korea'.
123. 27 Bde War Diary, 5 Nov 1950.
124. 27 Bde War Diary, 5 Nov 1950.
125. O'Dowd, p.22.
126. Gallaway, p.123.
127. Gallaway, p.120, reporting the recollection of the D Company radio operator, Stewart Duncan.
128. Algy Clark interview in Gallaway, p.118.
129. Walsh interview in Gallaway, p.124.
130. Beard interview, p.9.
131. Beard interview, p.9.
132. 1 ASH War Diary, Nov 1950, Appendix K, 'A Noisy Guy Fawkes Day'.
133. 'Enemy Tactics, Techniques and Doctrine', p.30.
134. *Voices from the Korean War*, p.91.
135. Wilson, p.177.
136. Ridgeway, p.58.
137. Willoughby Diary 3.9, 10 Nov 1950.
138. Willoughby Diary 3.9, 13 Nov 1950.
139. Wilson, p.174.
140. Willoughby Diary 3.9, 13 Nov 1950.
141. 3 RAR War Diary, Nov 1950.
142. 27 Bde War Diary, 14 Nov 1950.
143. 27 Bde War Diary, 22 Nov 1950.
144. Barry Reed interview, p.25.
145. Ridgeway, p.150.
146. 'Home by Christmas' statement, *Washington Evening Star*, 29 Nov 1950.
147. *Washington Evening Star*, 29 Nov 1950.
148. Ridgeway, p.60.
149. 27 Bde War Diary, 3 Dec 1950.
150. 27 Bde War Diary, 1 Dec 1950.
151. 27 Bde War Diary, 2 Dec 1950.
152. O'Dowd, p.49.
153. Gallaway, p.161.

154. 3 RAR War Diary, 12 Dec 1950.
155. Man, *Life Story*, p.68.
156. 3 RAR War Diary, Dec 1950, Routine Orders Part I.
157. 27 Bde War Diary, 1 Jan 1951.
158. 27 Bde War Diary, 1 Jan 1951.
159. 27 Bde War Diary, 7 Jan 1951.
160. Ridgeway, p.87.
161. Ridgeway, p.87.
162. Farrah-Hockley's official history, *The British Part in the Korean War*, was subtitled 'A Distant Obligation'.
163. McGibbon, Vol. 1, p.82.
164. McGibbon, Vol. 1, p.92.
165. McGibbon, Vol. 2, p.67.
166. Willoughby Diary, 20 Feb 1951.
167. Willoughby Diary, 12 Feb 1951.
168. Willoughby Diary, 15 Feb 1951.
169. Harrop Diary, Ch. 14.
170. Harrop Diary, Ch. 14.
171. Willoughby Diary, 15 Feb 1951.
172. Harrop Diary, Ch. 14.
173. 'Point 112', *British Army Journal.*
174. Coad Report, Appendix A.
175. 'Point 112', *British Army Journal.*
176. MacArthur, *A Soldier Speaks*, p.237.
177. Ridgeway, p.110.
178. *War of Patrols*, p.12.
179. Quoted in *War of Patrols*, p.14.
180. Quoting Gen Foulkes in *War of Patrols*, p.23.
181. Gray, p.xvi.
182. *War of Patrols*, p.66.
183. Stone, quoted in *War of Patrols*, p.59.
184. Grey, *Commonwealth Armies*, p.77.
185. PPCLI War Diary, 7 Jan 1951.
186. PPCLI War Diary, 18 Jan 1951.
187. Stone, 'Memoir: Kapyong'.
188. PPCLI War Diary, 20–21 Feb 1951.
189. Kolanchey, Interview Reel 2.
190. Junior Commissioned Officers, or JCOs, comprise a distinct rank group peculiar to the Indian Army. The direct descendant of the pre-independence Viceroy Commissioned Officers (VCO), JCOs can be roughly considered as occupying the rank of Warrant Officers and lieutenants in other Commonwealth armies.
191. COAD Report.
192. 27 Bde War Diary, 14 Dec 1950.

193. Banerjee MVC citation, 29 Mar 1951.
194. Farrar-Hockley, *The British Part in the Korean War Part 2*, p.64.
195. Peng De Huai speech at Fifth Enlarged Session of the Chinese People's Volunteers Party Committee on 6 Apr 1951, quoted in Farrar-Hockley Vol. 2, p.106.
196. Peng De Huai speech at Fifth Enlarged Session of the Chinese People's Volunteers Party Committee on 6 Apr 1951, quoted in Farrar-Hockley Vol. 2, p.106.
197. Peng Dehuai, quoted in Farrar-Hockley Vol. 2, p.109.
198. 'MacKenzie Report – 2 PPCLI Action Kapyong Area'.
199. 3 RAR War Diary, 20 Apr 1951.
200. 16 NZ War Diary, 22 Apr 1951.
201. Farrar-Hockley, Vol. 2, p.141.
202. *With the Australians in Korea*, p.91.
203. *The Battle of Kapyong*, p.33.
204. O'Dowd, 'The Battle of Kapyong: From the Inside', p.5.
205. NZ War Diary, 23 Apr 1951.
206. 'MacKenzie Report', para 64.
207. Desmond, *The War that Never Ended*, p.56.
208. 3 RAR War Diary, 23 April 1951.
209. Farrar-Hockley, Vol 2, p.143.
210. Stone, 'Memoir: Kapyong'.
211. Munro interview, quoted in Gray, p.63.
212. O'Dowd, 'The Battle of Kapyong: From the Inside', p.7.
213. Command Reports of the 2nd Chemical Mortar Battalion, April 1951.
214. 3 RAR War Diary, 24 April 1951.
215. O'Dowd, *In Valiant Company*, p.165.
216. O'Dowd, *In Valiant Company*, p.166.
217. O'Dowd, 'The Battle of Kapyong: From the Inside', p.8.
218. O'Dowd, 'The Battle of Kapyong: From the Inside', p.10.
219. Reed, MC citation.
220. 3 RAR War Diary, April 1951, Annex, 'Monthly Report by Regimental Medical Officer'.
221. 3 RAR War Diary, April 1951, Annex, 'Summary of Events – B Company night 23/24 April'.
222. Ray Parry would eventually be awarded the Military Medal for his defence of the B Company position on 23 April 1951 at Kapyong. His position is also the basis for a large diorama display of the battle shown at the Australian War Memorial in Canberra.
223. Knowles, *A Rifleman's View of Kapyong*, p.3.
224. Breen, *The Battle of Kapyong*, p.68.
225. Amazingly, Corporal Ray Parry was able to take a photograph of a group of five Chinese prisoners who were captured that morning. It is one of the few photographs that were taken during the Battle of Kapyong itself.
226. Breen, *The Battle of Kapyong*, p.73.

227. Breen, *The Battle of Kapyong*, p.76.
228. Breen, *The Battle of Kapyong*, p.77.
229. Breen, p.81.
230. Montgomerie, MC citation.
231. Breen, p.81.
232. Gray, p.77.
233. Mason, interview quoted in Gray, p.78.
234. Breen, *The Battle of Kapyong*, p.70.
235. Gallaway, *Last Call of the Bugle*, p.261.
236. Breen, *The Battle of Kapyong*, p.70, quoting an interview with Gravener.
237. Sgt Ray McKenzie, quoted in Breen, p.96.
238. O'Dowd, 'The Battle of Kapyong: From the Inside', p.17.
239. O'Dowd, 'The Battle of Kapyong: From the Inside', p.15.
240. Breen, *The Battle of Kapyong*, p.104, quoting O'Dowd.
241. Lieutenant Petrie's field notes, quoted in Gray, p.79.
242. Corporal Bill Shuler interview, quoted in Gray, p.88.
243. Gray, p.89.
244. Mitchell, DCM citation.
245. Stone, 'Memoir: Kapyong'.
246. Gray, interview.
247. 'MacKenzie Report', para 35.
248. McGibbon, p.134.
249. *Beyond the Danger Close*, p.113, quoting Levy.
250. *Beyond the Danger Close*, p.114, quoting Levy.
251. McGibbon, p.134.
252. Stone, 'Memoir: Kapyong'.
253. *Strange Battleground*, p.89.
254. 'MacKenzie Report', para 62.
255. O'Neill, Vol. II, p.151.
256. It has not been possible to get an exact count of 3 RAR's KIA and WIA for Kapyong. O'Neill's Official History places the numbers at 32 KIA and 59 WIA (Vol II, p.157), whereas Breen counts 34 KIA and 63 WIA (p.123).
257. *Strange Battleground*, p.89.
258. Stone, 'Memoir: Kapyong'.
259. O'Dowd, 'The Battle of Kapyong: From the Inside', p.1.
260. O'Dowd, 'The Battle of Kapyong: From the Inside', p.1.
261. Millar, quoted in Breen, p.83.
262. O'Neill, Vol. II, p.158.
263. Ferguson received his DSO on 1 May 1951. It was exceptionally rare for awards to be recommended, approved and awarded in such a speedy timeframe.
264. Special Order of the Day, 16 Field Regt War Diary, 29 Apr 1950.
265. Gray, interview.
266. Desmond, p.98.

267. Searl, Oral History.
268. Desmond, p.152.
269. Coad Report, Appendix B.
270. Searl, Oral History.
271. Willoughby Diary 3.9.
272. Kolanchey, Oral History, Reel 2.
273. Farrar-Hockley, *The British Part in the Korean War Part 2*, p.64.
274. McGibbon, p.362.
275. O'Neill, *Australia in the Korean War, Vol. 1*, p.402.
276. Parry interview.
277. Parry interview.

Military units

British and Commonwealth Units

United States Units

Republic of Korea Units

Index